Social Im/mobilities in Africa

Social Im/mobilities in Africa

Ethnographic Approaches

Edited by
Joël Noret

berghahn
NEW YORK · OXFORD
www.berghahnbooks.com

First published in 2020 by
Berghahn Books
www.berghahnbooks.com

© 2020, 2024 Joël Noret
First paperback edition published in 2024

Library of Congress Cataloging-in-Publication Data
Names: Noret, Joël, editor.
Title: Social im/mobilities in Africa : ethnographic approaches / edited by
Joël Noret.
Other titles: Social im/mobilities in Africa
Description: New York : Berghahn Books, 2020. | Includes bibliographical
references and index.
Identifiers: LCCN 2019037866 (print) | LCCN 2019037867 (ebook) | ISBN
9781789204858 (hardback) | ISBN 9781789204865 (ebook)
Subjects: LCSH: Social mobility--Africa. | Social status--Africa. |
Africa--Social conditions--1960-
Classification: LCC HN780.Z9 .S633 2020 (print) | LCC HN780.Z9 (ebook) |
DDC 305.5/13096--dc23
LC record available at https://lccn.loc.gov/2019037866
LC ebook record available at https://lccn.loc.gov/2019037867

British Library Cataloguing in Publication Data
A catalogue record for this book is available from the British Library

ISBN 978-1-78920-485-8 hardback
ISBN 978-1-80539-130-2 paperback
ISBN 978-1-80539-397-9 epub
ISBN 978-1-78920-486-5 web pdf

https://doi.org/10.3167/9781789204858

Contents

Introduction
Theorizing Social Im/mobilities in Africa

Joël Noret

> Initially, sociology presents itself as a *social topology*. Thus, the social world can be represented as a space (with several dimensions) constructed on the basis of principles of differentiation or distribution constituted by the set of properties active within the social universe in question.
> —Pierre Bourdieu, 'The Social Space and the Genesis of Groups'

This volume engages with the complex issue of social mobilities and immobilities in Africa at a time when the public debate about the continent is passionate but dichotomized – either portraying 'Africa Rising' or attending to huge levels of inequality epitomized by the poverty of shantytowns. As this book demonstrates, both of these realities are true simultaneously, depending on which segments of African societies are scrutinized. What is more, they intersect. In fact, broad stroke depictions of the continent are only made possible by the neglect of social positionality, and how it mediates and intertwines with political and economic dynamics. A central argument of this book thus resides in a plea for a more consequential and critical attention to the ways in which social positions matter when accounting for current changes, as some groups and individuals are always better positioned than others to appropriate opportunities, in Weber's famous terms.

Against this backdrop, the notion of social im/mobilities refers to the multifaceted dynamics of social structure in Africa today, and to the complex and sometimes paradoxical social trajectories they frame. These dynamics feature both social possibilities and social reproduction, social opportunities and social obstructions, in societies that are themselves subjected to rapid change – that is, in which the forces at play in the making of social positions are also in motion. Therefore, the idea of social im/mobilities emphasizes the limits, uncertainties and complexities of current social mobilities, since social trajectories can be marked by change without significant alterations of 'life chances', to refer once again to Weber. Considering a variety of situations, the chapters in this volume investigate the complex intersection of important social qualities – including levels of wealth and education, gender, autochthony or ethnicity – in the production and the distribution of social positions, and the correlative making of social divisions. Advocating a multifaceted view of African societies, they investigate the nature of the social powers that constitute the texture of societies, and that individuals confront or mobilize in the course of their existences.[1]

Thinking with Social Positionality

In what follows, social positionality is analysed from a multidimensional perspective, in which multiple factors intersect to produce more or less enduring social proximities among social subjects sharing similar conditions, but also, as a correlate, social divisions and social distances. In other words, the societies we scrutinize are here understood as 'social spaces', that is multidimensional and relational spaces of social positions structured by different, interlacing systems of inequality (Bourdieu 1979, 1984, 1994). The work of Pierre Bourdieu indeed offers a fertile framework to consider the intersection of social powers or qualities, potentially working as 'capitals', in the production of social positions and chances of social im/mobility. What is more, the idea of social space also allows us to avoid what might be considered a pitfall of unidimensional conceptions of the social ladder, along which social actors can only climb or fall. Contrastingly, a multidimensional analysis of social positions points to the entwinement of different social attributes or qualities in the production of social spaces, in which diagonal or horizontal moves, 'transverse movements' (Bourdieu 1979: 145–46), are also possible.

Consider, for instance, situations when people move from a condition of rural poverty to urban settings, but where they remain in the lower segments of urban society. This is a social move that cannot easily be understood through the prism of a unidimensional social ladder, or be referred to unequivocally in terms of 'gains' or 'losses'. Or consider when a slight increase in the formal education level between generations goes hand in hand with a general elevation in educational standards. This move will not necessarily translate into a notable change in economic position, albeit delivering the social profits of literacy, and therefore consisting in a form of social move in a relational space of social positions itself undergoing structural transformations. In this book, Fawzia Mazanderani analyses the 'undelivered promise of education' in a rural township of north-eastern South Africa, where higher levels of education haphazardly translate into the fantasies of success of the 'born free generation'. Some moves in fact are more significant than others. For instance, short moves in the lower regions of social space, those of the deprived and the excluded, cannot unambiguously be viewed as social mobility, insofar as they do not necessarily represent actual increases in living standards and 'life chances'.

From that perspective, the moves of social subjects between sectors of activity, tracked through massive databases by some development economists with an interest in social mobility (for instance Bossuroy and Cogneau 2013, Lambert et al. 2014), can actually represent ambiguous forms of social mobility – something returned to in the conclusion. On the one hand, the reduction of the share of the population involved in agriculture certainly represents a massive social change, and a significant social move for many rural youth, with cultural implications reaching far beyond the occupational structure, as lifestyles change dramatically. It also reminds us how closely strategies of social mobility and quests for a dignified life have been entwined with physical mobility on the continent, at least since the colonial period. On the other hand, if we consider social mobility as altered life chances, when the move away from agriculture brings poorly educated people into the poor strata of (peri)urban society, this does not unambiguously alter their chances of accumulating wealth or accessing sufficient income. Added to which there are the uncertainties and precariousness of social positionality in African states with generally poorly developed social rights. As Laura Camfield and William Monteith point out in their chapter, Ugandan small entrepreneurs of the informal sector often achieve only 'fleeting social mobility' in the challenging environment of Kampala.

As such, we focus in this volume on the variegated social powers producing social positionality and their intertwinements. This leads us to depict dynamics of social im/mobility in more complex ways by also taking into consideration processes of value conversion – such as when ethnicity is mobilized to access jobs, or when economic capital is converted into political notability, for instance through strategic practices of public generosity. What is more, we explore possible increases or decreases of the value of certain social forces shaping social positionality.

This is the case, for instance, in the current experience of many young Africans, who realize today in ever greater numbers that the distinctive power of education and their school qualifications have partly faded away and been devalued in parallel to the general increase in the level of formal education. In this volume, Gabriella Körling shows how in Niger, as in other African settings, 'the link between education and social advancement' has become 'increasingly tenuous' in the popular classes of peri-urban Niamey. In fact, such a change in the terms of trade between education and access to stable employment – in other words, the relational value of education – points very clearly to the importance of conceptualizing social im/mobilities in a way that accounts for both the multidimensionality of social positionality and the dynamics of the social forces distributing social positions and life chances.

Yet, since the late twentieth-century ebb of Marxism as a sociological force and the more or less concomitant push of both a 'cultural turn' and more 'phenomenological' approaches, a significant current across contemporary social sciences has been to put less theoretical effort into thinking about the complexities of social structure and social positionality, and to put more emphasis on thinking about agency and subjectivities. Some readers might find this judgement too hasty or too simple, and it is certainly formulated in very general terms here. Yet it is not a purely personal diagnosis, and several authors have already discussed in similar terms current evolutions in social theory more broadly (see Atkinson 2015, Chauvel 2001, Devine et al. 2005, Savage et al. 2015a, Wright 2005).

In African studies, this turn to agency and subjectivities has diversely led, among other possible examples, to the idea that the poor's 'immiseration' and 'fragile bare lives' could be 'somehow redeemed' through their inventive agency (Simone 2004: 428), or to the argument that a 'cultural analysis' of class focusing on boundary making offers a 'truer' picture of class, at least for the African middle class (Spronk 2014: 110). Alternatively, class can also be altogether dismissed as a relevant category of analysis in a city like Kinshasa, on the grounds that the Central African megalopolis' social stratification can be reduced to an opposition between a small elite and 'the poor', class therefore losing, from this perspective, 'most of its explanatory strength' (De Boeck 2015: S148).

In this book, without renouncing the incisive idea of situated agency, the following chapters adopt an ethnographic perspective that is immediately and consistently attentive to positioning social groups and actors in both their objective conditions of existence and the subjective divisions of the social space they confront and mobilize, which taken together inform their life chances as well as their multiple social strategies. As such, it remains essential to think with social positionality on a continent where multidimensional inequalities are glaring. Yet, this is in different respects hardly new, and already has a respectable genealogy. A detailed discussion of the different generations of scholarly works and paradigms that have organized the variegated accounts of African social stratification and its dynamics is obviously beyond the scope of this introduction. Still, before turning to what this book has to offer on the subject, a quick and inevitably selective retrospect might remind us of some essential milestones.

Social Im/mobilities in Africa in Restrospect

As Sally Falk Moore has convincingly argued, 'time-conscious' writing about a changing, 'living Africa' has been present in African anthropology almost since the beginnings of field research. It was first deployed in the interstices of the then theoretically dominant structural-functional (and more timeless) accounts of African 'tribal' societies, essentially famous for their concern with the political structure of precolonial states and the theory of segmentary lineage systems, as well as for their peripheral attention to social change (Moore 1994: 37–40). Yet, since 1940, the colonial situation was fully repatriated in Gluckman's seminal article on Zululanders – Blacks and Whites. Starting with a description of the inauguration of a bridge developing the infrastructure in a portion of rural Zululand, the text famously explores the dynamic workings of both the racial divide and the subdivisions of the black and white social worlds (Gluckman 1940).

However, it is the development of social research in urban settings, in the post-World War II context, that constituted the main trigger to the deployment on the continent of new discussions of social positionality and social change. There, perhaps more visibly than in rural settings, 'evidence of ongoing change existed everywhere' (Moore 1994: 52), and the challenge was both theoretical and methodological. Urban situations required anthropologists to think differently about social structure, and ethnographic fieldwork alone quickly appeared as not entirely satisfying when trying to work at the larger urban scale. Answers were sought on both fronts and took the form of methodological diversification and theoretical innovation. Mitchell's 'Kalela Dance' is emblematic of that moment. Grounded in ethnography, but also mobilizing quantitative data on occupational prestige and social distance between 'tribes', the argument is well-known, suggesting that the essential social divisions in the urban Copperbelt resided in reconfigured ethnicities and in occupational prestige, and is emblematic of that moment (Mitchell 1956).

Similarly emblematic, in francophone academia, is Georges Balandier's work on the dynamics of the 'black Brazzavilles' (Balandier 1955), which presents similar interdisciplinary concerns in both theory and methodology to grasp the dynamics of the late colonial urban scene.

The Rhodes Livingstone Institute researchers' well-tempered methodological eclecticism, alternating between in-depth studies of actual cases and more quantitative data, is well-known. However, the move was a more general one. From South Africa to Central Africa and from Uganda to Senegal (for instance Mercier 1956, 1960; Balandier 1955; Goldthorpe 1955), surveys were designed and implemented, leading to the production of various quantitative data, from measures of occupational prestige to household budgets. These complemented more classical ethnographic, and more broadly qualitative research (see Moore 1994: 62–73, Schumaker 2001: 171–89). Theory turned to sociology for inspiration. As for social positionality and its dynamics, social status and class quickly became central topics.

In the wake of the post-World War II intensification of political struggles in late colonial Africa, the new urban worlds gained both political and academic momentum. As Carola Lentz (2015) has recently reminded us, the notions of elite and of social class – both with diverse meanings and contours – became the central theoretical concepts to be mobilized in accounts of social positionality and im/mobility for several decades. The possible emergence of social classes – then essentially understood as status groups deriving from occupation – was discussed from around 1950, in works regularly (although diversely) haunted by a modernization paradigm (for instance Mercier 1954, Little 1953, Mitchell and Epstein 1959). Focused on urban society, these studies in fact regularly entwine concepts of class and of elites, as the latter term is mobilized on the African terrain almost concomitantly with 'class' (for instance Nadel 1956, and more generally UNESCO 1956).

The notion of 'elite' gained currency after P.C. Lloyd's edited volume on Africa's 'new elites' (1966). Lloyd argues against the relevance of class to capture the dynamics of African social stratification for essentially the same reasons that studies from the preceding decades had concluded that class was (still) of limited significance, emphasizing the importance of other social divisions and commitments (ethnic, regional or kinship-based) operating alongside and beyond class, and the correlative weakness of class identities or 'consciousness'. In fact, beyond the elite versus social class conceptual distinction, the works of the 1950s–1960s fundamentally acknowledge the challenging nature of interpreting African social stratification. The issue of class and elite boundaries emerges as central, as is the problem of what is to be made of the salient regional or ethnic identities and extended kinship networks. In the 1960s, the idea of 'plural societies' comes to be used as a way of theorizing African societies structured by variegated differentiation logics (Mitchell 1966, Balandier 1971). In a sense, the difficulty of accounting for African social stratification processes along a unidimensional social ladder has already become critical.

As the above paragraphs already suggest, research on social positionality also became more interdisciplinary. From the second half of the twentieth century onwards, not only did social anthropologists enrich their methodological apparatuses and theoretical arsenal, but other disciplines became increasingly present in discourses deployed about African social change. Sociologists, historians, political scientists, political economists and geographers made increasingly visible contributions to social theory in the African field. Since the time of independences, a relatively small but persistent strand of research also started to investigate social mobility through the prism of education, exploring the relations between social (and ethnic) origins, educational attainment and occupational outcomes (Foster 1963, 1965; Goldthorpe 1955, 1965; Clignet 1964; Clignet and Foster 1966).

Most significantly for the intellectual atmosphere of the next decades, and for reasons diversely related to the new possibilities of economic accumulation in post-independence Africa, as well as to the post-World War II resurgence of western Marxism (Young 1986), the 1960s saw the development of Marxist intellectual engagements with Africa, which consolidated (and diversified) in the 1970s and 1980s, before declining in the 1990s – with the notable exception of South Africa, where a stronger Marxist tradition persisted. This led to a rich body of literature, which left a durable imprint on approaches to social positionality and im/mobilities. Key debates took place around modes of production, class formation and class structure – as well as around the entwinement of the latter with uneven regional development and ethnicity. As with all paradigms, there were pitfalls and dead ends, and certain strands of work proved quite normative and teleological. There were also, however, significant new accents and directions (Freund 1984). At the times of independence, social positions were now commonly thought of at the scale of national spaces, but dependency theorists (Rodney 1972, Amin 1973) and world-system analysts (Wallerstein 1974) expanded on old invitations of Marxist political economy to think about social (and, especially, economic) positionality beyond the framework of the nation-state. Their views, however, were quickly criticized for their overly deterministic tone, as well as for downplaying the role of social struggles and of the complexities of local production processes and labour relations in the making of African economies and social formations (Cooper 1981).

Critically, Marxist works paid more systematic attention to inequality. For many, the state quickly emerged as the site *par excellence* of capital accumulation and a major channel for upward social mobility. The
'elite' had initially entered the field of African studies with a positive
connotation – would the elites not be at the forefront of the modernization process? The notion did remain in use in descriptions of the formation and lifestyles of dominant groups. Yet, the term also progressively
acquired a negative connotation, as it came to be associated with neo-
patrimonial politics, corruption and clientelism – a judgement that some
have suggested should be reconsidered, with more emphasis on the complexities of elites' moralities (Werbner 2004, Fumanti 2016).

In fact, Marxist-inspired scholars have deployed more critical accounts
of dominant groups since the 1960s (famously Fanon 1961) and throughout the 1970s and 1980s, often debating the contours of social classes
(for instance Cohen 1972, Berry 1985), class struggles, or the exploita-
tive role of a ruling or a state class, state or bureaucratic bourgeoisie, or
other similar expressions (for instance Sklar 1979). At the other end of
the social spectrum, discussions were taking place over the formation
of a working class, and around the potential class nature of the African
peasant masses.[2] In the same period, however, more sceptical voices were
heard on the appropriateness of class idioms to theorize African social
structures (notably Goody 1971, 1976). In fact, the class nature of African
societies, and the more or less (in)appropriateness of class terminologies
to analyse African society and multidimensional social divisions, had
been a disputed issue from the late colonial period onwards (see above).
Obviously, this introduction has no pretention to settle this debate, which
is further complicated by the fact that multiple understandings of class
and forms of class analysis coexist within the social sciences.

What is worth remembering, however, is that Marxist-inspired
approaches in African studies – a variegated constellation rather than a
monolithic block – not only put the political economy on the agenda and
deployed the analysis of economic positions and strategies far beyond the
mere distinction of income strata; they also promoted a relational gaze on
social positionality, as social classes in the Marxist tradition are not mere
juxtaposed entities, but form a dynamic set of positions related one to the
other, and in tension with one another.[3] To this day, these perspectives
have not only inspired relational accounts of poverty[4] – as 'the poor' have
now largely replaced the working classes in the making and the urban
and rural (sub)proletariats – but were also part of classic early perspectives on the 'informal sector' (Hart 1973), and remain key to some recent
critical understandings of the 'informal economy' (for instance Rizzo
2017).

The variegated Marxist-derived approaches, however, did not wipe out other lines of research, nor were they exclusive of additional influences or concerns. Beyond and besides the political economy, other discourses on social positionality and im/mobilities have represented significant contributions to African studies over several decades. Explorations of the generational condition of African youths in the wake of the Structural Adjustment Programmes represent a telling phenomenon here. Being barred from full access to social adulthood, a significant part of current African youths have been said to be stuck in a stage of 'waithood' (Honwana 2012), translating into experiences of boredom and shame (for instance Mains 2007, Masquelier 2013), and of 'killing time' (Ralph 2008) – though also feeding the generational protests currently multiplying across the continent. Indeed, the combination of the debt crisis and increasing education levels have added a layer of complexity to the exploration of the educational avenues to social mobility that a few scholars had started to analyse a few decades earlier. Shrinking life chances 'across class' (Hansen 2005), in what has even been called a 'lost generation' by some (Cruise O'Brien 1996), have attracted a lot of comments on the uncertain entanglements of education and social im/mobilities on the continent.

Yet, still other currents of research have developed important discourses on social positionality and im/mobilities grounded in what Roger Brubaker refers to as 'categories of difference',[5] that is socially salient 'ascribed statuses' and ascriptive identities such as gender or ethnicity, not to mention race – in the southern African situation especially – or slave descent – particularly in Sahelian Africa. These categorical differences have been researched in different theoretical guises, in and of themselves or in conjunction with other social dynamics. In fact, the emergence of gender as an analytical lens has represented a major advance in African studies and in the analysis of social positionality in Africa, most fruitfully mobilized when its intersections with other social divisions are considered. The various ways that a gender bar works have now been evidenced through different methodological apparatuses and disciplinary perspectives, and in various domains of social life, from the legal barriers still preventing women from inheriting land and material property, to the dynamics of unequal education and access to white-collar, 'formal' occupations, and more diffuse forms of discrimination.

Lastly, as a major 'ground for difference' (Brubaker 2015) in contemporary Africa, the role that ethnicity has played in framing African postcolonial national spaces cannot be ignored when one considers social positionality. There are significant national differences, however, in the way in which ethnicity is politicized, and relates to 'regional disparities in economic well-being and social mobility opportunities' (Young 1986: 471). Here again, entire libraries have been published on the historicity of ethnic divisions and belongings, their contextual dimension, their relative salience in a variety of settings, their entwinement with regional identities, as well as their articulation to economic and political processes. Most prominently, the important body of literature revolving around the 'neo-patrimonial state'[6] has elaborated the complex intersections of the economic and political dimensions of social positionality with ethnicity through the idea of patronage networks organized along ethno-regional lines. Once more, the intersection of different social divisions in the production of African societies – and the correlative importance to think beside and beyond the model of a unidimensional social ladder (only) – emerges as crucial.

Bayart's 'State in Africa' (1989) can probably be considered as a milestone in this respect. Indeed, despite its primary focus on the nature of African states, the book also deploys a keen interest in issues of social positionality. As others have before him, Bayart posits access and distance to the state as a major stratifying force throughout the continent – the state being a major site from which political actors can deploy 'strategies of extraversion', as he further elaborates later (Bayart 2000). From this perspective, the fundamental process which accounts for the formation of African ruling classes is that of the 'reciprocal assimilation of segments of the elite' under the auspices and through the channels of the postcolonial state – the political field being the site *par excellence* where the postcolonial 'system of inequality' is forged (Bayart 1989). Essentially, 'reciprocal assimilation', a formula he borrows from Gramsci, refers to the encounter and the entwinement of heterogeneous types of elites, supported by various forms of capital and legitimacy (material resources, school titles, traditional nobility, political credentials, etc.) in the state arena, and to the multiple processes of conversion of value and straddling taking place in these circumstances. The focus is undisputedly on the (re)production of the postcolonial ruling class. The rest of the social field is essentially considered as made of factions aligned to the elites and their redistributive power, and dominated by regional identities and 'terroirs'. In sum, in Bayart's 1980s 'State in Africa', the combination of reciprocal assimilation and factional struggles provides the key to the dynamics of the social space.

Significant changes have taken place throughout the continent since the 1980s. The state itself has undergone a series of transformations under the effects of (neo)liberalization and, in many countries, decentralization processes in the post-cold war era, not to mention the diverging trajectories that African states have experienced in uneven democratization experiences or (semi-)authoritarian persistence. Beyond the state, the last decades have also witnessed, among other things, further growth of cities and secondary towns, an expansion of education in terms of both access and general level, and unevenly distributed new foreign investments. This account is brief and many other important works of the last three decades could be cited that attempt to think of the intersecting systems of difference and social powers that produce social positionality on this changing African scene. But a few key issues emerge in the brief retrospect above, such as the plural differentiation principles of African societies – alongside and beyond class –, the importance to think both with the political economy and without losing sight of other social divisions and categorical differences, and the productivity of a relational perspective on social positionality.

Perhaps especially relevant for this volume, the growing interest in African middle class(es) has witnessed renewed attempts at thinking about the production and distribution of social positions in African societies. Besides economic approaches that work mainly with income or expense strata,[7] the social sciences have insisted on the need to grasp the cultural side of class, especially in the form of middle class 'boundary work'.

Yet, beyond the recognition of the difficulties in agreeing on the contours of the African middle classes and of the importance of the cultural side of class, two directions appear of particular interest for a reflexion on social im/mobilities. First, there is the call by (still) Marxist-inspired scholars to extend the current interest in middle classes towards a renewed class analysis, and an appreciation of the relational positionalities of African middle classes (Melber 2017, Southall 2018): how are the middle classes located in a space of social positions? How (dis)continuous is such a space? What forces of differentiation are there at work, and how do they intersect?

Second, the focus on the cultural side of (middle) classes, on class as identity or subjectivity, should not result in analyses dropping more or less altogether the objectivist side of class – that of the access to, and the possession of, economic powers, a concern shared (though in different guises) by both Marxist and Weberian traditions (Wright 2005: 25–27). Considering that class is first and foremost about 'modes of sophistication' and 'signifying practice' (Spronk 2014), or that 'classes – middle or otherwise – emerge from the complexity of individual choices and actions' (Scharrer et al. 2018: 24), only tells one side of the story.

As Claire Mercer has recently put it, middle classing in suburban Dar es Salaam revolves largely around 'building the right kind of house in the right part of the suburb' (Mercer 2018: 10), but this in turn is closely associated to the economic capacity to access land, and to secure it. So, 'boundary work' is here 'first and foremost a set of material practices concerned with accessing and securing one's claim to a plot of land' (2018: 10). And accessing land in a context of growing land scarcity and pricing has to do with more than culture, signifying practice and individual choices, but crucially with 'mechanisms of accumulation' (Savage et al. 2015b: 1017). Social im/mobilities need to be considered besides and beyond identities and subjectivities.

Social Im/mobilities and Social Space

Against this backdrop, a thread running through the chapters of the book suggests that Bourdieu's notion of social space (notably Bourdieu 1979, 1984, 1994) offers a promising framework to think about these issues together. Most chapters therefore build on the idea of social space in creative and critical ways. In that, the contributions to this volume stress the importance of thinking about the dynamics of social positions – that is, about social im/mobilities – in a multidimensional and relational way, as well as with sustained attention to both their objective side as a set of conditions of existence, and their subjective side as a sense of one's place in the (social) world. In this respect, precariousness and uncertainty, for instance, are not only defined by objective, 'material' conditions, but also need to be considered as 'a structure of feeling' (Cooper and Pratten 2015).

So, what are Bourdieu's key views on social spaces? And what do we make of them? First, Bourdieu approaches social space – that is, the space of social positions – as a continuous space of positions. This space is structured by the unequal distribution – both in terms of volume and of structure – of different forms of capitals and other social powers, attributes or properties.[8] In order to work as 'capitals' (Bourdieu 1986) and become social powers, these social qualities or properties need to ensure those endowed with them a form of social advantage that can provide the basis for a mechanism of accumulation, and be convertible into other advantages. To mention just a few obvious examples, this is the case when money facilitates access to education, or education to income opportunities, or when social relationships, working as 'social capital', facilitate access to economic resources. This endowment with different volumes and structures of capitals is crucial to understanding how different social subjects are (un)able to negotiate their everyday life and, more decisively, the 'vital conjunctures' they face, that is these 'critical durations when more than usual is in play, when certain potential futures are galvanized and others made improbable' (Johnson-Hanks 2006: 3).

In this way, the idea of social space accounts for social reality beyond emic categorizations. Indeed, despite the fact that Bourdieu's theory of class is regularly referred to as a 'cultural turn' in class analysis, the idea of social space is actually designed to think of the objective and subjective structures of the social world together. Hence, Bourdieu always assigned a major role to economic capital in the distribution of social positions and in the making of (objective) conditions of existence. Economic capital is essential in drawing the contours of 'classes on paper' (Bourdieu 1984). This is what makes Bourdieu's style of class analysis converge with historical styles of class analysis inspired by Marx and Weber which, although organized around different issues, nonetheless have a common interest in the power of economic resources to draw major social divisions.

What is more, another key idea conveyed by the notion of social space arises from its ambition to account for social positionality as a multidimensional and relational phenomenon. Social space is relational insofar as, in good structuralist fashion, it invites us to look at social positions as the product of a system of differences. In other words, social positions exist through the differences they represent with other positions and the social distances they establish, both in the objective order of the conditions of existence and in the subjective order of the habitus – the schemes of thought, feeling and action that social agents practically mobilize in the course of everyday life. It is multidimensional in that it invites us to explore social dynamics beyond (and beside) the idea of a unidimensional social ladder.

There are obviously upper and lower regions or segments in social space – where people are endowed with a bigger or smaller global volume of capitals – but there is also the potential, to a certain extent, for different orders of worth and plural social hierarchies. Bourdieu's account of the French social space in the 1960s–1970s is famous for its analysis of the space of social positions mainly grounded in the unequal distributions (and the interplay) of economic and cultural capitals, which he deemed to be the most decisive social properties in his case study. Yet, late twentieth-century French society represents only one possible case. As Ben Page puts it in his chapter, while exploring the forces at play in the making of social positionality in Buea, the idea of social space has an 'assertively idiographic' quality that makes it a productive tool to 'locate social differences' and explore relations of power in a variety of settings. Therefore, building on Bourdieu to think of African situations inevitably results in recognizing other social forces that prove to be key in other instances. The vast majority of students of Africa would recognize that money and economic capital more generally distribute social positions in powerful ways across the continent, and all the more since economic and social rights remain poorly developed in most African countries. Examples abound in the literature, of how money frames both polarizing objective conditions of existence on the one hand, and subjectivation processes and internalized senses of one's place on the other, contributing in decisive ways to the making of 'unequal lives' (Fassin 2018). In many African settings, wealth is not only a major social power in the production of objective inequalities, but also recognized as legitimate, and therefore working as symbolic capital, endowing its owners with social recognition.

African situations, however, prove immediately more complex when we confront them with Bourdieu's understanding of 'cultural capital'. For instance, the historical sedimentation of schools and formal education as legitimate institutions capable of producing cultural domination is not the same as in the West. As Max Bolt suggests in this volume, on the South African-Zimbabwean border, the overall transient character of the border society makes 'symbolic orders' precarious and uncertain, with little room for the recognition of the cultural capital of educated, former white-collar migrants in search of better futures away from the Zimbabwean economic crisis. In that sense, there is no 'unification of the market in cultural capital', and the legitimate forms of cultural capital can change depending on the situation (Hilgers and Mangez 2015). Education has long been recognized as a powerful stratifying force on the continent. In this, school capital is certainly relevant for thinking about life chances in many social situations. Yet other forms of cultural capital can be recognized as well. Take the case of forms of religious capital deriving from a religious education or status – being a priest, a pastor or a Muslim cleric endows one with social recognition in many situations – or from the mastery of 'tradition' or 'custom'. These can also represent powerful social forces and credentials.

In fact, there is no reason to assume that African social spaces are invariably structured everywhere and in any decisive way by the same sort of blend of economic and cultural capitals as late twentieth-century France. A secondary point of attention in Bourdieu's discussions of French society, social capital for instance might well deserve more sustained attention in explorations of the production of social positionality in Africa. In fact, social capital has been discussed extensively in economic sociology and development studies in recent decades. Notable discussions have taken place around the merits and limits of the distinction between 'strong' and 'weak' ties, and the value of social networks, as these can be alternatively envisioned as social capital or liabilities (Meagher 2006). In fact, serious empirical investigation of African social networks reveals that their nature and contributions to African institutional worlds and production of social positions can differ significantly depending on situations (Meagher 2006, 2010). Yet, despite its ambiguities, social capital – resources deriving from membership in groups themselves more or less endowed with different forms of capital (Bourdieu 1986) – is regularly regarded as a major structuring force in African social spaces. As Benjamin Rubbers points out in this volume, social capital proves 'crucial to account for the dynamics of inequality' in the Congolese Copperbelt in the last decades. More broadly still, the ways in which people are able to navigate their relations with the state, the distribution of business and job opportunities, the importance of various types of associations and religious communities, are but a few of the scenes in which the (in)capacity to mobilize social relationships and networks proves to be key to the conduct of social life.

Yet, another range of social forces also need some consideration here, when thinking of life chances and social im/mobilities in African social spaces. Categorical differences and inequalities deriving from ascribed identities – such as ethnicity or gender – typically receive less attention in Bourdieu's characterizations of social space. Passing mentions of ethnicity and citizenship can be found in *Distinction* as secondary phenomena, yet they can work as 'capitals' too (see for instance Hage 1998, Hilgers 2011). *Masculine Domination* contains no detailed discussion of gender in relation to social positionality, beyond a few pages on the uneven social effects of feminist struggles across social classes and general statements suggesting that male dominance is at work 'in the whole set of social spaces and sub-spaces' (Bourdieu 2002: 102). In this volume, Inge Tvedten explores how Maputo's women endowed with the status of household heads and daily domestic independence, are in a better position than those with a marital commitment to engage in informal economic activities: they do not have to live with quotidian masculine pressures on their time, movements in urban space and economic resources. In fact, exploring African spaces of social positions without seriously considering ethnicity, gender or other categorical 'grounds for difference' is inconceivable.

Indeed, besides gender, other 'grounds for difference', as Brubaker puts it, such as forms of 'traditional' historical nobility – or conversely of slave descent – for instance, or ethnic claims relying on an ideology of autochthony, or refugee status and restricted citizenship, can all be powerful social forces and sources of categorical inequalities shaping uneven chances of social im/mobility. This is not to imply that all possible forms of categorical differences work in the same ways and can be merged altogether. There are indeed 'different kinds of difference' within categories of difference (Brubaker 2015: 18). Categorical inequalities deriving from citizenship work, for instance, largely through legally governed processes, while gender exclusion can work through both legal barriers (preventing inheritance for women, for instance) and in more diffuse – though not necessarily less pervasive – ways. Categories of difference are thus 'inhabited', internalized and embodied in variegated ways, and their workings diversely regulated (ibid.: 19–47). Yet, a range of African situations shows very clearly that social divisions grounded in categories of difference can have deep structuring effects on the distribution of social positions and chances of social mobility.

However, the fertility of the idea of social space probably proves most attractive to think about how forms of capitals and social forces of the sort evoked in the above paragraphs entwine in intimate and complex ways in the production of social positionality and chances of social im/mobility. As Hannah Hoechner shows in this volume, the life chances of students of 'traditional' Quranic schools in northern Nigeria suffer from a double exclusion: these children and youngsters are not only poor, but also looked down upon by many urban dwellers because of the cultural illegitimacy of their style of religious education, to the point that they now 'epitomize the alleged "backwardness" of the rural poor'. In fact, against a 'reproductionist bias' in Bourdieu's reception (Gorski 2013), it is worth remembering that Bourdieu's framework was largely conceived in order to theorize the dynamics of social positions in situations of social change, that is in circumstances of 'motion within motion', to borrow Henrik Vigh's elegant formula (2009).[9] Considering the entwining of social forces, the notion of social space underlines how different social powers combine in the production and distribution of social positions. It also draws attention to the concomitant possibility of processes of value conversion, such as when ethnic traditions are turned into identity economics and the 'ethno-preneurialism' of 'Ethnicity Inc.' (Comaroff and Comaroff 2009), when money and social capital appear to be mutually constitutive and intimately entwined, as observed in the petty criminal networks of Abidjan's street economy (Newell 2012), or when forms of nobility or slave descent continue to constrain labour relations and/or patterns of actual physical mobility (Rossi 2009, Pelckmans 2012) – to take just three short examples among many other possibilities.

Still, working with the idea of a multidimensional space of social positions invites us to scrutinize social im/mobilities beyond the idea of a unidimensional social ladder. Indeed, besides conventional understandings of social climbing and descending, social moves can be characterized by changes in the structure of capitals rather than in their overall volume. Channelling the attention to the interplay between forms of capitals – and their fluctuating relations – a multidimensional analysis of social positions also invites us to think about the 'reconversion strategies' through which social subjects and domestic groups strive to maintain their position amidst changing circumstances (Bourdieu 1979: 145–85). In fact, the challenge of accounting for the complex regimes of social im/mobilities on the continent requires us to consider both the trajectories of social subjects and the dynamics of the forces at play in the making of social positions.

Following this theoretical skeleton, it is time we put some ethnographic flesh on these conceptual bones. Grounding the discussion in empirical materials and putting theory to work is precisely what the coming chapters offer. The first site we use to explore current social im/mobilities is education. Largely considered as a key for African futures, education is on everyone's lips when considering the challenges facing the continent today. Still, its impacts on social space are multifarious and more convoluted than what is sometimes presented as a direct relationship with the Holy Grail of development.

In the opening chapter, Hannah Hoechner explores the contours of the changing social position of 'traditional' Qur'anic students in northern Nigeria. Historically a respectable, religious-centred style of education for boys from an early age and through their youth, traditional Qur'anic schools now largely recruit in the most deprived strata of society, among impoverished urban households or, most notably, from among peasant families. What is more, they now represent a socially devalued schooling style on the education market, in which formal lay education – private or public – has become dominant. Having to hustle for their own food, as well as for their lodging in many cases, during their stays in Qur'anic schools the boys combine their religious learning with various forms of unskilled labour. Those with a rural background also regularly return to their families to help with farm labour during the rainy season. Once considered as religious students disciplining themselves in the pursuit of a pious life, traditional Qur'anic students now face social judgements that see them as backward, illiterate, rural poor boys. This of course bears heavily on their work arrangements with better off families or patrons in search of cheap labour, in which they are at pains to be treated as the pious religious subjects they claim they are.

Shifting to the meanders of secular education, Fawzia Mazanderani takes us to a rural township in the north east of South Africa. Her research focuses on students in their last year of secondary school and aspiring to upwardly mobile futures. She explores how the emphasis put on individual responsibility and hard work in their curriculum affects their experiences and projects. In fact, few of these young people from rural backgrounds will ever go to university. Yet, despite persisting attachments to the rural and an ambivalent imagination of urbanity, their aspirations are largely framed by ideologies of social mobility and desires to access the urban, deemed as the place *par excellence* of both a desirable modernity and moral corruption. Black rural youth have today more possibilities than their parents had under the apartheid regime. Yet, education hardly delivers the type of social mobility that young people from disadvantaged backgrounds are taught to dream of, leading to 'paradoxical forms of social mobility' marked by both an objective increase in the level of education and simultaneous feelings of failure.

The next chapter shifts the attention from southern Africa back to West Africa, while continuing to explore similar issues. Grounded in an ethnography of youth engagements with education, work and the state on the outskirts of Niamey (Niger), Gabriella Körling accounts for the ambivalent commitment to school among young people in peri-urban areas, between strong aspirations to an educated status and a better future, consciousness of the uncertain outcomes of educational investment, and absence of tangible, auspicious alternatives. After a few decades of systematic hiring of university graduates in the state apparatus, with its advantageous salaries and economic security, the 1990s have witnessed a progressive decline of the social benefits of education, with cuts in state recruitments in the wake of the Structural Adjustment Programme, and the simultaneous general increase of the level of education, at least in urban areas. In this new Nigerien order, Körling argues that the prestige of education in itself does not provide much ground for social distinction when it remains disconnected from minimal economic resources – opinions about unemployed school graduates can be severe, and lack of economic autonomy constitutes a serious obstacle on the sinuous path to social adulthood. Like Mazanderani's, Körling's chapter evokes the delicate moment of transition to adulthood. In the Nigerien families she interviewed, the prospect of becoming a civil servant is limited, and a significant proportion of young people with little educational background at some point try their luck in the informal economy. They then work either as precarious wage labourers – as African informal economies are far from being made of independent businesses only (for instance Rizzo et al. 2015) – or, for those in a position to access some capital, as self-employed workers or small-scale business(wo)men.

Laura Camfield and William Monteith take us from West to East Africa, and to the heart of the practicalities and indeterminacies of small-scale entrepreneurship in Uganda. The last two decades have seen a lot of emphasis put on entrepreneurship in Africa, which has become, together with education, one of the most celebrated ways of salvation in African development. Among Kampalan small-scale entrepreneurs and self-employed workers with whom Camfield and Monteith have conducted research since the beginning of the 2010s, uncertain economic prospects and difficulties accessing funds to start a business only allow those endowed with enough economic and social capitals to reach forms of 'precarious prosperity' and relative protection from the spectre of poverty. Access to property and commitment to building one's own house – before other possible investments – is key here. Yet, beyond a general consciousness of provisionality, and open-ended economic strategies, unequal access to capital is what appears to stratify owners of small businesses most clearly. Such access in turn presupposes the capacity to rely on family and other social networks, in a context of high interest rates in the official banking circuit.

Camfield and Monteith's chapter touches briefly on gender issues in entrepreneurs' access to capital. Returning to southern Africa, the next chapter now focuses on the gendered dynamics of social space in Maputo (Mozambique). Combining quantitative and qualitative data on gender and class inequalities, Inge Tvedten emphasizes how the agency of urban dwellers is framed by 'structural conjunctures'. Historically, race and gender have been the main social forces organizing the divisions of the colonial city. In the last decades however, class and gender have probably drawn the main dividing lines in the urban space of the contemporary metropolis. Yet, in the popular classes of poor suburban districts, economically independent women – who are not members of male-headed households – tend to get by better, economically speaking, than male-headed households. In fact, single or divorced women, though still regularly stigmatized, crucially access more diverse jobs in the urban informal economy than both men and their married counterparts. This partial subversion of gendered economic roles – men are expected to be breadwinners – coupled with the political emergence of a growing number of women as elected heads of neighbourhoods as well as in other community-level political structures, has led to a significant evolution of the gendered distribution of social positions in urban social space in the last decade. Women are now increasingly recognized as fully capable, and independent economic agents in the urban popular classes.

The next chapter turns to essentially masculine professional worlds. Mobilizing fifteen years of research in Katanga – the mining region of south-eastern Democratic Republic of the Congo – Benjamin Rubbers discusses the local dynamics of inequality and social im/mobilities in the Congolese Copperbelt. His analysis of the evolution of Katangese social space shows how the relative values of social, cultural and economic capital have changed over the last decades, as the promises of upward mobility through education have somewhat faded. His ethnography focuses on the postcolonial trajectory of two socio-professional groups, namely white businessmen and former employees of the state-owned, national mining company (Gécamines). In the late 1990s, the collapse of the national mining company led to a major redistribution of economic opportunities. In this process, white entrepreneurs have mobilized extraverted social networks to forge new economic avenues, while the largely company-bound social capital of Gécamines' workers and managers has left them without many social resources once the company stopped paying them. Yet, following years of unpaid salaries, unequal compensations in cash for former managers on the one hand, and former workers on the other, have led to diverging opportunities for reconversion strategies after the demise of the company.

After the contrapuntal trajectories of white entrepreneurs and public companies' employees in the Copperbelt, Max Bolt's chapter takes us to the South African side of the border with Zimbabwe, where Zimbabwean migrants with different social origins and labour arrangements – some being permanent workers, others much more temporary – engage in agricultural work on large, white-owned farms. Bolt explores both the complexities of social positionality in the black workforce and how they are partly framed by unequal regimes of physical mobility. Migrant seasonal workers' daily mobilities in the border society are in fact more constrained and restrained than the possibilities to move enjoyed by permanent workers, endowed with the legal status and social networks that allow them to live more extraverted lives. Yet, labour hierarchies and unequal mobility regimes do not necessarily translate into unambiguous social hierarchies. For instance, seasonal workers, often with more uncertain, but also more open-ended strategies of social mobility, can also be more educated and retain some sense of 'middle-class' social distance in daily practice, performing a form of abstention from communal life in the barracked world of the farm where permanent workers enjoy the most enviable lifestyle.

We return to West Africa for the last chapter. While retaining an interest in the making of objective conditions of existence, Ben Page departs from the central foci of the volume on education and labour, to explore how different forms of upward social mobility, namely 'state-led, migration-led and business-led', provide useful lenses to explore the boundary-making practices of the now famous 'new African middle classes'. Grounded in empirical work conducted in Buea in south-western Cameroon, where building a house is one of the key ways to assert economic success, his chapter scrutinizes how architecture and home decoration materialize variegated ways to inhabit middle classness. A general 'neophilia' broadly frames these visual materializations of success. Yet, the social trajectories of different types of successful, upwardly mobile individuals also translate into differing displays of social status through architectural achievements and home aesthetics. Finally, beyond 'the public *play* of class' and the staging of social identity, the discourses of the owners of these properties about their intimately invested creations also reveal, hovering in the background of their strategies of social mobility, their quasi-existential quests for social recognition and legitimate personhood.

The chapters will now speak for themselves. From different angles, they will explore how a multidimensional approach to social positionality and social im/mobilities can help to grasp the present, multifaceted changes in African social spaces. In this way, they contribute to theorizing how people navigate the structural constraints which inform their positions and form their grounds for action. How the resulting social im/mobilities represent a key part of what takes place on the continent today seems relatively obvious to us. How critical these issues are to make sense of the current African moment will ultimately be for the reader to decide.

Joël Noret is Associate Professor of Anthropology at the Université libre Bruxelles. He has conducted most of his fieldwork in southern Benin, where he worked on funerals, religious change and the memory of slavery. In the last few years, he has started investigating social inequalities in education, combining ethnography with survey research to explore the making of unequal lives. His publications include *Deuil et Funérailles dans le Bénin Méridional: Enterrer à Tout Prix* (2010), *Mort et Dynamiques Sociales au Katanga* (co-authored with Pierre Petit, 2011), and *Funerals in Africa: Explorations of a Social Phenomenon* (co-edited with Michael Jindra, 2011).

Notes

1. For their diverse contributions to this introduction and/or this volume as a whole, I would like to thank Kate Fayers-Kerr, Sasha Newell, Hannah Hoechner, Corentin Chanet, Benjamin Rubbers, Pierre Petit, Anneke Newman, Ben Page, Inge Tvedten, Claire Mercer and Noémie Marcus, as well as two anonymous reviewers from Berghahn Books. They have all been incredibly generous with their time. Yet, the views expressed here are mine alone, and I remain solely responsible for the arguments conveyed in this text, and for any possible deficiencies.
2. As Crawford Young put it in a review of the literature in the mid-1980s, 'the number of contributions relevant to a consideration of class analysis in Africa now runs into the thousands' (1986: 457). The rough sketch outlined in this introduction is thus inevitably highly selective, its sole ambition being to remind readers of some essential landmarks. In the 1970s and 1980s, entire journal issues were full of these debates, for instance in the *Review of African Political Economy* or *The Journal of Peasant Studies*.

3. Despite an overall decline of Marxist-inspired perspectives in the social sciences, there have been recent vigorous calls to revisit what Marxian views have to offer (for instance Neveling and Steur 2018).
4. Studies of poverty in Africa represent another complex corpus that is hardly touched upon here, despite the important questions it raises and the significant theoretical and epistemological challenges that poverty analysis represents (for instance Jones and Tvedten 2019).
5. Categories of difference are differences organized as 'discrete, bounded, and relatively stable categories' (Brubaker 2015: 11).
6. As class analysis, neopatrimonialism represents a field of research and a space of debate in itself, with significant disagreements on the scope and depth of this regime of political regulation, which cannot be reviewed here.
7. The will to synthesis should not lead to oversimplification, and it is worth noting here that the focus on expense (rather than income) strata can be complemented by minimal characterization of the type of occupation, such as the importance of stable employment (see Bannerjee and Duflo 2008), and the correlative opportunity to invest beyond the satisfaction of necessity. Also, it is worth noting that another current of research has attempted to produce a substantive definition of the middle class, identifying its minimal substance with standards of living (access to electricity and 'flush toilets', that is 'decent housing'), education ('completed secondary schooling'), and occupation ('skilled employment outside the agricultural sector') – even though these scholars recognize that metrics can shift 'over time' (Thurlow, Resnick and Ubogu 2015, Resnick 2015).
8. It should be made clear here that 'space' in a notion like that of 'social space' is used as a metaphor, spatial metaphors being one of the most regular metaphors used by social scientists, from social 'mobility' to social 'distance', social 'dynamics' and social 'movements', to evoke just a few of the most common ones. This of course can (and actually needs to) combine with the analysis of how social distance can be correlated (or not) with geographical/physical distance, and of how social inequalities are spatialized in various ways.
9. Surprisingly, Vigh's reading of Bourdieu rests on the idea that the latter has essentially dealt with the 'stable ground' of 'relatively stable class-structured states' that he himself contrasts with the transience and instability of the Guinea-Bissauan society (Vigh 2009: 426–27). This might be reconsidered in a less 'reproductionist' perspective when one remembers for instance the works on the changing matrimonial market in the Bearn (Bourdieu 2002) or the attention devoted to changing generational circumstances in *Distinction* (Bourdieu 1979).

References

Amin, S. 1973. *Le Développement Inégal*. Paris: Minuit.
Atkinson, W. 2015. *Class*. Cambridge: Polity Press.
Balandier, G. 1955. *Sociologie des Brazzavilles Noires*. Paris: Armand Colin.
_____. 1971. *Les Dynamiques Sociales*. Paris: PUF.
Bannerjee, A.V., and E. Duflo. 2008. 'What is Middle Class about the Middle Classes around the World?', *Journal of Economic Perspectives* 22(2): 3–28.
Bayart, J-F. 1989. *L'Etat en Afrique: La Politique du Ventre*. Paris: Fayard.
_____. 2000. 'Africa in the World: A History of Extraversion', *African Affairs* 99(395): 217–67.

Berry, S. 1985. *Fathers Work for their Sons: Accumulation, Mobility, and Class Formation in an Extended Yoruba Community*. Berkeley: University of California Press.
Bossuroy, T. and D. Cogneau. 2013. 'Social Mobility in Five African Countries', *Review of Income and Wealth* 59(1): 84–110.
Bourdieu, P. 1979. *La Distinction*. Paris: Les Editions de Minuit.
_____. 1984. 'Espace Social et Genèse des Classes', *Actes de la Recherche en Sciences Sociales* 52–53: 3–14.
_____. 1985. 'The Social Space and the Genesis of Groups', *Social Science Information* 24(2): 195–220.
_____. 1986. 'The Forms of Capital', in J. Richardson (ed.), *Handbook of Theory and Research for the Sociology of Education*. New York: Greenwood, pp. 241–58.
_____. 1994. *Raisons Pratiques*. Paris: Seuil.
_____. 2002 [1998]. *Masculine Domination*. Stanford: Stanford University Press.
Brubaker, R. 2015. *Grounds for Difference*. Harvard: Harvard University Press.
Chauvel, L. 2001. 'Le Retour des Classes Sociales?', *Revue de l'OFCE* 79: 315–59.
Clignet, R. 1964. 'Education et Aspirations Professionnelles', *Revue Tiers-Monde* 5(17): 61–82.
Clignet, R., and P. Foster. 1966. *The Fortunate Few: A Study of Secondary Schools and Students in the Ivory Coast*. Evanston, IL: Northwestern University Press.
Cohen, R. 1972. 'Class in Africa: Analytical Problems and Perspectives', *The Socialist Register* 9: 231–55.
Comaroff, J., and J. Comaroff. 2009. *Ethnicity Inc*. Chicago: The University of Chicago Press.
Cooper, E., and D. Pratten. 2015. 'Ethnographies of Uncertainty in Africa: An Introduction', in E. Cooper and D. Pratten (eds), *Ethnographies of Uncertainty in Africa*. New York: Palgrave, pp. 1–16.
Cooper, F. 1981. 'Africa and the World Economy', *African Studies Review* 24(2–3): 1–86.
Cruise O'Brien, D. 1996. 'Youth Identity and State Decline in West Africa', in R. Werbner and T. Ranger (eds), *Postcolonial Identities in Africa*. London: Zed Books, pp. 55–74.
De Boeck, F. 2015. '"Poverty" and the Politics of Syncopation: Urban Examples from Kinshasa (DR Congo)', *Current Anthropology* 56(11): S146–S158.
Devine, F., M. Savage, J. Scott and R. Crompton. 2005. *Rethinking Class: Cultures, Identities and Lifestyles*. London: Palgrave.
Fanon, F. 1961. *Les Damnés de la Terre*. Paris: Maspero.
Fassin, D. 2018. *La Vie: Mode d'Emploi Critique*. Paris: Seuil.
Foster, Philip. 1963. 'Secondary Schooling and Social Mobility in a West African Nation', *Sociology of Education* 37(2): 150–71.
_____. 1965. *Education and Social Change in Ghana*. London: Routledge & Kegan Paul.
Freund, B. 1984. 'Labor and Labor History in Africa: A Review of the Literature', *African Studies Review* 27(2): 1–58.
Fumanti, M. 2016. *The Politics of Distinction: African Elites from Colonialism to Liberation in a Namibian Frontier Town*. Canon Pyon: Sean Kingston Publishing.
Gluckman, M. 1940. 'Analysis of a Social Situation in Modern Zululand', *Bantu Studies* 14: 1–30.

Goldthorpe, J.E. 1955. 'An African Elite: A Sample Survey of Fifty-Two Former Students of Makarere College in East Africa', *The British Journal of Sociology* 6(1): 31–47.

_____. 1965. *An African Elite: Makerere College Students 1922–1960*. Nairobi: Oxford University Press/East African Institute of Social Research.

Goody, J. 1971. *Technology, Tradition, and the State in Africa*. London: Oxford University Press.

_____. 1976. *Production and Reproduction: A Comparative Study of the Domestic Domain*. Cambridge: Cambridge University Press.

Gorski, P. 2013. 'Bourdieu as a Theorist of Change', in P. Gorski (ed.), *Bourdieu and Historical Analysis*. Durham, NC: Duke University Press, pp. 1–18.

Hage, G. 1998. *White Nation: Fantasies of White Supremacy in a Multicultural Society*. Annandale: Pluto Press.

Hansen, K.T. 2005. 'Getting Stuck in the Compound: Some Odds against Social Adulthood in Lusaka, Tanzania', *Africa Today* 51(4): 2–16.

Hart, K. 1973. 'Informal Income Opportunities and Urban Employment in Ghana', *The Journal of Modern African Studies* 11(1): 61–89.

Hilgers, M. 2011. 'Autochthony as Capital in a Global Age', *Theory, Culture & Society* 28(1): 24–54.

Hilgers, M., and E. Mangez. 2015. 'Afterword: Theory of Fields in the Postcolonial Age', in M. Hilgers and E. Mangez (eds), *Bourdieu's Theory of Social Fields: Concepts and Applications*. London: Routledge, pp. 257–73.

Honwana, A. 2012. *The Time of Youth: Work, Social Change and Politics in Africa*. Boulder: Kumarian Press.

Johnson-Hanks, J. 2006. *Uncertain Honor: Modern Motherhood in an African Crisis*. Chicago: The University of Chicago Press.

Jones, S., and I. Tvedten. 2019. 'What Does it Mean to Be Poor? Investigating the Qualitative-Quantitative Divide in Mozambique', *World Development* 117: 153–66.

Lambert, S., M. Ravallion and D. van de Walle. 2014. 'Intergenerational Mobility and Interpersonal Inequality in an African Economy', *Journal of Development Economics* 110: 327–44.

Lentz, C. 2015. *Elites or Middle Classes? Lessons from Transnational Research for the Study of Social Stratification in Africa*. Mainz: Working Papers of the Department of Anthropology and African Studies.

Little, K. 1953. 'The Study of "Social Change" in British West Africa', *Africa* 23(4): 274–84.

Lloyd, P.C. (ed.). 1966. *The New Elites of Tropical Africa*. London: Oxford University Press.

Mains, D. 2007. 'Neoliberal Times: Progress, Boredom, and Shame among Young Men in Urban Ethiopia', *American Ethnologist* 34(4): 659–73.

Masquelier, A. 2013. 'Teatime: Boredom and the Temporalities of Young Men in Niger', *Africa* 83(3): 470–91.

Meagher, K. 2006. 'Social Capital, Social Liabilities, and the Political Capital: Social Networks and Informal Manufacturing in Nigeria', *African Affairs* 105(421): 553–82.

_____. 2010. *Identity Economics: Social Networks and the Informal Economy in Nigeria*. Woodbridge: James Currey.

Melber, H. 2017. 'The African Middle Class(es) – In the Middle of What?', *Review of African Political Economy* 151: 142–54.

Mercer, C. 2018. 'Boundary Work: Becoming Middle Class in Suburban Dar es Salaam', *International Journal of Urban and Regional Research*, early view 18 Dec. 2018: 1–16. DOI:10.1111/1468-2427.12733

Mercier, P. 1954. 'Aspects des Problèmes de Stratification Sociale dans l'Ouest Africain', *Cahiers Internationaux de Sociologie* 17: 47–65.

_____. 1956. 'Un Essai d'Enquête par Questionnaire dans la Ville de Dakar', in D. Forde (dir.), *Aspects Sociaux de l'Industrialisation et de l'Urbanisation en Afrique au Sud du Sahara*. Paris: UNESCO, pp. 543–56.

_____. 1960. 'Etude du Mariage et Enquête Urbaine', *Cahiers d'Etudes Africaines* 1 (1): 28–43.

Mitchell, J.C. 1956. *The Kalela Dance: Aspects of Social Relationships among the Urban Africans in Northern Rhodesia*. Manchester: Manchester University Press.

_____. 1966. *Tribalism and the Plural Society: An Inaugural Lecture Given in the University College of Rhodesia and Nyasaland*. Salisbury: University College of Rhodesia.

Mitchell, J.C., and A.L. Epstein. 1959. 'Occupational Prestige and Social Status among Urban Africans in Northern Rhodesia', *Africa* 29: 22–40.

Moore, S.F. 1994. *Anthropology and Africa: Changing Perspectives on a Changing Scene*. Charlottesville: University Press of Virginia.

Nadel, S.F. 1956. 'The Concept of Social Elites', *International Social Science Bulletin* 8: 413–24.

Neveling, P., and L. Steur. 2018. 'Marxian Anthropology Resurgent', *Focaal: Journal of Global and Historical Anthropology* 82: 1–15.

Newell, S. 2012. *The Modernity Bluff: Crime, Consumption, and Citizenship in Côte d'Ivoire*. Chicago: The University of Chicago Press.

Pelckmans, L. 2012. '"Having a Road": Social and Spatial Mobility of Persons of Slave and Mixed Descent in Post-Independence Central Mali', *Journal of African History* 53(2): 235–55.

Ralph, M. 2008. 'Killing Time', *Social Text* 26(4): 1–29.

Resnick, D. 2015. 'The Political Economy of Africa's Emergent Middle Class: Retrospect and Prospects', *Journal of International Development* 27: 573–87.

Rizzo, M. 2017. *Taken for a Ride: Grounding Neoliberalism, Precarious Labour, and the Public Transport in an African Metropolis*. Oxford: Oxford University Press.

Rizzo, M., B. Kilama and M. Wuyts. 2015. 'The Invisibility of Wage Employment in Statistics on the Informal Economy in Africa: Causes and Consequences', *The Journal of Development Studies* 51(2): 149–61.

Rodney, W. 1972. *How Europe Underdeveloped Africa*. London and Dar es Salaam: Bogle - L'Ouverture Publications and Tanzania Publishing House.

Rossi, B. 2009. 'Slavery and Migration: Physical and Social Mobility in Ader', in B. Rossi (ed.), *Reconfiguring Slavery: West African Trajectories*. Liverpool: Liverpool University Press, pp. 182–206.

Savage, M. et al. 2015a. *Social Class in the 21st Century*. London: Pelican.

_____. 2015b. 'On Social Class, Anno 2014', *Sociology* 49(6): 1011–30.

Scharrer, T., D. O'Kane and L. Kroeker. 2018. 'Africa's Middle Classes in Critical Perspective', in L. Kroeker, D. O'Kane and T. Scharrer (eds), *Middle Classes in Africa: Changing Lives and Conceptual Challenges*. New York: Palgrave, pp. 1–31.

Schumaker, L. 2001. *Africanizing Anthropology: Fieldwork, Networks, and the Making of Cultural Knowledge in Central Africa*. Durham, NC and London: Duke University Press.

Simone, A. 2004. 'People as Infrastructure: Intersecting Fragments in Johannesburg', *Public Culture* 16(3): 407–29.

Sklar, R.K. 1979. 'The Nature of Class Domination in Africa', *The Journal of Modern African Studies* 17(4): 531–52.

Southall, R. 2018. '(Middle-) Class Analysis in Africa: Does it Work?', *Review of African Political Economy* 157: 467–77.

Spronk, R. 2014. 'Exploring the Middle Classes in Nairobi: From Modes of Production to Modes of Sophistication', *African Studies Review* 57(1): 93–114.

Thurlow, J., D. Resnick and D. Ubogu. 2015. 'Matching Concepts with Measurement: Who Belongs to Africa's Middle Class?', *Journal of International Development* 27: 588–608.

UNESCO. 1956. *African Elites*, special issue of the *International Social Science Bulletin* 8(3).

Vigh, H. 2009. 'Motion Squared: A Second Look at the Concept of Social Navigation', *Anthropological Theory* 9(4): 419–38.

Wallerstein, I.M. 1974. *The Modern World-System*. New York: Academic Press.

Werbner, R. 2004. *Reasonable Radicals and Citizenship in Botswana: The Public Anthropology of Kalanga Elites*. Bloomington: Indiana University Press.

Wright, E.O. 2005. 'Foundations of a Neo-Marxist Class Analysis', in E.O. Wright (ed.), *Approaches to Class Analysis*. Cambridge: Cambridge University Press, pp. 4–30.

Young, C. 1986. 'Nationalism, Ethnicity and Class in Africa: A Retrospective', *Cahiers d'Etudes Africaines* 26(103): 421–95.

Chapter 1

Inequality from Up Close
Qur'anic Students in Northern Nigeria Working as
Domestics

Hannah Hoechner

In the Service of the Better-Off

Aminu enters the courtyard, a bulging black plastic bag in hand. The
boy, in his early teens, greets politely and bows as he hands the bag over
to a woman, visibly in charge of the house, then remains forward-bent,
waiting for a sign of dismissal from her, while she inspects the contents
of the bag. She, however, starts querying him: he bought only onions?
How dare he bring her only onions? Is she supposed to eat onions on
their own? Aminu bends further forward as he apologizes in a low
voice, explaining that he had been told to buy onions. The woman orders
Aminu, who is still bent over, to instantly buy her tomatoes, chilies and
peppers. She is about to turn her back on him when he summons the
courage to point out that he will be late for his Qur'an class if he returns
to the market now, and that his teacher will not be pleased. Will she
please give permission for him to leave? At this point, the woman's fury
boils over: time for Qur'an class? How dare he tell her it's time for class
now that he starts looking well-fed! He is only jealous of her children,
who at this very moment are studying in school. Dropping the plastic
bag full of onions forcefully at Aminu's feet, she tells the boy in a scath-
ing voice that his parents have failed, sending him away like this to earn
his own upkeep, and that he better immediately buy the remaining vegetables. With that said, she turns on her heel, leaving a desperate-looking

---

Notes for this chapter begin on page 45.

Aminu behind who now needs to find a way out of his dilemma on his own.

Aminu's real name is Ikiramatu, and together with eight other classical Qur'anic school students, or *almajirai* as they are called in Hausa, northern Nigeria's lingua franca, he wrote the script for the film scene described here. The woman is a professional actress whom we engaged (with funds from the Goethe Institute Kano, which supported our 'participatory' film project) to play a spiteful employer of *almajirai*. The storyline is fictional; the characters are acted. Yet, both storyline and characters are also to some extent real. Ikiramatu, the protagonist, is an expert domestic worker, who has been employed in various households in the neighbourhood since his arrival at the Qur'anic school there. The grievances depicted in the film scene (albeit in somewhat overstated, 'movie-like' fashion) correspond to the *almajirai*'s actual grievances about their relationships with the better-off people in the urban neighbourhoods of their schools. The boys and young men I conducted my research with felt that the better-off in society often treat *almajirai* condescendingly. Most *almajirai* are from poor rural peasant families and have a low status in the urban areas where they come to study. For many urban dwellers, they epitomize the alleged 'backwardness' of the rural poor.[1] They stand for a lack of family planning and 'oversized' families unable to care for all their children. They are also taken to symbolize the presumed disinterest and even hostility of the rural poor for 'modern' education. The emergence of 'modern' Islamic schools has, moreover, led many to doubt whether the *almajiri* system is still able to provide an appropriate religious education today.

Many *almajirai* are highly mobile and both individual students and entire schools move between urban and rural areas in accordance with agricultural work cycles. This chapter is interested in the experiences the *almajirai* have in urban areas. Even though far from all urban schools of *almajirai* are in 'rich' neighbourhoods, most students will, throughout their sojourns in urban areas, come into contact with people from more privileged segments of society, not least because such households are more likely to afford domestic workers. Despite the risk of bad treatment, many young *almajirai* seek domestic employment.

Most *almajiri* schools, where boys and young men from primary school age to their early twenties live with a Qur'anic teacher or *malam* to study the Qur'an, do not have the means to provide for their students' upkeep. This means students must earn their own living. While older students wash clothes, carry loads and engage in petty trade or handicrafts, younger students have few options to earn a living in urban areas but to beg for food and money in their neighbourhoods and on the streets – or to accept work as domestics.

Domestic Work and the Social Space

Domestic work arrangements bring people at opposite ends of the socio-economic spectrum intimately close together, and thus reverse trends towards the increasing spatial segregation of different socio-economic strata, as they are spurred for instance by processes of gentrification and ghettoization. According to Dickey, 'domestic service interactions constitute the most intense, sustained contact with members of other classes that most of their participants encounter' (2000: 463). What is more, domestic work arrangements matter for a number of what Bujra (2000: 4) calls 'class projects'. Arguably, domestic service contributes to the reproduction of class relations not only materially – when the work of domestics is appropriated – but also symbolically in that having domestics serves to display a particular class status. Dickey for example argues about South Asia that domestic service 'provides one of the clearest markers of class distinctions. The ability to hire servants is a sign of having achieved middle- or upper-class status' (2000: 466). Through domestic service interactions, members of different strata negotiate, enact and potentially contest their relative positions within society. By looking at domestic work arrangements, we can trace how reduced physical distance affects the social, emotional and economic distance between members of different segments of society.

While 'class' thus is a powerful lens through which to consider domestic work arrangements, we cannot apprehend them fully if we do not also pay attention to the roles played by other vectors of social division, such as gender, race/ethnicity, rural/urban origin, age or religion. Some of these factors have received a considerable amount of scholarly attention, including in the African context. Gender and race or ethnicity have been the focus of studies of domestic work for example in Eastern and Southern Africa, where often European and Asian households have employed both African women and men as domestic workers (see e.g. Bujra 2000, Cock 1980, Gaitskell et al. 1983, Hansen 1986).[2] In the case of the *almajirai*, employers and domestic workers are of the same ethnicity. Ethnicity is thus not a pertinent characteristic in this context. Gender is, though, as domestic work is a predominantly female activity in northern Nigeria. Having to perform 'female' work, moreover under the authority of women, adds to the *almajirai*'s discontent about their domestic work roles (see Hoechner 2014a).

The burgeoning literature on childhood and youth has laid emphasis on the fact that many domestic workers are children, thus bringing the age hierarchies structuring domestic work arrangements to the fore, including in the African context (Jacquemin 2004, Klocker 2011, Thorsen 2012). UNICEF estimates that at the turn of the century, child domestic workers constituted 'the largest group of child workers in the world' (1999: 2). Many children possess the skills required for domestic work because they carry out similar tasks in their own homes (e.g. Bourdillon 2009). They are likely to work for lower pay and be more malleable than adult employees (e.g. Klocker 2011). This is also true in the case of the *almajirai*, whose employers often wield powers similar to those a parent would have over her/his children (see Hoechner 2014b).

Alongside 'class' or socio-economic status, gender and age are thus fairly well established categories in the analysis of domestic work arrangement. Building on this work, this chapter explores factors also influencing the *almajirai*'s domestic work relationships that have been less prominent in the literature. One of them is religion. The *almajirai*'s identities as religious students matter enormously for their employment relationships as religion provides these boys with a vocabulary with which to make claims on their employers and other potential 'benefactors'. Religion also supplies them with an idiom to evaluate critically the treatment they receive and to pass judgement on employers they consider to be stingy. Conversely, *almajiri* education has lost some of its sway today with the rise of Islamic reformist movements and the 'modern' forms of Islamic schooling promoted by these. Reformist Islamic ideas receive support especially in urban areas, which is also where most 'modern' Islamic schools are located. Many urban dwellers consider the religious practices and beliefs of the rural population as 'traditionalist'. In this context, urban employers can play on the waning legitimacy of *almajiri* education as they limit the material contributions they make to the system and its students.

Finally, this chapter also pays attention to the role of rural/urban divides and of educational status for domestic work arrangements. Rural/urban and educational divides and a generalized condescension towards poor rural peasants without exposure to 'modern' education matter in two ways. Firstly, they make it possible for the *almajirai*'s urban employers to conceive of themselves as accomplishing a 'civilizing' mission by employing *almajirai*. Secondly, they matter for the self-definitions and future aspirations the *almajirai* come to embrace. Having been in close contact with urban households, many of them come to aspire to 'cosmopolitan' lifestyles which are very much at odds not only with the frugal and ascetic ethos their schools seek to instil, but also with their realistic life chances. Most *almajirai* are unable to act upon their 'cosmopolitan' aspirations. This draws attention to the ways in which domestic work can shape not only material opportunities but also aspirations and imaginaries (see e.g. Thorsen 2012: 10), leaving young people trapped between high-flying hopes and highly limited opportunities.

The various vectors of social divisions sketched out here are of course not static. As the *almajirai* come of age, and transition from the category of 'boys' into that of 'young men', inevitably the terms of their participation in domestic work relations change. For young men, it becomes inappropriate to enter the compound of another man, putting an end to most domestic work arrangements. As hinted at above, 'religion' is not a static variable either. Islamic reform movements – which challenge the religious legitimacy of the *almajiri* system – garner increasing support in northern Nigeria, to the effect that the *almajirai*'s religious discourses progressively lose their sway.

How can we conceptualize the social dynamics underpinning domestic work relationships like those of the *almajirai* in a way that acknowledges these different vectors as well as their interactions and their evolution over time? The Bourdieusian notion of a multidimensional 'social space' can provide a conceptual starting point. It seeks to capture people's endowment with different forms of economic, cultural, social and symbolic 'capital' which, in turn, allow people to appropriate certain 'scarce goods' (Bourdieu 1989: 16–17). The metaphor of a multidimensional 'space' makes it possible to take into account various different axes of social division simultaneously, to imagine an infinite number of social positions (thus safeguarding against the reification of social identities), and to envisage that over time people 'move' through space as the quantity, composition – or value – of their 'capital' changes. This chapter explores the domestic work performed by Qur'anic students in northern Nigeria through the notion of 'social space', paying particular attention to how not only socioeconomic status, age and gender, but also religion and rural/urban and educational divides shape this space.

The next section elaborates how the data was collected. After that, I take a closer look at the literature on child domestic workers in West Africa and explore the specificity of the domestic work performed by the *almajirai* in this context. The second part of the chapter sheds light on the *almajirai*'s experiences of their domestic work roles, paying particular attention to how religion, rural origins and differential access to education structure the domestic work encounter. It also sketches the *almajirai*'s likely economic futures, highlighting tensions between aspirations and available opportunities.

Methods and Data

This chapter builds on thirteen months of fieldwork carried out in Kano
State in northern Nigeria between 2009 and 2011 with current and former
almajirai, their parents and caregivers, teachers, and employers. My fieldwork included four months in Albasu, a small rural town in Albasu
Local Government Area (LGA) in the east of Kano State. Albasu, largely
dependent on agriculture, is among the poorest areas in Kano State. For
the remaining nine months, I lived close to the city gate Sabuwar Kofa
within Kano's Old City. I collected data in the form of fieldwork observations, semi-structured interviews, group conversations and casual
interactions.

My data also includes material from 'participatory' research, e.g.
discussions of the photographs that young *almajirai* took with dispos-
able cameras, and 'radio interviews' they conducted amongst each other
with my tape recorder. In addition, I draw on data from the production process of a 'participatory' documentary film/docu-drama, which
I organized during my research about the perspectives of *almajirai* on
their lives and the challenges they face. This includes stories narrated or
written down during the script writing process, as well as discussions
about the way they would like to see their lives and identities represented
on screen. The nine participating youths were aged between fifteen and
twenty years and came from three different Qur'anic schools in which I
had previously taught English.[3]

If the *almajirai* get more of a hearing in the pages to follow than their
employers, this is firstly an effect of my data. I collected data on employers' views and behaviours during over a year of ethnographic fieldwork
largely 'along the way'. Data with *almajirai* on the other hand was collected through a wide range of methods, including participatory methods, which generated powerful and nuanced insights into their concerns.
Secondly, perspectives on domestic work arrangements are necessarily
subjective. This chapter is interested in showing the *almajirai*'s perspectives. The next section embeds the *almajirai*'s experiences within the wider
context of child domestic work in West Africa.

Child Domestic Work in West Africa

West Africa has a long history of children working in households other
than their own. In fosterage arrangements, children are placed with
members of the extended family or other acquainted adults. Children

are 'circulated' for a number of reasons: to provide childless households with children, to reinforce bonds between different households, so they can attend school or pursue apprenticeships, to facilitate their acquisition of housekeeping skills (girls), or for 'character training' (Bledsoe 1990, Goody 1982, Hashim 2005, Jonckers 1997, Notermans 2008, Pilon 2003). Fosterage serves 'to distribute the economic costs and benefits of children' (Bledsoe 1990: 74). Most fostered children are expected to perform certain domestic and other tasks for their guardians, for which they or their parents receive material and symbolic support from the foster household.

The historical practice of fosterage to procure domestic workers has undergone considerable transformation over recent decades and has given way to commodified and market-based arrangements. Arguably, today many households in West Africa eschew the reciprocal relationships underpinning fosterage arrangements. The labour of fostered children is not free, as Jacquemin (2009: 13) notes for example for Côte d'Ivoire: 'the reciprocity expected has a considerable financial cost in a period of recession and also has a high symbolic cost'. According to her, today many urban households therefore 'prefer to employ an unrelated girl that they pay a salary as this is much cheaper ... than using the services of a "little niece"' (ibid.). In many cases the distinction between familial and employment relationships is kept deliberately blurry (Jacquemin 2004, Klocker 2011, Thorsen 2012).

In some cases, domestic service can open up access to economic, social or cultural capital for young workers. Employers may for instance pay school fees, provide support during difficult circumstances, or help their domestic workers find better-paying jobs as they grow older (Thorsen 2012, Wasiuzzaman and Wells 2010). These potentially positive effects should, however, not detract our attention away from the fact that for many young domestic workers, the changes described above have resulted in poor and precarious working conditions.

The large majority of young domestic workers in West Africa – an estimated 80 per cent – are girls (Thorsen 2012: 4). In northern Nigeria, on the other hand, mostly young male Qur'anic students are employed as domestic workers. While girls may be fostered to members of the extended family, female live-in domestic workers without family connections, as they can be found in the households of the better-off in other parts of West Africa, are rare. Concerns about protecting female sexuality play a role in this. What is more, given the ubiquity of classical Qur'anic schools, *almajirai* constitute an alternative readily available pool of cheap labour for domestic tasks. The next section presents the *almajirai* and their education system in more depth.

Qur'anic Students in Northern Nigeria

The *almajirai* live with a Qur'anic teacher, often for several years, learning to read, write and recite the Qur'an. 'Modern'/secular subjects do not form part of their curriculum, and specialized Islamic fields of study other than the Qur'an are the preserve of advanced learners. Most classical Qur'anic schools operate informally and outside the purview of the state. Teachers receive no salary but live off the support given by the local community, the alms received in exchange for their spiritual services, the contributions of their students and supplementary income-generating activities. Most teachers are themselves products of the classical Qur'anic education system. The classical Qur'anic education system exists primarily in the Sahel and follows the seasonal rhythms of the region in that individual students, and entire schools, migrate in accordance with agricultural work cycles.

The *almajiri* system once catered primarily to boys and young men from privileged households. However, changes during the past century increasingly relegated the system to the economic, social and political margins. The introduction of 'modern' education by the British, who conquered what is today northern Nigeria at the beginning of the twentieth century, gradually undermined the religious scholars' 'monopoly over literacy' and thus their access to prestige, positions and resources (Umar 2001: 129). Upon independence in 1960, the first generation of modern-educated Muslims inherited power from the British.

Profound changes in the political economy during the colonial period also altered the social recruitment base of the Qur'anic education system. The gradual ending of slavery, which had been a central pillar of economic life in Hausaland until then (see Lovejoy and Hogendorn 1993), created novel opportunities for social mobility for freed slaves, many of whom turned to religious education as an avenue to a higher status (Last 1993: 120; cf. Ware 2014: 163–64 on Senegal). What is more, with slave labour becoming unavailable, households struggled to produce enough grain to feed all their members during the agriculturally idle dry season. Under these circumstances, more teachers and students left their homes during the dry season to move to urban areas (see e.g. Smith 1954: 132).

Socio-economic change during the second half of the twentieth century contributed to the transformation of the *almajiri* system from a high-status education system into a system mostly catering to the rural poor. Since the 1970s the income of students and teachers has declined as more affluent Muslims, swayed by Islamic reformism and the individualization of society, have increasingly ceased to support the system through alms and accommodation, and as those segments of society still endorsing it were hard hit by the economic downturn in the aftermath of the oil boom of the 1970s and by structural adjustment that began in 1986 (e.g. Ya'u 2000).

Today, classical Qur'anic school students have become the subject of much public concern across West Africa in the context of increased attempts to achieve universal primary education and concerns about child welfare. Children's rights' advocates tag them as 'abandoned,' 'trafficked' and 'exploited' (Perry 2004). The push by Islamic reform movements for the formalization of religious learning has put classical Qur'anic schools under strain to assert their legitimacy (e.g. Ware 2014). Today, many Muslim parents educate their children in 'modern' Islamic educational institutions (called *Islamiyya* schools in Nigeria, or *écoles franco-arabes* e.g. in Senegal). In Nigeria, the presumed role of Qur'anic schools as recruitment grounds for radical groups has become a recurrent theme in the context of the Boko Haram crisis.

Meanwhile, demand for *almajiri* education persists. The decline of the rural economy due to the oil boom and structural adjustment combined with the onset of massive demographic growth in Nigeria, with the population more than quadrupling since 1950 (United Nations 2009). This has contributed to the perpetuation of both poverty and educational disadvantage, especially in rural areas. While basic education is officially free, in reality it implies recurrent costs: for textbooks, writing materials and uniforms, as well as in the form of opportunity costs of foregone children's work. 'Investing' in 'modern' schooling is both burdensome and risky in a context where the pay-offs of 'modern' education in terms of future opportunities are more than uncertain, especially as the 'modern' education available to poor rural children is of extremely poor quality (Johnson 2008).

In addition to the difficulties families face in accessing quality education, poverty also matters more directly for *almajiri* enrolments in the sense that some families struggle to feed all of their members. Enrolling children as *almajirai* alleviates the subsistence burden of poor peasant households. At the same time, parents do not lose their sons' labour force completely when they enrol them as *almajirai*, as *almajirai* can be (and frequently are) summoned back home during the farming season to help. In a context of limited alternatives, a high regard for Qur'anic learning, and belief in the educational value of a certain degree of hardship for the social and moral training of children underpin families' decisions to send their children to live as *almajirai* in the urban centres (e.g. Last 2000, Ware 2014, and below).

An Employment Relationship Fraught with Tensions

As Qur'anic students who come to town first and foremost to pursue their religious education, the *almajirai* used to be the habitual recipients of alms, and townspeople could gain religious standing by supporting them. Yet, as the religious merit of the classical Qur'anic education system has increasingly come under attack by those calling for Islamic reform and the modernization of Islamic education, the *almajirai*'s role as legitimate recipients, and even claimants, of charity is being redefined (see below). It has become largely impossible today for *almajirai* to survive on charity alone. Begging, moreover, exposes *almajirai* to abuse. Almost all *almajirai* have already been insulted and chased away when begging. Some even describe physical assaults. Domestic work for neighbouring households can constitute a comparably easy way of earning money.

Socio-economic inequalities, educational change and strict female seclusion (*purdah*) across the social spectrum in Kano foster demand for children's labour (see Robson 2004, Schildkrout 2002). As many women are largely confined to their compounds, children make the daily activities of the household possible. Unencumbered by the gender norms restricting the movements of adults, they can be called upon to clean, shop or run errands. The fact that most of the urban households that can afford to do so educate their own children in 'modern' secular (*boko*) and 'modern' Islamic (*Islamiyya*) schools today reinforces the demand for the labour of the *almajirai*. During schooldays, children of school age are away for most of the morning and afternoon. 'We, that's the time we are free', says Ibrahim, Ikiramatu's schoolmate at Sabuwar Ƙofa, explaining the timetable of their Qur'anic school. Most classical Qur'anic schools hold sessions early in the morning right after the dawn prayer, then break to let their students pursue their morning work obligations. Many schools have another session in the late morning, but then go on break over lunch time and resume sessions only in the late afternoon or at night, when the day's work is done (cf. Bano et al. 2011).

Some households establish durable relationships with individual *almajirai*, who may be in charge of washing and ironing clothes, of cleaning around the house, of fetching water each day, and of doing the daily shopping. Others employ *almajirai* on an ad-hoc basis for all sorts of odd jobs and errands, e.g. to catch run-away chickens, to repair a mud wall that has crumbled under the rain or to clear out a blocked sewer. *Almajirai* are also engaged to provide basic spiritual services. They say prayers/supplications, recite Qur'anic verses, or fabricate 'potions' (*rubutun sha*), which aim to improve the fortunes of a particular employer or household. Almost all *almajirai* I met had some experience working as domestics.

Towards the end of puberty, however, gender norms governing adult behaviour begin to apply fully, highlighting how the *almajirai*'s position within the 'social space' changes over time. Young men then stop entering the houses of other men and seek other forms of employment. But until that age, domestic employment is one of the most accessible ways of earning a living, or of earning at least an occasional meal or a place to sleep in a neighbour's entrance room. As many schools lack facilities to shelter all of their students, young *almajirai* may have little choice but to seize such bargains. Many *almajirai* do not receive a regular wage for the domestic services they provide, but have to content themselves with donations in kind.

Unfortunately, these work arrangements are often anything but a happy symbiosis between the *almajirai* and the households in the neighbourhoods of their schools. As indicated in the introduction to this chapter, for the *almajirai* in my research, their relationship with urban employers was a major source of frustration. They felt their employers paid them too little and asked for too much of their time, they treated them as 'labour power' rather than as human beings, and did not assume (enough) responsibility for the provision of care when they fell ill or wished to further their education (see Hoechner 2014b).

A first reason for the *almajirai*'s frustration lies in the fact that they and their employers have different expectations for their relationship. The *almajirai* seek to establish long-term, intimate personal relationships akin to patronage and even family-like bonds, which hold the promise of longer-term livelihood support. The latter, by contrast, assume more ambiguous positions. Employers benefit from vague arrangements, e.g. regarding working hours and pay, which are possible within more personalized arrangements. At the same time, limiting their commitment to cash-for-service exchanges allows them to eschew longer-term obligations (for a more extensive discussion, see Hoechner 2014b). For some households, this may be a necessity given their own constrained resources; others may conceive of the *almajirai* simply as being beyond the scope of their responsibilities. Also, with changing definitions of what an appropriate religious education is, fewer people think it worthwhile to support and sustain the *almajiri* system on religious grounds (see below). Finally, given their young age and the vast supply of potential domestic servants, the *almajirai* are in a rather weak bargaining position vis-à-vis their employers.

How does the *almajirai*'s specific position within the 'social space' shape their experiences of domestic work? The remainder of this chapter explores this question, paying particular attention to the roles that their (contested) religious identities as well as their rural origins and educational status play with regard to how the *almajirai* experience domestic work, and how they relate to their employers. It has been argued that the juxtaposition of a spatial and emotional intimacy resulting from a worker's integration into his employers' private space and a distance resulting from class and other hierarchies triggers a 'dynamic of self-other contrast' as ways must be found to justify workplace hierarchies (Adams and Dickey 2000: 2–3, 17). As we will see in the following, ideas about what it means to be moral, pious or 'civilized' play an important role in contestations over the relative status of both sides (see e.g. Bujra 2000: 134ff on the 'micro-politics of domestic employment' in Tanzania).

Looking at Domestic Work Arrangements through the Lens of Religion

How does religion matter for the *almajirai*'s experiences of domestic work? In this section I argue that it provides the interpretative framework through which the Qur'anic students both justify their own presence in the urban areas they move to, and the support they expect from other members of society. What is more, they evaluate the treatment they receive from others, including from their employer-patrons, through a religious framework.

In a context where for many people the term *almajiri* has negative connotations, the *almajirai* in my research endeavoured to emphasize their religious credentials, and to portray themselves as *matafiyi mai neman ilimi*, those who have left their homes in search of knowledge. Some *almajirai* told me that the syllable AL in *almajiri* stood for Allah, whereas MA was short for the Prophet Muhammad, and JIRI for the angel Jibril. This interpretation does not reflect the word's actual etymology – the word *almajiri* derives from the Arabic term *al-muhajir* (migrant), a term echoing the Prophet's *hijrah* from Mecca to Medina. Yet, this interpretation shows how eagerly the *almajirai* sought to embrace pious self-conceptions.

To some extent, the *almajirai* perceived themselves to be trained to be more strictly practising Muslims than other people, as evidenced for example by Buhari's (early twenties) comments on the role of Qur'anic schools in ensuring that students pray regularly: if children stay with their parents, Buhari argued, prayer time comes and goes, and children keep roaming about. No one makes them say their prayers. *Almajirai*, on the other hand, would be beaten if they are late for prayer. The boys/young men involved in the film-making, with whom I spent long stretches of time, persisted with their fast during Ramadan even when feeling ill, added voluntary fasting days outside Ramadan and were unlikely to be late for any of their daily prayers.

As religious students, the *almajirai* can conceive of themselves as legitimate recipients and even claimants of charity and support, meaning that they can assess the treatment they receive in religious terms. This was particularly apparent in the context of their begging where a religious interpretation of begging helped them to maintain some self-respect in the face of denigrating treatment. Danjuma (aged fifteen) for example argued that 'some people think ... you come out to beg [because you don't have food in your house]. But it's not like that; it's because you're searching for knowledge'.

Recourse to religion thus helped the *almajirai* justify their begging, which is often disparaged in northern Nigeria. Yet, religion also offered them a vocabulary with which to pass judgement more widely on better-off Muslims, who often fail to provide the support the *almajirai* feel they deserve. In our film, for example, the *almajirai* criticize their domestic employers for not treating them with the respect and generosity appropriate to the 'religious mission' they are on. After some time of absence from work due to an injury, the protagonist Aminu visits his female employer to plead with her to let him take up his work again. When she sneeringly tells him that she has no intention of taking him back, he informs her composedly: 'what I want you to know, we also have people who care about us. To search for knowledge, that's why we've left our parents. That's why you see us struggling like this'.

The *almajirai* I got to know during my research accused those denying them support and respect of lacking religious knowledge. One *almajiri* at Sabuwar Ƙofa (aged fifteen) argued in a 'radio interview' that *almajirai* in urban areas are treated worse than in rural areas because 'most of the village people are [Qur'anic] teachers, they know the Qur'an and its importance very well. In Kano, some of them are illiterate. They only have the *boko* ['modern' secular] studies'.

The *almajirai* also stressed that the pious-minded ought to support them generously, not merely out of pity, but for fear of God. Bashir (aged eighteen) and Nura (aged about nineteen) for example equated supporting *almajirai* with having strong faith – and a failure to do so with a lack thereof:

Bashir: In Nigeria, how many *almajirai* do the rich take responsibility for?
Nura: Actually, the rich in Nigeria, not all of them have faith [*imani*]. Out of a hundred, you can only get 1% that have faith.

Unsurprisingly, the *almajirai*'s employers did not see their relationship with the Qur'anic students in quite the same light as the boys concerned. The wider religious context in northern Nigeria is important to consider in this regard. As hinted at above, the classical Qur'anic schools of the *almajiri* system have been the subject of fervent controversies and harsh critiques by reform-oriented Muslims who see the system as a cultural aberration and distortion of Islam (see Hoechner 2014a). Islam permits begging only in acute emergencies, they claim. Bambale (2007: 7), lecturer at Bayero University Kano, for example, accuses the *malamai* of the *almajiri* system of having 'misunderstood or manipulated' Islamic injunctions 'to suit their personal needs'. This resulted in 'an atmosphere of unnecessary begging among a vast number of people including those that are not even almagirai [*sic*] or needy' (ibid.: 8). The *almajirai*, as other powerless groups, are at the receiving end of arguments about religious differences. The youths involved in the film project, for example, told me about the followers of the Islamic reform movement *Izala* that 'if an *almajiri* begs at their house, they don't give to him, they might even beat him'.

Even people not otherwise sympathetic to the reformist agenda have come to doubt whether the hardships and deprivations of an *almajiri* education are appropriate to the religious upbringing of the young. Most of the urbanites who can afford it prefer to educate their children in secular and 'modern' Islamic schools (*Islamiyya* schools) today. In this context, support for the *almajiri* system has been dwindling. The people housing or employing *almajirai* I interacted with sometimes interpreted their actions as a means of honouring their religious commitments through 'facilitating' the *almajirai*'s religious studies. More often though, they presented it as a way of taking responsibility for the 'needy', and thus a sign of their own 'largesse'. Not many subscribed to the *almajirai*'s claim that offering them generous support was a religious duty.

The better-off employers of *almajirai* with whom I interacted frequently cast themselves as granting rather than seizing opportunities when I asked them about the *almajirai* in their households. Some people support *almajirai* unconditionally. Yet, most *almajirai* are expected to reciprocate the 'charity' they receive in some way or the other, be it through prayers for a 'benefactor's' advantage or the provision of other spiritual services, or by carrying out domestic work. In one scene in our film, two upper-class women discuss their opinions on *almajirai*. One of them states: 'their parents grew tired of them, they farm, grow food, sell it to us, then they send their children and want us to feed them?'

While the protagonist of the film Aminu is providing crucial services to her household, his employer dismisses this, and casts their relationship as one in which she is expected to feed him magnanimously. Surely, this scene caricatures upper-class behaviour. Nonetheless, it originates from a shared understanding between the *almajirai* and the professional actresses involved, of how some people define themselves vis-à-vis the *almajirai* working for them: notably as 'philanthropists' rather than as partners to a labour contract.

Rural Origins, Urbane Aspirations

What difference does it make to the *almajirai*'s experiences of domestic work that they originate mostly from poor, rural, peasant households with little exposure to 'modern' education and that they sustain continued links with these? As indicated above, the *almajiri* system chimes well with the seasonal work rhythms of peasant households, and many boys spend the months of the agriculturally active rainy season away from school to help their parents or teachers farm. Yet, by going away, the *almajirai* put their employment status at risk: many a boy comes back to find his job has been taken by someone else during his absence.

Yet, their rural origins also matter in more subtle ways. Rurality connotes negatively for most urban dwellers. Frequently, the *almajirai* are labelled backward, gullible and dirty. Tellingly, Aminu's employer in our film admonishes him when he first comes to her house and is offered employment on the condition that 'from now on, you'll bathe, and wash your clothes, so you too look like other people'. The employment arrangement is thus garnished with 'civilizing' overtones.

How do the *almajirai* position themselves in this respect? I have cited Adams and Dickey (2000) earlier who posit that the juxtaposition of physical closeness within the domestic space and social distance due to class and other hierarchies sparks a 'dynamic of self-other contrast'. How do the *almajirai* react to being associated with filth, dirt and rural backwardness?

I have described elsewhere (Hoechner 2015b) how the *almajirai* embrace an ascetic ethos to moderate feelings of inadequacy and shame triggered by experiences of exclusion. Rural parents enrolling their sons as *almajirai* hold hardship to be educative and indispensable for the social and moral maturation of boys into men. On some occasions, the *almajirai* embrace this discourse about the educative value of hardship and frugality, for example when they seek to justify their deprived living conditions in a context where poverty attracts shame.

However, I also found that the *almajirai* come to adopt aspirations for an urbane and cosmopolitan lifestyle, and seek to create images of themselves as worldly wise and conversant with Western-style modernity.

Thorsen (2012: 10) argues about girl domestic workers in West and Central Africa that '[i]n the course of living in the city, girls get new ideas about their identities and about the kind of life they would like to live'. This is equally true for the *almajirai*.

'Cosmopolitan' aspirations and imaginaries transpired for instance from the snappy postures the *almajirai* assumed when taking photographs, from fashion accessories they flaunted (such as sunglasses, wrist watches and finger rings), and from making proud and public use of (borrowed or owned) electronic appliances like MP3 players and mobile phones. During the film production process, the participating *almajirai* seized the opportunity to snap each other behind the computer we used for editing, pretending to be busy working, with headphones on, a hand on the mouse and a concentrated look on their face – even though most of them hardly knew how to type.

Many of the *almajirai* I met in my research entertained high-flown future aspirations, which will probably be difficult for them to achieve, given their limited curriculum and the generally very difficult economic conditions in northern Nigeria. When Abbas, a student at Bayero University Kano who supported our film project for a brief period, asked the participating *almajirai* what they wanted to become in life, the majority of youths present declared they aspired to a formal sector job (e.g. soldier, customs officer, or simply 'government worker', *ma'aikatan gwamnati*). The circumstances of the conversation may have influenced the *almajirai's* answers: in the eyes of the *almajirai*, studying at university made Abbas a likely candidate for future formal sector employment I think, and therefore an appropriate audience for such aspirations.[4] But aspirations for formal sector employment came up far too often in my interviews for me to dismiss them as merely a passing fancy. Several students in a Qur'anic school I visited regularly in urban Kano, for example, expressed the wish to become a judge, soldier, primary school teacher, or government official, which reflects the respect society accords these professions.

Ferguson (1999: 207ff) describes how rural migrants on the Copperbelt try to distance themselves from their rural origins by adopting particular 'cosmopolitan' styles. Similarly, the ways in which the *almajirai* fashioned themselves in the situations described here reveal reveries that sit uneasily with the rural realities in which most of their families live (and to which many of them are likely to return). And indeed, the *almajirai* talked with some condescension about people who lacked exposure to urban life, including parents who failed to understand the purpose of our film project. On one occasion, after a quarrel, some students insulted each other as 'villagers' (*dan/'yan kauye*). Aliyu (aged fifteen) grumbled that the behaviour of a crowd of children who, attracted by the sight of a white person, came running after us in his home neighbourhood, was *kauyanci*, village behaviour. In a context where rurality connotes negatively, the *almajirai* had little to offer in reply to discourses denigrating them as country bumpkins. Instead, they thought to portray themselves as urbane, and to hide their rural origins as well as they could. Arguably, this is an endeavour with limited prospects of success, given that the *almajiri* system encourages the sustenance of continued links with peasant life and that many former *almajirai* have little choice but to return to a rural livelihood.

In urban Kano, I met ex-*almajirai* who, through their former employers, had found work (such as factory work) that paid enough to sustain a family in an urban area. I met others who, incrementally, had expanded the business they had engaged in already as *almajirai* (tailoring, capmaking, retail sale) to the extent that it could just about sustain a family. Predictably, all the *malamai* of the schools I interacted with were former *almajirai*. Yet, we have reason to believe that for many recent *almajiri* graduates, an urban 'cosmopolitan' future may not be in the cards.[5] Returning to a rural livelihood, on the other hand, is an option available to most, even though conveniently located farmland is increasingly becoming scarce. In my rural field site Albasu, I met numerous young men who had spent part of their boyhood and youth as *almajirai*. Yet, to launch adult careers they had returned to their home village. This is where they built a house, or at least a room, often inside or bordering their father's compound, to accommodate their wife or wives and children. Some returned to their rural home to support ageing parents, but many others did so because they failed to find ways of setting themselves up as married men in the city.

Conclusion

Domestic work arrangements juxtapose the physical closeness of workers and employers with a social distance resulting from class and other hierarchies. This makes them an intriguing setting to study how the relationships between different segments of society are enacted, negotiated and potentially contested in everyday life. Scholars of domestic work have been interested in the role of various vectors of social division for the relationships between workers and employers, most prominently among them class, race or ethnicity, gender and age. This chapter has paid particular attention to social properties that have received little attention in the literature so far. To understand the intricacies and implications of the domestic work performed by migrant Qur'anic students in northern Nigeria, it is helpful to pay attention not only to the dynamics of class, age and gender, but also to the role that religion and rural/urban and educational divides play with regard to how the *almajirai* are positioned within the 'social space'. It is important, moreover, to note how different vectors of social division interact to produce particular power constellations.

With the general decline of Marxism and class analysis, studies of religion have paid less and less attention to the ways in which religion relates to socio-economic inequalities and to questions of class (e.g. Raines 2002: 12). The analysis in this chapter has sought to show the added value of doing so. In the case of the *almajirai*, religion provides an idiom for the poor to demand support and better employment conditions. At the same time, religious change and reformation have altered the 'social space'. They have strengthened the position of domestic employers who dispute the religious legitimacy of the *almajiri* system, as well as of the support claims of the boys enrolled in it.

Rural/urban and educational divides have often been subsumed under the wider category of 'class' in the literature. What can we learn from paying closer attention to such divides? First of all, they can reveal how different vectors of social division interact to produce particular power constellations. Their rural origins, their poverty and their lack of 'modern' education all play together to make the *almajirai* particularly weak bargaining partners in the contest over the meaning of and material rewards for the domestic work they perform. Secondly, paying closer attention to rural/urban divides can uncover seasonal dynamics related to agricultural work cycles that impact domestic work arrangements. Many *almajirai* participate in farm work during the rainy season. Seasonal absences weaken their position vis-à-vis their employer-patrons. Finally, paying attention to rural/urban and educational divides can reveal potent imaginaries which likely strengthen the position of employers. Socialized into 'urban ways', the *almajirai* came to share the perspective of many urbanites that life in the countryside is both 'boring' and 'backward' – even though many of them may eventually have to return to rural life. Simultaneously, however, discourses equating rurality with backwardness strengthen the position of employers who can conceive of themselves as completing a 'civilizing' mission by employing *almajirai* of rural origin.

Hannah Hoechner is a lecturer in education and international development at the School of International Development, University of East Anglia. She holds a PhD from the University of Oxford, and has held postdoctoral positions in Brussels and Antwerp. Her book *Qur'anic Schools in Northern Nigeria: Everyday Experiences of Youth, Faith, and Poverty* has recently been published with Cambridge University Press in the International African Library. Debunking stereotypes about Qur'anic schools as recruitment grounds for Boko Haram and other violent groups, Hannah explores what it means to be young, poor and Muslim in a context of pervasive inequality.

Notes

1. Not every rural dweller is poor of course, and there actually exists a quite successful stratum of agricultural entrepreneurs (see Meagher 2001).
2. Bujra (2000) points out that during the colonial period, demand for male domestic servants was high in many parts of Africa, not least because relying on the – more expensive – labour of men signalled high status more effectively. Most historical labour migration was moreover male.
3. The film (*Duniya Juyi Juyi*, 2016) is available online at: https://www.youtube.com/watch?v=A-SDeFX5rfI&t=2083s (last accessed 18 July 2019). I reflect on my filmmaking experiences in Hoechner (2015a).
4. How privileged the *almajirai* considered Abbas to be became apparent when they laughed at his proclamation that the government ignored not merely the rights (*'yanci*) of the *almajirai* but also the rights of university students like him. 'It's your parents who gives you [the financial support needed]! [*sic*]', one of the youths retorted.
5. For a more detailed discussion of *almajirai*'s future prospects, see Hoechner (2018: 203ff).

References

Adams, K.M., and S. Dickey. 2000. *Home and Hegemony: Domestic Service and Identity Politics in South and Southeast Asia*. Ann Arbor: University of Michigan Press.

Bambale, A.J. 2007. 'Almajiranchi and the Problem of Begging in Kano State: The Role of Shekarau Administration (2003–2007)', *7th BEN Africa Annual Conference, 1–3 August 2007*. Addis Ababa: Business Ethics Network of Africa.

Bano, M., M. Antoninis and J. Ross. 2011. *Islamiyya, Qur'anic and Tsangaya Education Institutions Census in Kano State: Final Draft Report*. Kano: ESSPIN.

Bledsoe, C. 1990. '"No Success Without Struggle": Social Mobility and Hardship for Foster Children in Sierra Leone', *Man* 25(1): 70–88.

Bourdieu, P. 1989. 'Social Space and Symbolic Power', *Sociological Theory* 7(1): 14–25.

Bourdillon, M. 2009. 'Children as Domestic Employees: Problems and Promises', *Journal of Children and Poverty* 15(1): 1–18.

Bujra, J. 2000. *Serving Class: Masculinity and the Feminisation of Domestic Service in Tanzania*. Edinburgh: Edinburgh University Press.

Cock, J. 1980. *Maids & Madams: A Study in the Politics of Exploitation*. Johannesburg: Ravan Press.

Dickey, S. 2000. 'Permeable Homes: Domestic Service, Household Space, and the Vulnerability of Class Boundaries in Urban India', *American Ethnologist* 27(2): 462–89.

Duniya Juyi Juyi, 2016, film produced by H. Hoechner, Kano, distributed by Goethe Institut, 69 mins. Retrieved 19 June 2019 from https://www.youtube.com/watch?v=A-SDeFX5rfI&t=4s.

Ferguson, J. 1999. *Expectations of Modernity. Myths and Meanings of Urban Life on the Zambian Copperbelt*. Berkeley: University of California Press.

Gaitskell, D., et al. 1983. 'Class, Race and Gender: Domestic Workers in South Africa', *Review of African Political Economy* 27/28: 86–108.

Goody, E.N. 1982. *Parenthood and Social Reproduction: Fostering and Occupational Roles in West Africa*. Cambridge: Cambridge University Press.

Hansen, K.T. 1986. 'Household Work as a Man's Job: Sex and Gender in Domestic Service in Zambia', *Anthropology Today* 2(3): 18–23.

Hashim, I.M. 2005. *Exploring the Linkages between Children's Independent Migration and Education: Evidence from Ghana* (Working Paper No. 12). Sussex: Development Research Centre on Migration, Globalisation and Poverty. Retrieved 26 August 2019 from http://www.childmigration.net/MigartionDRC_Hashim_05.

Hoechner, H. 2014a. *Ambiguous Adventures: 'Traditional' Qur'anic Students in Kano, Nigeria*, PhD Dissertation. Oxford: University of Oxford.

_____. 2014b. 'Experiencing Inequality at Close Range: Almajiri Students and Qur'anic Schools in Kano', in A.R. Mustapha (ed.), *Sects and Social Disorder: Muslim Identities and Conflict in Northern Nigeria*. Woodbridge: James Currey, pp. 98–125.

_____. 2014c. 'Traditional Quranic Students (Almajirai) in Nigeria: Fair Fame for Unfair Accusations?', in M.-A. Perouse de Montclos (ed.), *Boko Haram: Islamism, Politics, Security and the State in Nigeria*. Leiden: African Studies Centre & Institut Français de Recherche en Afrique, pp. 63–84.

_____. 2015a. 'Participatory Filmmaking with Qur'anic Students in Kano, Nigeria: "Speak Good about us or Keep Quiet!"', *International Journal of Social Research Methodology* 18(6): 635–49.

_____. 2015b. 'Porridge, Piety and Patience: Young Qur'anic Students' Experiences of Poverty in Kano, Nigeria', *Africa* 85(2): 269–88.

_____. 2018. *Quranic Schools in Northern Nigeria: Everyday Experiences of Youth, Faith, and Poverty*. Cambridge: Cambridge University Press.

Jacquemin, M. 2004. 'Children's Domestic Work in Abidjan, Cote D'Ivoire: The Petites Bonnes have the Floor', *Childhood* 11(3): 383–97.

_____. 2009. '(In)Visible Young Female Migrant Workers: "Little Domestics" in West Africa. Comparative Perspectives on Girls and Young Women's Work', *Workshop Child and Youth Migration in West Africa: Research Progress and Implications for Policy*, 9–10 July 2009. Accra: Development Research Centre on Migration, Globalisation and Poverty University of Sussex and Centre for Migration Studies, University of Ghana. Retrieved 13 May 2018 from http://www.migrationdrc.org/news/reports/Child_and_Youth_Migration/papers/Jaquemin%20Accra%20English.pdf.

Johnson, D. 2008. *An Assessment of the Development Needs of Teachers in Nigeria: Kwara State Case Study*. Report No. KW 301. Kano: ESSPIN.

Jonckers, D. 1997. 'Les Enfants Confiés', in M. Pilon et al. (eds), *Ménages et familles en Afrique: Approches des dynamiques contemporaines*. Lomé: Centre Français sur la Population et le Développement, pp. 193–208.

Klocker, N. 2011. 'Negotiating Change: Working with Children and their Employers to Transform Child Domestic Work in Iringa, Tanzania', *Children's Geographies* 9(2): 205–20.

Last, M. 1993. 'The Traditional Muslim Intellectual in Hausaland: The Background', in T. Falola (ed.), *African Historiography*. Harlow: Longman, pp. 116–31.

_____. 2000. 'Children and the Experience of Violence: Contrasting Cultures of Punishment in Northern Nigeria', *Africa: Journal of the International African Institute* 70(3): 359–93.

Lovejoy, P.E., and J.S. Hogendorn. 1993. *Slow Death for Slavery: The Course of Abolition in Northern Nigeria, 1897–1936*. Cambridge: Cambridge University Press.

Meagher, K. 2001. 'The Invasion of the Opportunity Snatchers: The Rural-Urban Interface in Northern Nigeria', *Journal of Contemporary African Studies* 19(1): 39–54.

Notermans, C. 2008. 'The Emotional World of Kinship: Children's Experiences of Fosterage in East Cameroon', *Childhood* 15(3): 355–77.

Perry, D.L. 2004. 'Muslim Child Disciples, Global Civil Society, and Children's Rights in Senegal: The Discourses of Strategic Structuralism', *Anthropological Quarterly* 77(1): 47–86.

Pilon, M. 2003. *Foster Care and Schooling in West Africa: The State of Knowledge*. Preparation of the UNESCO 2003 EFA Monitoring Report. Ouagadougou: IRD and UERD.

Raines, J. (ed.). 2002. *Marx on Religion*. Philadelphia: Temple University Press.

Robson, E. 2004. 'Children at Work in Rural Northern Nigeria: Patterns of Age, Space and Gender', *Journal of Rural Studies* 20(2): 193–210.

Schildkrout, E. 2002. 'Age and Gender in Hausa Society: Socio-economic Roles of Children in Urban Kano', *Childhood* 9(3): 342–68.

Smith, M.F. 1954. *Baba of Karo: A Woman of the Muslim Hausa*. London: Faber and Faber.

Thorsen, D. 2012. *Child Domestic Workers: Evidence from West and Central Africa*. Dakar: UNICEF.

Umar, M.S. 2001. 'Education and Islamic Trends in Northern Nigeria: 1970s–1990s', *Africa Today* 48(2): 127–50.

UNICEF. 1999. *Child Domestic Work. Innocenti Digest*. Retrieved 26 August 2019 from https://www.unicef-irc.org/publications/265-child-domestic-work.html.

United Nations. 2009. *World Population Prospects: Population Database. The 2008 Revision, Highlights*. Department of Economic and Social Affairs, Population Division No. 210. Retrieved 13 May 2018 from http://esa.un.org/unpp/index. asp?panel=1.

Ware, R. 2014. *The Walking Qur'an: Islamic Education, Embodied Knowledge, and History in West Africa*. Chapel Hill: University of North Carolina Press.

Wasiuzzaman, S., and K. Wells. 2010. 'Assembling Webs of Support: Child Domestic Workers in India', *Children and Society* 24(4): 282–92.

Ya'u, Y.Z. 2000. 'The Youth, Economic Crisis and Identity Transformation: The Case of the Vandaba in Kano', in A. Jega (ed.), *Identity Transformation and Identity Politics under Structural Adjustment in Nigeria*. Uppsala: Nordiska Afrikainstitutet, in collaboration with The Centre for Research and Documentation, Kano, pp. 161–80.

Chapter 2

'Born Free to Aspire'?
An Ethnographic Study of Rural Youths' Aspirations in
Post-Apartheid South Africa

Fawzia Mazanderani

Introduction

In October 2015, the state of higher education in South Africa came under
immense flame. This flame was ignited by crowds of disappointed university students, who, mobilising under the banner of '#Fees must Fall',
were protesting the 10.5 per cent fee increase and 6 per cent registration
fee increase proposed by South African universities for 2016. These dem-
onstrations, which spread across the country and led to the shutdown of
numerous universities and technical colleges, encompassed the largest
South African student movement(s) since the 1976 Soweto Riots. While
students succeeded in obtaining a 0 per cent fee increase for 2016 alone,
further demands included the end of outsourcing of workers on cam-
puses and an appeal for free tertiary education, a call which has received
continued momentum to date. These protests have formed part of a new
wave of student activism across the country, whereby the generation
born after the dismantling of apartheid have come to question the extent
to which they remain immobilized by an educational system that favours
those coming from historically privileged backgrounds.

This 'born free generation', who account for over half the country's
population (Cronje et al. 2015: 2), were raised in a democracy that officially offers them 'free and equal access to education' (South African
Schools Act, 1996). The pervasive discourse of 'freedom and a better life

Notes for this chapter begin on page 66.

in the new South Africa' has created a general belief in upward mobility for 'previously disadvantaged' youth. The expectation is that they will build a life different from and better than their parents' generation, who endured gross discrimination under the apartheid regime (De Lannoy 2008: 168). Existing studies indicate ambitious future aspirations (in normative terms) among young black[1] South Africans who typically express a desire for white-collar rather than blue-collar work (Swartz et al. 2012; De Lannoy 2008). However, studies on youth aspirations across global contexts indicate that the impact of social structures, particularly the social class, race and educational background of parents, continues to have great bearing on what is and what is not possible to achieve, however high ones' aspirations (Ball, 2003). While young people may express a language of individual choice and agency, it is only for some that the necessary resources and opportunities accompany the rhetoric (Furlong and Cartmel 2007). In the case of South Africa, this is indicated through how, despite being twenty-four years into democracy, 60 per cent of South Africa's youth have no educational qualifications (Spaull 2015: 36).

Given the influential role of the school on the development of young people's aspirations, this chapter considers how the circulation of ideologies of social mobility, such as 'progress' and the promotion of university education, affect experiences of social mobility and inequality. Drawing upon ethnographic observations conducted within one secondary school between September 2015 and June 2016, I explore how the neoliberal discourses that pervade this learning environment perpetuate notions of individual responsibility. As such, they neglect to interrogate the role of history, politics and economics in the making of South Africa's highly divided social space as well as in the shaping of young South African's trajectories. This leaves students dreaming of success but with little sense of how to locate themselves within a particular historical legacy as well as how to navigate significant structural obstacles. By exploring young people's own representations of their situations, I argue that such discourses inadvertently provide the grounds upon which experiences of social im/mobility are cultivated.

Locating the Study

In the context of post-apartheid South Africa, expectations of social mobility intertwine with spatial mobility. Given that the young people in this study are still living in the zones allocated to the previous generation, it is important to consider the ways that apartheid geographies continue to structure the opportunities available in the post-apartheid era (King

2007). Mobilities are especially significant for rural youth, who experience a kind of mobility imperative created by the 'accelerating concentration of economic and cultural capital in cities' (Farrugia 2016: 836). For this reason, I am interested in the largely neglected experiences of young South Africans residing in rural areas and will be focusing on a township in Mpumalanga province, situated on the borders of the Kruger National Park. The term 'township' refers to the settlements set aside for non-white inhabitants of South Africa as part of the apartheid government's ruthless racial segregation and deliberate organization of space to benefit the minority white population.

The data to inform this research consists of classroom observations, in-depth interviews, focus groups, curriculum analysis and general observations within the area. My core observations took place in one school, Inyoni High,[2] located in Intaba township, although I engaged, and conducted interviews with students and teachers from across other local schools. My key research participants were students in their final year of schooling (known as grade twelve or matric) as well as young people who had left school one to three years previously (post-matrics). With the exception of the post-matrics, whom I had known from previously working in the region, key participants were selected through focus groups held on the school premises. My approach towards the research has been informed by post-structural, feminist theories that deconstruct the notion that researchers are capable of providing objective accounts. I thus acknowledge the partial, relational and inherently fragmentary nature of any construction of the 'other' and the implications of my positionality upon the account that I produce (see Mazanderani 2017).

Due to my interest in young people's aspirations, this chapter will pay particular attention to the curriculum and teaching of the subject 'Life Orientation' (LO), a learning area concerned with the personal, social, intellectual, spiritual and physical development of learners, so that they can 'achieve their full potential' in the new democracy of South Africa (South African Department of Education 2003: 9). LO, which became a compulsory part of the secondary school curriculum in 2008, aims to prepare students to 'make informed decisions about subject choices, careers, and additional and higher education opportunities' (ibid.). While the decision to introduce LO was timely, the effectiveness of the curriculum and its teaching remains unclear and it is a learning area that has been beset with criticisms (Jacobs 2011).

This research regards LO as a site through which to explore how my research participants negotiate dominant neoliberal discourses. Following Foucault, 'discourse' is interpreted as 'a system of representation' with the rules and practices that provide a language for talking about 'a particular topic at a particular historical moment' (Hall 2001: 72). In this sense discourse can be defined as consisting of 'laws of possibility, rules or existence for the objects that are named, designated or described within it, and for the relations that are affirmed, or denied in it' (Foucault 1972: 91). Discourses not only demarcate what it is possible to say, know and do, but also determine what kind of person one is entitled/obliged 'to be' (MacLure 2003: 176). This provides a useful conceptual tool to explore how young rural South Africans draw upon available discourses in order to narrate, but not necessarily move themselves into social spaces deemed desirable.

A 'Good Education'

In order to understand the value attached to education in the social space of post-apartheid South Africa, it is pertinent to consider how, during apartheid, a ceiling was set on black South African's upward mobility. The Bantu Education Act of 1953 designed a separate curriculum for 'whites' and 'non-whites', providing them with technical rather than academic skills and ensuring the creation of a low skilled labour pool for the apartheid economy. After the dismantling of apartheid in 1994, education was to be the cultural vehicle for the realization of the new constitution – 'to heal the divisions of the past and establish a society based on democratic values, social justice and fundamental human rights' (The Republic of South Africa 1996).

Despite numerous reforms, to improve access, quality, equality and redress for learners (Pandor 2008: 17), increases in expenditure for schooling have not resulted in an equal improvement in outcomes. For 20–24-year-olds, 16 per cent remain in school, 12 per cent are in post-school education, 21 per cent in employment, and 51 per cent are not in employment, education or training (Branson et al. 2015: 42). As such, growing up in post-apartheid South Africa is for many 'a journey of a dream denied' (Soudien 2003: 64), a reflection which the previously mentioned student protests attest towards.

The 'dreams' of my research participants typically involved attending university and alternative trajectories were rarely articulated. The desire to study medicine was prevalent, followed by aspirations towards engineering and IT related fields. Most students perceived higher education as a necessary step in securing employment, forming an implicit association between 'a good education' and 'a good life'. While education is not a guarantee for improving young peoples' circumstances, South Africans with some form of tertiary education are more than twice as likely to be formally employed when compared to those with incomplete schooling (Cloete 2009). The possession of a university degree remains 'a ticket of entry to the black middle class in times of precarious employment prospects' (Southall 2016: 119).

In South Africa, 'Higher Education' includes education for undergraduate and postgraduate levels, certifications and diplomas and incorporates universities and universities of technology. 'Further Education' or Technical Vocational Education and Training (TVET)[3] includes vocational training, career-oriented education and training offered in technological colleges, community colleges and private colleges. There are three ways of passing the government assessed matric examinations. A 'bachelor degree pass' provides entrance into universities, a 'diploma pass' grants entrance into any university of technology or diploma course and a 'higher certificate pass' allows students to attend colleges or complete a certificate course. While universities are typically the most desired option for South African youth across different contexts, traditional universities have the most stringent entrance requirements, requiring a bachelor degree pass in addition to specific subjects depending on the programme chosen, and, in most cases, a pass on an internal entrance examination. Most school leavers do not achieve high enough grades to allow them entrance into universities, and, of those who are admitted, less than half eventually graduate (Wilson-Strydom 2011).

The matric pass rate is in itself not an indicator of the state of education in South Africa, as the matric class refers to only the 'best' 50 per cent of learners who remain in the schooling system. While South Africa has high levels of school enrolment and attendance amongst children aged seven to thirteen, schooling is compulsory only until the age of 15 (the end of Grade Nine) and the attendance rate decreases rapidly from there onwards. To illustrate: of 100 learners who started school in 2003, only 49 made it to matric in 2014; 37 passed; and 14 are qualified to go to university (Spaull 2015: 36). The students in my study represent those who have remained within the schooling system and are thus, on a relative scale, high academic achievers. Approximately half of the matric year group at Inyoni High had repeated a school year (sometimes more than one) in order to stay within the school system. Yet while passing matric is in itself an achievement, it is generally not enough to enable entry into aspired for professions.

Further educational programmes are therefore positioned as the 'more realistic' option for many young people whose academic achievements do not permit university entrance. Studies indicate, however, that black students often associate vocational work with the degrading working conditions their parents had to endure during apartheid (Ramphele 2002) and the preference for 'white collared jobs' and university degrees is a marked trend in the aspirations of previously disadvantaged young people (Needham and Papier 2011). Such aspirations need to be located within the social space of post-apartheid South Africa, where the emerging black middle classes serve as agents of modernity and hope. When attempting to motivate students to work towards their futures, the LO curriculum promotes a visualization exercise which involves imagining oneself at university, not heading towards graduation at a vocational or technical college.

> If you cannot motivate yourself to study, then try to: imagine yourself in an academic gown walking up the steps of a university to obtain your degree, with your family and friends cheering for you. Imagine yourself finding your name in the newspaper – you have got seven distinctions for your grade 12 exams. (Rooth et al. 2013: 102)

Throughout my fieldwork, I did not hear a teacher recommend attending an FET college to any of the students. In confidence, however, one of the school administrative staff, Portia, told me that attending a FET college was the best decision she had ever made. She had initially been studying at a technical university in Pretoria but dropped out because it was 'too fast' for her. Portia waxed lyrical about how all her friends who went to an FET college had jobs and did not have to pay the more expensive fees required by universities. When I asked her whether she ever shared these thoughts with students, she was dismissive, saying that none of the students wanted to attend a FET college because they looked down on them. It may also be that Portia did not want to admit to students that she had gone to a FET college, internalising the stigma attached to attending FETs, despite regarding it to have been an ideal option for herself.

Although initially all of the students I met expressed little to no interest in pursuing studies at a FET college, an underlying interest in attending FETs emerged once deepened rapport had developed between participants and myself. Two students, Petal and Pearl, approached me one school afternoon to say that although they knew their teachers thought going to a FET college was not 'what we are supposed to be thinking of' (Petal), they wanted to apply anyway. Their reasoning was that they did not feel they would manage the academic requirements of university and feared the high dropout rates. This perception stemmed from witnessing neighbours within the area return home without completing their degrees, an observation in keeping with South African statistics which indicate that some 51 per cent of students are unlikely to graduate (Cronje et al. 2015: 2). They worried that if they did not attend an FET college they would be stuck doing 'township maintenance', a humorous local expression used to refer to unemployed young people who hang around the township, 'maintaining' it through the absence of any other formal occupation. Petal explicitly mentioned how she felt her teachers would not help her pursue studies at a FET college: 'I asked Mr Silinda about whether he had any forms for the FET and he looked at me and said "Do I look like someone who knows about FETs?" So eish, yah, we are not supposed to be thinking of those places…'. I wanted to see whether the stigmatized view of FETs was unique to Inyoni, or was a view widely spread across the township and so I probed this point with my post-matric research participants, who represent five schools across the township.

> Fawzia: When you were at school, did people want to go to university or FETs?
> Pauline: If people don't go to university they think maybe you are not that good, they don't even think of a technikon[4] … they think varsity[5] is the place to be if you want to succeed. Yah when I was at school everybody was looking forward to going to varsity, nobody at that time had an application form for technnikon, everyone had application forms for varsity.
> Fawzia: But did that changed after they got their matric marks?[6]
> Pauline: Yah that affected them so then they had to go to technikons if anywhere. But you still looked down on yourself, you don't think that technikon is the right place to achieve, you still stereotype, you still focus on one thing, you have been channelled.

The idea of being 'channelled' into going into university is not something that only Pauline mentioned, but was illustrated through numerous conversations with matrics and post-matrics. It is reinforced through the comments made, in a focus group, by post-matrics Thabo and Felicia:

> Thabo: 'When you come home in the holidays, the neighbours and stuff ask you what university you are studying at. They don't ask about colleges… they only want to know the name of a university. And then even if you didn't go to one, or maybe you dropped out, you and your family have to make up a lie'.
> Felicia: 'When people see their marks are low, they can't apply for university, they don't consider technical colleges, they just think the only way to achieve is university…and if they don't get good marks they must get some other jobs. Most of the time we blame ourselves, because I was the one who wrote the exam'.

Rather than blaming their parents, their schooling systems or the government, there was a tendency for students to blame themselves when life did not work out as they had envisioned. Such neoliberal discourses of meritocracy 'project responsibility for failure away from social structures and institutions and onto individuals' (Francis and Hey 2009: 226).

The concept of 'misrecognition' and 'symbolic violence', defined as 'the violence which is exercised upon a social agent with his or her complicity' (Bourdieu and Wacquant 1992:167) can offer insight here. The normalization of aspiration can be seen as a form of symbolic violence, as it downplays the 'systemically unequal strategies and tactics involved in realising aspiration that school students adopt in their everyday lives' (Kenway and Hickey-Moody 2011: 152).

A 'Good Life'

My observations and conversations with students and teachers, reinforced this idea of young people being 'channelled' into going into university, or at least feeling the need to express a desire to go to university in the face of others. While there are numerous reasons why a university degree may have been desirable to my participants, one of the most significant reasons is that it is deemed a gateway into financial success. Material objects generally served as signifiers of this success, specifically, big, beautiful homes and fancy cars. The conspicuous consumption of material objects, and especially clothes, has become an important identity marker for post-apartheid South African youth.

Bearing in mind that any analysis of consumption needs to be viewed in historical perspective, it is important to view people's modes of consumption as integral to their senses of self (Posel 2010: 61). When talking to my participants about the kind of life they wanted to live and the work they wanted to do, what often emerged was the clothes they wanted to wear when doing this work. One of my participants, Percy, the son of a panel beater and a domestic worker, told me 'whatever I'm going to do when I leave school, I'm going to wear a suit and people are going to respect me'. Swartz (2009: 41) has noted that 'for impoverished young people branded clothing is perhaps even more important than for their wealthy peers, since their contexts provide few opportunities for enhancing self-esteem.

While material acquisition appeared as a key marker of success, the ideal kind of success involved a combination of materialistic consumption and a strong notion of giving back to their families and communities. My research participants often expressed hopes to return to the township and buy their family members new houses, new kitchens and cars and to pay for the private education of younger family members. This sentiment of 'giving back' and 'returning to one's rural area' occurs repeatedly in the LO curriculum and is a clear representation of when someone has 'made it'. The importance of wealth, not just for individual gain, resonates with Deborah James' (2015) study on indebtedness in South Africa which reveals that people borrow considerable sums of money, as much in order to acquire flashy goods and branded clothes, as to invest in the likes of education, marriage and bride wealth, and funerals.

As well as desiring to retain connections to family members residing in rural areas, a number of students spoke about wanting to return to the rural locations themselves, once they had made a success of their lives. In making locational choices, the aspiring African 'middle class' are responding to the opportunity to move into high amenity residential suburbs previously reserved for white people, but also to the desire to remain physically connected to social networks and cultural experiences found within the townships (Harrison and Zak in Southhall 2016: 182). Mobilities are thus not merely about migration. Rather, they indicate the desire to mobilize social resources unevenly distributed across diverse spaces in order to 'construct biographies that extend taken for granted urban/rural dichotomies' (Farrugia 2016: 840).

Within South Africa and indeed elsewhere, young people typically leave rural areas in search of better employment or income-generating opportunities, better education, and access to health care, housing and welfare services. Yet as young people with the requisite cultural and economic capital migrate to the city, an inability to move due to lack of resources often means that immobilized young people are positioned as failures within definitions of success based on the valorization of mobility (Farrugia 2016: 839). This happened within my own field site, where I encountered young people moving to nearby townships and staying with relatives in order to give the impression of having left for university in the city.

My observations within the LO classroom illustrated to me why students may have felt the need, or indeed, a pressure, to leave the area upon graduation. The LO teacher frequently repeated the statement, 'You have to see yourself somewhere'. This 'somewhere' was not constructed as a rural space, despite the fact that many students indicated a preference for a 'rural' lifestyle. The 'somewhere' was a place marked with the symbols of modernity and the urban. Discursive separations between the rural and the urban position the city as the place where modern life happens. If young people wish to take up the subjectivities offered by contemporary youth culture, they must become mobile, either imaginatively or through actual migration (Farrugia 2016: 842–843). Social and spatial mobility entwine with the aspiration to 'go far', as classed fantasies of self-improvement map onto the mobility imperative of rural education, whereby schooling is constructed as a means of exiting rural spaces (Corbett 2007: 772).

Yet rather than assuming a move to the city would automatically pave the way for the 'good life', I found that ideas of the 'urban' was met with equal parts excitement and horror. Among my participants, there were those who desired to attend universities located in the major cities and those who wanted to go to the more 'rural' universities. These 'urban' centres of learning are typically the historically white institutions, whereas the 'rural' universities are the formerly black only institutions. The fear attached to moving to urban spaces was generally a response to a wariness of the 'fast life' and its embodiment of activities considered as morally dubious (be it sexual promiscuity, excessive partying, alcohol and drug consumption etc.). At the same time, the opportunities for consumption and leisure experiences available in cities has come to define 'youth culture' internationally, and the reach of these mobile cultural flows creates what Katz describes as 'a transnational burgeoning of desire' (1998: 131) for the identities and ways of life offered by these symbols.

In contrast, rural areas were constructed as rustic and conservative, idyllic sanctuaries from the complexities of modernity (Valentine 1997). There was a dominant association between the 'rural' and 'traditional' culture, with 'urban' life corresponding with modernity. In a focus group with five male participants, they explained to me how their 'rural' and 'traditional' upbringing enabled not only the expression of their 'African' identity but of their worth as men. As stated by Paul: 'In a rural area, we learn more things as a man. I know if I am a man I have to wake up in the morning and go and fetch water, go to collect some roots and collect fire'. Zinhle, one of my female participants who aspired to be a doctor, constructed the rural as a safe haven, saying 'a rural area teaches me to be a good girl, and to be an African, doing those things that your grandfathers have done before you. You won't waste your money like you would in an urban area and there are no fights here, it is safe'. Ideas of immorality were entwined with cityscapes, where students perceived rural spaces as implying connections to local communities, their families, their ancestors, 'tradition', and a way of life that promoted equality and mutuality, with less disparities in income and no one competing with one another. As cities were celebrated as a source of enterprising and cosmopolitan citizens, rural spaces were often represented as sites of traditionalism and decline. By reclaiming their rural identity in the image of the romanticized rural, students such as Zinhle resist the pathologies that are projected onto the social space of Intaba.

In juxtaposition to this, many participants expressed a vehement desire to leave their rural locales and never return. Life here was 'too slow' and 'too quiet'. On more than one occasion a participant mentioned a desire to live in a place with 'no cows', as this was seen as the dominant symbol of the rural. As well as being rife with cows, rural areas are the sites of witchdoctors or 'sangomas', whose huts are scattered across the landscape and who exert a strong influence on rural lives in particular within South African. Several of my participants expressed a desire to leave rural areas to avoid the infliction of 'witchcraft' upon their lives. As noted by Geschiere (1997), writing about Cameroon, discourses about witchcraft are particularly pertinent in situations of social inequality. In this context, witchcraft provided support for elites to accumulate greater wealth and power but could also be a weapon of the weak, enabling the poor to level inequalities. Several of my participants pointedly expressed wanting to move to urban areas so as to not be exposed to the levels of witchcraft associated with rurality, where their potential future successes may be susceptible to heightened forms of jealousy. These contrasting views regarding the spaces deemed worth aspiring towards indicate the need to attend to people's broader emotional geographies, their attachments to or exclusions from particular social spaces.

Moving beyond 'Rural Backgrounds'

When I inquired to various teachers as to why most students did not end up studying at university, despite expressing a desire to do so, the majority of responses I received referenced the problem being students' 'backgrounds'. As well as regarding students' low levels of achievement as a reflection of their familial background, teachers regarded it to be a reflection of their geographical location, and staff room discussions often involved laments about the barrenness of the schools' surrounding landscape. In contrast to the elevated aspirations that students expressed to me, all of the teaching staff bar one viewed the students as having low aspirations, which they reasoned as being a result of their 'rural backgrounds'. The Head LO teacher, Zinky, told me as follows: 'The majority of them, if you look at their social background, some of them they don't have the idea of going to tertiary. I think they don't have those role models at home, they don't have people who actually push them, who say it is good to go to this university or that. We have to do all the motivation at school'. Teachers frequently complained about the students' parents or guardians, who they regarded as uneducated, 'traditional' and generally unable to support their children due to their low educational levels.

Yet while the teachers referenced how students' social and geographic locations influenced their abilities, they rarely situated these as historically informed factors or explicitly acknowledged the lingering effects of apartheid on their students' lives. They instead expressed that the students 'have opportunities now', while it was different in the time when the teachers themselves were navigating post-school opportunities and faced with a limited range of what was possible. This is particularly relevant given that most of teachers at Inyoni were educated under the apartheid regime. Tim, the Geography teacher, told me that while there was a 'chance' that students could go to universities because of the opportunities nowadays, 'unlike before', he considered this an unlikely prospect.

Any study which pays attention to 'discourse' needs to take heed of the silences and grey points of discussion – in this case, the absence of any explicit mention of the lingering effects of apartheid on young people's present realities. Yet given my positionality, as a non-white outsider, conducting research within the seemingly 'post-racial' landscape of post-apartheid Africa, the omissions within teachers' narratives are not to be taken solely as a lack of insight from their part. They could also be viewed as an illustration of how speech is constructed and produced within a particular historical moment and under certain historical conditions, in this instance the framing of their narratives with the audience of a white outsider in mind.

While the silences within the LO curriculum are extensive, what is relevant for the purposes of this chapter is how the curriculum helps cultivate this notion of moving beyond ones' disadvantaged background, feeding into the idea that 'anything is possible' if you 'believe in your dreams'. The curriculum generally describes these difficult circumstances as being part of the experiences of those living in townships and/or rural areas. An example of a case study taken from the curriculum illustrates this point:

> 'My name is Nhlakanipho Colin Mkhize and I come from the township of Imbali in Pietermaritzburg. I am the eldest of four children and I have a bursary. I am currently in my third year of study for a Bachelor of Science degree with Physics and Chemistry as my major subjects at Rhodes University. *University was a far-off dream for me as a child growing up with a single mother.* She struggled to put me through primary school. Fortunately in high school I was awarded a *full scholarship* at Carter High School. But even with this financial burden lifted, the struggle continued. When I was in matric, my LO teacher gave me a form to *apply for a bursary*...The childhood dream of university was becoming a reality. This opportunity has allowed me to *dream even bigger!*' (Rooth et al. 2013: 53)

According to the LO curriculum, the primary means to move beyond one's disadvantaged background is through hard work, which will ultimately lead to acquiring a bursary for further studies. The primary text used to teach LO, the 'Focus' textbook, is rife with examples of students receiving bursaries to fund their studies, often with the aid of a LO teacher. However, in my field site, both current and post-matrics unanimously expressed not finding their LO teacher helpful in providing them with specific information. This was also reflected through my observations of the LO teacher at Inyoni not being familiar with the relevant bureaucratic systems. Application forms can be lengthy and complex to fill out and financial aid applications require supporting documentation that were not generally readily available (such as parents' payslips or death certificates). While the curriculum provides basic information regarding how to approach applications for further studies, for details on admission and funding, internet access is required. Many institutions want applications to be submitted online and charge an application fee, which makes multiple applications costly and for young people who do not have access to a computer or basic computer literacy, a difficult if not impossible task (Branson et al. 2015: 45).

At Inyoni, there were no computers for student use and the majority of students were computer illiterate and unable to set up the email addresses required to send an electronic application. While there was one library that had computers in Intaba, it was a 15-minute drive/1 hour walk from the school and was only open at times when the students were expected to attend school. Although nine out of ten households in South Africa have mobile phones (Cronje et al., 2015: 4) and mobile phones were prevalent within my field site, students lacked the money for data and they often did not have phones with internet access. Despite these obstacles, both students and teachers spoke frequently about being able to apply for a bursary without discussing the specifics of such. When asked how they intend to fund their future studies, the majority of students said that they would work hard, do well in matric and get 'a bursary'. Leon, a matric student, told me, 'to reach my career goals the only thing to do is to study. What I know is that wherever you are, the minute you get good marks they are going to want to sponsor you, for everything'.

Students' general lack of practical information regarding post-school pathways was further demonstrated through the influence of media on their aspirations. This became apparent to me with the case of Lucilla, who aspired to become a detective because of her love of watching criminal investigations on television. Lucilla, a single mother and orphan, was not aware of any place where she could study to be a detective or what the name for this degree was but it remained her primary plan throughout her matric year. She is not the only one of my participants who received their career guidance from television. The film 'Transformers' inspired

Thulani to aspire towards becoming a pilot, and 'Iron Man' drew Leon
into his interest in mechatronics. Such aspirations are perhaps not surprising in themselves, given the lofty ideals that typify the experience
of being young (Swartz et al. 2012). What is unsettling about the influence of television on career aspirations is that, in the case of most of the
young people in my study, there are few potential mentors with whom to
discuss these abstract dreams, in order to assess whether they have any
potential to materialize.

As mentioned earlier in this chapter, throughout the duration of my
fieldwork, my matric participants expressed future aspirations for university courses that required academic results far higher than their own,
yet were positive that they would receive these results in due course.
The need to be positive has echoes of Christianity within it, especially
the positive thinking that is historically embedded in the prosperity
Gospel of the Charismatic Churches. This is unsurprising given the high
presence of religious institutions my field site, with approximately fifty
churches within Intaba and new ones emerging continually. The most
rapidly growing churches appear to be Evangelical/Pentecostal, which
seem to draw youthful congregations (Johnson 2009). Writing about other
contexts within sub-Saharan Africa, Gifford argues the one of the new
(charismatic) churches' main characteristics is an emphasis on success,
wealth and the power of positive thinking (2004: 171).

Several of my participants directly linked their optimism with their
religious beliefs, as they considered a lack of positivity to symbolize an
absence of faith in God's plan for them. Sipho, a post-matric who had
spent one year immobilized upon leaving school due to not having the
correct identification documents to apply to university, told me that he
was not concerned about the future, as his faith would provide for him.
He explained, 'I am a Christian, so I believe in God. He keeps his promises. So whenever I face any problems I know my God is my source'. In
a similar vein, students often drew upon God as a resource when reflecting on the other difficulties in their life, thus acknowledging some of the
obstacles they were facing, while simultaneously expressing that these
would be overcome, not necessarily through practical support or innovation, but through the love of God. Sihle explained this, 'I am always positive that I can do it, even though I can see financially I am not stable, but
I always say that it can happen because I know God will help me. I feel
like when I am at church everything becomes good. I have to maybe pray
hard or work hard in order to achieve whatever I want'.

Ramphele's ethnography of the struggles waged by young people who
are not yet benefitting from the 'fruits of post-apartheid South Africa'
indicates that the 'presence of a dream' is an important factor in young

people's narratives (Ramphele 2002: 11). Hopes and dreams, have 'survival value' within contexts of adversity and preserving hope can be a coping strategy for daily experiences of deprivation. While 'positive dreams' may have their own power, as studies on the role of resilience in contexts of adversity (Dass-Brailsford 2005) would indicate, my findings show that the discourse of 'anything is possible' perpetuates a cycle whereby young South Africans high aspirations may be coupled with slim chances of success. As such, there is a 'quiet violence' at work within their dreams (Swartz et al. 2012).

The Myth of Meritocracy

The data discussed thus far echoes Swartz et al.'s (2012) perception that while young people from a township in South Africa may be subjected to forms of violence (treated as inferior, denied resources, limited in their social mobility etc.), they might not perceive it that way. Rather, their situation may seem to them to be 'the natural order of things' (Danaher et al. 2002: 25). Young South African's strong sense of personal responsibility reflects the 'meritocracy myth' (Swartz et al. 2012), invoking the idea that by hard work and personal responsibility a person is able to achieve their aspirations, without concern for social and political contexts. My participants spoke the language of individual choice, corresponding with empirical literature which indicates that black youth residing in townships deem themselves individually accountable for their future (Newman and De Lannoy 2014, De Lannoy 2008). An excerpt from an interview with Leon alludes to as much:

> Fawzia: Do you ever think the government is responsible for helping you?
> Leon: I think nobody is responsible for my future but me. I honestly don't think a lot about the government since I cannot just expect anything from them as they have provided free schools and free clinics and stuff. I cannot blame them if things don't work out, I can only blame me.

In order to substantiate my findings, I explored whether a different narrative arose from among the post-matric group, given that the majority of their peers were not at the tertiary institutions they had aspired towards, but were studying at local technical colleges, working in local retail outlets or as cleaners, or not working at all. One of my unemployed post-matric participants, Sipho, mentioned earlier in this chapter, did not have the finances to obtain an identity document that would allow him to apply for further studies or work. I asked him what he considered were the biggest challenges preventing both himself and his fellow students from achieving the goals they had aspired to when still at school. His response:

> 'Friends will give you different opinions about what you are expected to do, like if you want to be a doctor they will say, ooh, you are going to take many years before you start working. That corrupts your mind so you end up doing other things that you were not intending to do...The ones who went to university, they have a positive mind'.

Sbusiso, another post-matric from the area, similarly spent his first year after leaving school 'hanging around' the neighbourhood, without a plan and without any work. He had wanted to study to be a graphic designer, but failed to achieve the necessary academic grades. He told me that while he had intended to re-write his matric exams, he had ended up being too busy to do so, because of 'going to the gym and stuff'. Both Sipho and Sbusiso did not refer to any broader structural forces at play but expressed the belief that individuals could do anything if they were motivated enough. While their plans had not worked out, this also did not influence the immense positivity they expressed about the future, a future in which their success was still yet to come. My findings illustrate that my participants were evidently not lacking aspirations but instead lacking the economic, social and cultural resources, which can enable them to realize these aspirations.

My participants' account of poverty, as something that happens to people who do not work hard enough, draws on an individuated understanding of inequality that blames poor people for their own marginalization. Given LO's emphasis on hard work, future-planning and personal responsibility, young people's investment in this narrative is not surprising. LO erases class divisions through discourses of individual responsibility and thus obscure the 'distinctive ways in which particular landscapes of poverty are formative of thought, feeling, imagination, and identity' (Hicks and Jones 2007: 57). For example, Leon, when speaking about wealthy black South Africans, told me, 'they are living their dreams because they worked for them'. This understanding of success, similarly espoused by the LO curriculum and teaching instruction, disregards the lingering influence of history upon present socioeconomic circumstances. When the students reference 'working hard' as the process for obtaining success, this narrative takes the place of a tangible plan for the future, which would require specific details about action required. When the 'working hard' narrative proves not to be enough to obtain this aspired for success, students are able to give up their dreams with greater ease, given the abstract nature of the dreams themselves.

The embodiment of this meritocratic myth became particularly visible to me through how my research participants responded to student protests calling for the end to university fees in South Africa, events mentioned at the start of this chapter. When I arrived at my field site, I assumed that my participants would identify with the student movements and see something of their own impending struggle for higher education echoed in the struggle of their peers. I found this to be far from the case, perhaps because students did not think of their post-school trajectories as rife with the difficulties that I predicted them to be. On the contrary there appeared to be a trend towards viewing the 'struggle' of fellow young South Africans to access higher education to be the result of them simply *not working hard enough*. Instead, my participants expressed immense optimism about their futures and espoused the belief that anything was possible if they worked hard enough. Petal, a matric student, encapsulated the views of many of her peers when she told me, 'if they [the protestors] had worked hard enough, they wouldn't have had to pay fees in the first place, they would have got a bursary'. As my fieldwork progressed, I found that most of the young people I met expressed a similar sentiment, indicating that those who were protesting the injustices of the higher educational system did not reflect the views of South African youth at large. This chapter shows that these expressions of frustration are especially disconnected from the views of secondary school students residing in isolated rural regions.

Conclusion

The students within this study, working with the discourses circulating within the LO classroom as well as the general school environment, typically adopted an individualized approach to the future whereby they consider themselves personally responsible for transcending the constraints of their rural locations. As a subject that emphasizes the importance of flexibility, independence and mobility, LO fits within a set of educational discourses that have been widely critiqued as technologies of neo-liberalism (Bradford and Hey 2007). Given the limited scope of the research to inform this work, the intention of this chapter is not to make generalizable claims concerning the aspirations of rural youth in South Africa. Rather, by looking closely at the curriculum and teaching of LO, it demonstrates how the LO classroom can be argued as inadvertently aiding the production of social im/mobilities in post-apartheid South Africa.

This chapter has focused upon the interrelationship between schooling and the development of aspirations of young people residing in a rural township in South Africa. It has demonstrated how, although born free students are subject to greater job prospects and social mobility than experienced by the older generation, their higher level of education remains rarely able to deliver its promise of upward mobility at the level expected by young people themselves. While students born after 1994 have been given the tools to aspire in ways that their parents were not permitted, the substantial socio-economic factors that continue to impede the realizations of their aspiration indicate that paradoxical forms of social mobility are at play. This undelivered promise of education is key to understanding the social space of South Africa today.

Fawzia Mazanderani is a Teaching Fellow in the School of Global Studies at Sussex University. She has a background in Social Anthropology (The University of Cape Town), The Anthropology of Development (SOAS) and International Education (Sussex). Her PhD research, which informed this chapter, looks at how South African youth, born post-apartheid and living in a rural township, develop aspirations towards the future. Her research interests include race and identity in post-colonial contexts; history and critical consciousness; the relationship between gender, class and food consumption and ethnographic research methods.

Notes

1. Throughout this chapter, I use the socially constructed categories of 'black' and 'white' because they are the terms people use to describe themselves. 'Youth' or 'young people' refers to all those born post the 1994 democratic elections.
2. This study uses pseudonyms to refer to people and places.
3. TVET colleges were originally referred to as FET (Further Education and Training) colleges and are still called this by my participants, despite a name change in 2014. For this reason, TVET and FET will be used interchangeably throughout this text.
4. 'Tecknikon' is another way of referring to a technical college.
5. 'Varsity' is a colloquial expression for 'university'.
6. 'Matric marks' is a reference to the final year national senior certificate examinations.

References

Ball, S.J. 2003. *Class Strategies and the Education Market: Middle Classes and Social Advantage*. London: Routledge.
Bourdieu, P., and L. Wacquant. 1992. *An Invitation to Reflexive Sociology*. Cambridge: Polity Press.

Bradford, S., and V. Hey. 2007. 'Successful Subjectivities? The Successification of Class, Ethnic and Gender Positions', *Journal of Education Policy* 22(6): 595–614.

Branson, N., et al. 2015. 'Post-school Education: Broadening Alternative Pathways from School to Work', in A. De Lannoy, et al. (eds), *South African Child Gauge 2015*. Cape Town: Children's Institute, University of Cape Town, pp. 42–50.

Cloete, N. 2009. *Responding to the Education Needs of Post-School Youth*. Wynberg: Centre for Higher Education Transformation.

Corbett, M. 2007. 'Travels in Space and Place: Identity and Rural Schooling', *Canadian Journal of Education* 30(3): 771–92.

Cronje, F., et al. (eds). 2015. *Born Free but Still in Chains: South Africa's First Post-Apartheid Generation*. Johannesburg: South African Institute of Race Relations. Retrieved 17 April 2018 from https://irr.org.za/reports/occasional-reports/files/irr-report-2013-born-free-but-still-in-chains-april-2015.pdf/view.

Danaher, G., T., Schirato and J. Webb. 2002. *Understanding Bourdieu*. Crows Nest: Allen & Unwin.

Dass-Brailsford, P. 2005. 'Exploring Resiliency: Academic Achievement among Disadvantaged Black Youth in South Africa', *South African Journal of Psychology* 35(3): 574–91.

De Lannoy, A. 2008. 'Educational Decision Making in an Era of AIDS', PhD dissertation. Johannesburg: University of Cape Town.

Farrugia, D. 2016. 'The Mobility Imperative for Rural Youth: The Structural, Symbolic and Non-Representational Dimensions Rural Youth Mobilities', *Journal of Youth Studies* 19(6): 836–51.

Foucault, M. 1972. *The Archaeology of Knowledge*. London: Routledge.

Furlong, A., and F. Cartmel. 2007. *Young People and Social Change: New Perspectives*, 2nd edn. New York: Open University Press.

Francis, B., and V. Hey. 2009. 'Talking back to Power: Snowballs in Hell and the Imperative of Insisting on Structural Explanations', *Gender and Education* 21(2): 225–32.

Geschiere, P. 1997. *The Modernity of Witchcraft: Politics and the Occult in Postcolonial Africa*. Charlottesville: University of Virginia Press.

Gifford, P. 2004. 'Persistence and Change in Contemporary African Religion', *Social Compass* 51(1): 169–76.

Hall, S. 2001. 'Foucault: Power, Knowledge and Discourse', in M. Wetherell, S. Taylor and Y. Yates (eds), *Discourse Theory and Practice*. London: Sage, pp. 72–81.

Harrison, P., and T. Zack. 2014. 'The Wrong Side of the Mining Belt? Spatial Transformations and Identities in Johannesburg's Southern Suburbs', in P. Harrison, et al. (eds), *Changing Space, Changing City: Johannesburg after Apartheid*. Johannesburg: Wits University Press, pp. 269–92.

Hicks, D., and S. Jones. 2007. 'Living Class as a Girl', in J.A. Van Galen and G.W. Noblit (eds), *Late to Class: Social Class and Schooling in the New Economy*. Albany: Suny Press, pp. 55–86.

Jacobs, A. 2011. 'Life Orientation as Experienced by Learners: A Qualitative Study in North-West Province', *South African Journal of Education* 31(2): 212–23.

James, D. 2015. *Money from Nothing: Indebtedness and Aspiration in South Africa*. Stanford: Stanford University Press.

Johnson, T.M. 2009. 'The Global Dynamics of the Pentecostal and Charismatic Renewal', *Society* 46: 479–83.

Katz, C. 1998. 'Disintegrating Developments. Global Economic Restructuring and the Eroding of Ecologies of Youth', in T. Skelton and G. Valentine (eds), *Cool Places: Geographies of Youth Cultures*. London: Routledge, pp. 130–43.

Kenway, J. and A. Hickey-Moody. 2011. 'Life Chances, Lifestyle and Everyday Aspirational Strategies and Tactics', *Critical Studies in Education* 52(2): 151–63.

King, B.H. 2007. 'Developing KaNgwane: Geographies of Segregation and Integration in the New South Africa', *The Geographical Journal* 173(1): 13–25.

MacLure, M. 2003. *Discourse in Educational and Social Research*. Buckingham: Open University Press.

Mazanderani, F. 2017. '"Speaking Back" to the Self: A Call for "Voice Notes" as Reflexive Practice for Feminist Ethnographers', *Journal of International Women's Studies* 18(3): 80–94.

Newman, K. and A. De Lannoy. 2014. *After Freedom: The Rise of the Post-Apartheid Generation in Democratic South Africa*. Boston: Beacon Press.

Needham, S., and J. Papier. 2011. *Practical Matters: What Young People Think about Vocational Education in South Africa*. London: City & Guilds Centre for Skills Development.

Pandor, G. 2008. *Preface in Reviews of National Policies for Education: South Africa*. Organisation for Economic Co-operation and Development, 20. Retrieved 17 April 2018 from http://www.oecd.org/southafrica/reviewsofnationalpolicie sforeducation-southafrica.htm.

Posel, D. 2010. 'Races to Consume: Revisiting South Africa's History of Race, Consumption and the Struggle for Freedom', *Ethnic and Racial Studies* 33(2): 157–75.

Ramphele, M. 2002. *Steering by the Stars: Being Young in South Africa*. Cape Town: Tafelberg.

Rooth, E. et al. 2013. *Focus CAPS Life Orientation Grade 12 Learner's Book*. South Africa: Maskew Miller Longman.

Spaull, N. 2015. 'Schooling in South Africa: How Low-Quality Education Becomes a Poverty Trap', in A. De Lannoy, et al. (eds), *South African Child Gauge 2015*. Cape Town: Children's Institute, University of Cape Town, pp. 34–41.

Soudien, C. 2003. 'Routes to Adulthood: Becoming a Young Adult in the New South Africa', *IDS Bulletin* 34(1): 63–71.

Southall, R. 2016. *The New Black Middle Class in South Africa*. Auckland Park: Jacana.

South African Department of Education 2003. *National Curriculum Statement Grades 10–12 Life Orientation*. Pretoria: Government Printer.

Statistics South Africa 2015. *National and Provincial Labour Market: Youth Q1: 2008– Q1: 2015. Statistical release P0211.4.2*. Pretoria: Stats SA.

Swartz, S. 2009. *The Moral Ecology of South Africa's Township Youth*. London: Palgrave Macmillan.

Swartz, S., J.H. Hamilton and A. De Lannoy. 2012. 'Ikasi Style and the Quiet Violence of Dreams: A Critique of Youth Belonging in Post-Apartheid South Africa', *Comparative Education* 48(1): 27–40.

The Republic of South Africa 1996. 'Act no.108 of 1986: The Constitution', Pretoria: Government Printers.

Valentine, G. 1997. 'A Safe Place to Grow Up? Parenting, Perceptions of Children's Safety and the Rural Idyll', *Journal of Rural Studies* 13(2): 137–48.

Wilson-Strydom, M. 2011. 'University Access for Social Justice: A Capabilities Perspective', *South African Journal of Education* 31: 407–18.

Chapter 3

Great Expectations and Uncertain Futures
Education and Social Im/mobility in Niamey, Niger

Gabriella Körling

Introduction

Inspired by Bourdieu's theory of social space, in this chapter I explore education as one of many other factors that structure social positions in Niger.[1] I focus especially on the increasingly tenuous relation between state schooling and social mobility as experienced by youth in Niamey. In Niger, as in many other African countries, this type of formal education has historically played an important role as a path to social advancement through the economic privilege and political power associated with formal employment, mainly in the state apparatus. However, in recent decades, economic crisis, cuts in the public sector (limiting recruitment), increasing enrolment rates, and a correlative economic devaluation of the value of school diplomas, has made the link between education and social advancement increasingly tenuous. In this context, the historically important role of education in conferring cultural capital is thus being challenged. In Niger one can observe the paradox described by authors in other contexts, namely that increasing access to school has occurred at the same time as opportunities to benefit from education through social and economic mobility have crumbled (Camfield 2011, Jeffrey 2008). Understanding the impact of this change on social stratification requires a relational and dynamic understanding that pays attention not only to structural conditions but also to representations (Bourdieu 1985). For

---

Notes for this chapter begin on page 88.

instance, in the introduction to a special issue on models of success (*figures de la réussite*) and political imaginaries, Banégas and Warnier point out that the figure of the intellectual (*figure de l'intellectuel diplômé*), exemplified by the salaried civil servant, is losing its social value in competition with other models of success and economic accumulation that are not centred on formal education, such as the trader, musician and informal operator (Banégas and Warnier 2001).

Against this background, I explore the place of education in young people's imaginations of the future and in their experiences of social im/mobility. Much has been written on the precarious situation of youth in Africa in a context of financial crisis and widespread unemployment, which has made it difficult for (especially male) youth to reach social maturity (Abbink and Kessel 2005, Cruise O'Brien 1996, Diouf 2003). Cruise O'Brien has pointed to the marginalization of youth in the 1990s as young people had finished school but were unemployed and thus unable to set up an independent household, in contrast to the 'boom years' of the 1960s and 1970s when the path to economic independence was more straightforward (Cruise O'Brien 1996: 57–58). In a study of youth in Lusaka, Hansen describes how in the face of circumscribed economic opportunities youth find themselves 'stuck in the compound' (and unable to reach social adulthood), a phrase which reflects both social and spatial immobility and exclusion (Hansen 2005). In order to explore these widely shared experiences of immobility I argue that it is important to focus on education. As Pype argues, 'in order to deepen our knowledge about contemporary practices of social growth and mobility for youth in urban Africa – with their moments of distress and uncertainties, but also desire and joy, we need to take into account the space of formal education' (Pype 2015: 7). In urban areas, school is a central part of children's and young people's lives and contributes to shape imaginations of desired futures.

In Niger as in many other African countries, urban areas have always stood out with high enrolment rates in contrast to rural areas where access to school, despite significant improvements, is still far from guaranteed. Niamey as the capital city has since the colonial period been the centre (*pôle central*) of education (Tidjani Alou 1992: 341), characterized by an earlier establishment and concentration of schools, including secondary education. While at the national level enrolment rates in primary education reached 70 per cent in 2014 (United Nations Data 2015), in Niamey they had reached 98 per cent already in 2000 (Ministère de l'Education Nationale 2007). Likewise, gender differences in access to school is less pronounced in Niamey. In Niamey education inequalities appear in particular in the possibility of succeeding in school. In urban areas the social and economic stakes of schooling are high and parents with financial means are willing to invest in the education of their children by paying for after-school classes, private tutoring and private schooling in order to ensure educational achievement. Economic capital plays an important role in accessing (quality) education, and in ensuring 'education success', that is the achievement of sufficient grades and test scores to progress through the education system in order to get a diploma. At the same time, given the high unemployment rates, even a successfully completed education career crowned by a diploma is far from a guarantee of an economically secure future, as entry into the public and 'formal' private job market often depends on the ability to draw on personal relations and social networks. In other words, school capital is now less easily converted into upward social mobility, reliance on social capital being essential in order to transform education into a minimally secure economic position. Additionally, given its historical association with social mobility, school is a space where social immobility becomes especially palpable when dreams of a potential upward mobility remain unfulfilled, necessitating the search for alternative paths to social recognition.

A Brief History of Schooling and Social Mobility in Niger

The 'modern' education system in Niger, that is, formal education modelled on the French system, was introduced by the colonial power. However, as documented by Tidjani Alou, the education system put into place in Niger was extremely limited (Tidjani Alou 1992). Niger, alongside Mauritania, registered the lowest enrolment rates in French West Africa (ibid.: 197). Initially only elementary primary education was made available in Niger and it was not until 1960 that the first upper secondary school (*lycée*) was created in Niamey (ibid.: 243). Given that the colonial education system was quite limited in its reach, Tidjani Alou argues that one of its most important impacts was the creation of a new social category, the *évolués* or educated elite, who through their mastery of the French language and codes of government went on to form a new dominant political class (ibid.: 202). Significantly, education also provided a route to social mobility for people from commoner or slave decent in otherwise highly stratified societies/communities, formal education offering a new means of social promotion and access to a new sphere of political power in the state apparatus (Meunier 2000: 75).

Given the limited investments in education during the colonial period, the expansion of the school system was a pressing necessity for the newly independent regime, along with the training of teachers and state officials

(Meunier 2000: 109). Graduates were more or less guaranteed employment in the civil service upon graduation. This led to the 'mythification' of school as the main engine of economic, social and political mobility through advancement into the political and administrative elite (Meunier 2009: 22). In the 1970s the economy grew, buoyed by the intensification of uranium exploitation and the accompanying expansion of the public and private sectors, providing a number of job opportunities. During this period, important investments were also made in the education sector and enrolment rates steadily increased. However, with the fall of uranium revenues and the rise of debt, Niger was drawn into the economic recession and world debt crisis of the 1980s. Previously students had been fairly privileged but now drastic budget cuts were made in the education sector as resources were directed away from higher education to primary education (Robinson 1994: 600). Career opportunities were definitely curtailed with the cessation of automatic hiring of university and professional school graduates into the civil service in 1991 (Wynd 1999: 106) and the introduction of a competitive examination (*concours*) for recruitment to different parts of the civil service. This had the greatest impact on students from rural backgrounds whose chances of being hired were reduced given that they had a more limited social and cultural capital than students from more privileged backgrounds (Meunier 2009: 32).

The situation in Niger mirrored that of many other countries in Africa, where budget cuts in the public sector reduced employment opportunities and weakened public school systems. Working in Mali, Lange and Diarra point to decreasing school enrolments and increasing number of pupils withdrawn from school – *déscolarisation* – as evidence of a silent protest on the part of parents of the fact that social advancement was no longer possible through school (Lange and Diarra 1999: 165–66). In Niger as well, the increase in enrolment rates slowed during much of the 1990s.[2] The bleak employment prospects especially discouraged people in rural areas from enrolling their children in school as the negative consequences of schooling, such as the loss of labour and a more general disconnection from the rural way of life, were no longer counterbalanced by the potential benefits of employment (Meunier 2009: 25). Ever since, the 1990s public education system has been perceived to be in a perpetual state of crisis due to underfunding.

Yet, in recent years (since the year 2000) there has been a dramatic increase in donor funds in an effort to ensure progress towards the global goal of achieving universal primary education. Subsequently education infrastructure has been extended through the construction of schools and classrooms particularly in rural areas, and enrolment rates have increased.

Between 2000 and 2005 enrolment rates in primary school increased from
34 to 52 per cent (Meunier 2009: 30) and in 2014 they had reached 70 per
cent.[3] However, support and public spending has been geared largely
towards primary education, considered by donors as the most efficient
and cost-effective way to expand access to public education and increase
enrolment rates, leading to the neglect of secondary, technical and higher
education. Enrolment rates in secondary school have increased only
slightly. In 2014, at the national level the enrolment rate in secondary
school was only 18.82 per cent, additionally revealing a continuation of
gender disparity between boys (22.08 per cent) and girls (15.56 per cent).[4]
Moreover, these quantitative achievements have been offset by concerns
about the quality of education. As described by Welmond in the case of
neighbouring Benin, in Niger there is also an evident tension between, on
the one hand, the policies of mass education for economic development
promoted by international donors and by national governments, and on
the other hand local perceptions of education as a path to social mobility
(Welmond 2002: 57).

Precarious Education Trajectories

As an introduction to the relation between education and social im/
mobility in the urban periphery of Niamey I start with a discussion of
common education trajectories. Significantly, education trajectories collected during fieldwork reveal the often uneven and tortuous paths (e.g.
grade repetition, exclusion, etc.) that are central to many young people's
experience of formal schooling. This is especially the case for pupils from
disadvantaged urban backgrounds who have limited access to social, cultural and economic capital (e.g. family support network, language spoken
at home, financial resources) that in other contexts have been identified as
central factors in determining progression through school and education
achievement (Buchmann 2002).

In order to illustrate the unevenness of education trajectories I start
with the narrative of one young man who I will call Ibrahim. Ibrahim
came from a relatively poor background. He lived in a large family compound, made up of one- and two-bedroom houses in *banco* (mud brick),
located next to the river in a former village, which had gradually been
integrated into the urban agglomeration. Like in many other families
in this peripheral neighbourhood, Ibrahim's parents had not gone to
school. The household made a living mainly from agricultural activities.
Ibrahim's father had a rice field and his mother grew vegetables on a borrowed plot next to the rice fields. The family kept livestock in a pen in one

corner of the yard. Ibrahim and his siblings helped with cultivating the rice field and did their own gardening and fishing as well.

At the time of our first interview Ibrahim, who was in his early twenties, was attending the last year of upper secondary school (*terminale*) pursuing the *baccalauréat* in literature and philosophy (*baccalauréat A*) in the local public school. On the verge of successfully graduating with a *baccalauréat*, he was the only one of his siblings to have continued his education beyond primary school. Ibrahim's older sister Djamila had been excluded from the public school system after twice failing the final exam at the end of primary school. Ibrahim's older brother Ousseini dropped out of school in fifth grade (CM1) and his younger brother Yacouba had dropped out in the last year of primary school.

As we talked through Ibrahim's 'school biography' the picture that emerged was that of a gifted and motivated student but whose time in school had been filled with ups and downs, accomplishments and setbacks. Ibrahim recalled that he learned quickly and easily in primary school: 'I was like a devil, things were easy for me'. In the final exam in primary school he even had the second best results in the examination centre, which regrouped several schools, a feat for which he was rewarded with gifts. In the first two years of lower secondary school he continued to be among the best pupils in his class. This is especially important in a context in which pupils, starting already in primary school, are continuously ranked according to their grade point average. The ranking, which is closely followed by pupils and also by some parents, is a source of pride and motivation for those in the top of the class and a source of shame and demotivation for pupils who find themselves in the bottom half of the class. After having spent most of his time in school at the top of his class in ninth grade (*en quatrième*) Ibrahim had started to slip behind and when he did not achieve the average needed to continue to the next grade, he was held back and had to repeat the year. At this point what Ibrahim referred to as adolescent carelessness, which made girls and having fun seem more important than school, combined with frequent teacher strikes, demotivated him from making an effort in school. However, in tenth grade he said that he got back on track (*j'ai pris conscience*) but failed the final exam (*brevet*). He finally passed the exam and was able to enter upper secondary school. Everything had gone well in upper secondary school until the final year which Ibrahim was repeating, after having failed the final exam for the *baccalauréat* the previous school year. In fact, only seven pupils in his overcrowded class of several dozens of students had managed to pass the exam and 'get the *bac*' (*décrocher le bac*). At the national level the overall success rate of the *baccalauréat* that year was only 14 per cent. The *bac* is a stumbling block for many pupils, often necessitating several attempts and a successful *bac* is a source of family pride and celebration.

The *bac* was important in fulfilling Ibrahim's ambition to continue his studies. He had planned to enrol at the national university in Niamey, although he would have preferred to attend a private professional school or institute if he had been able to pay the tuition fee. For many young school leavers, the national university in Niamey, which was over-crowded, underfunded and plagued by a series of unfinished semesters, was not a very attractive option. In comparison, the rapidly expanding offer of private professional schools that ran one- or two-year degree programmes in accounting, marketing and administration, or manage-ment, promised a quick entry into the formal (although saturated) labour market. The following year Ibrahim made another ultimately unsuccess-ful attempt to pass the final exam.

Many aspects of Ibrahim's and also his family's experience of a highly uncertain progression through school are widely shared in these peri-urban neighbourhoods. In conversations and interviews about education, it was striking how many school careers resembled those of Ibrahim's sib-lings, which ended early as pupils were excluded from the public school system (after repeating a grade twice or after failing a final exam twice) or dropped out due to a difficult family situation, marriage, financial troubles, a lack of motivation or despondency in the face of poor school results. For many families with modest means, like Ibrahim's family, interrupted school careers was a central part of their encounter with formal education.

In fact, the education system in Niger is extremely selective as evi-denced by high attrition rates, which are in part a result of the role of national exams in determining progression from primary to lower sec-ondary school, from lower secondary school to upper secondary school and in determining the successful completion of upper secondary school. A study of adolescents in Niamey showed that the number of young ado-lescents in school decreases as one moves up the age bracket. Whereas eight out of ten adolescents (in the age bracket ten to twelve years) are in primary school, in lower secondary school only two out of ten adoles-cents (in the age bracket thirteen to sixteen years) are in school, and in upper secondary school (in the age bracket seventeen to nineteen years) only one out of ten adolescents are still in school (Institut National de la Statistique 2015: 47). Hence while a majority of adolescents are liter-ate after having attended primary school, and possibly lower second-ary school, a minority manage to continue to higher levels of education (upper secondary school and university/professional schools or insti-tutes). For pupils who manage to stay in school, education trajectories

are unstable, uncertain and far from straightforward. Against this background it would be fair to say that Ibrahim was both an exceptional and
an ordinary pupil. He had made it all the way to the last year of secondary school in a highly selective education system without much external
support but was now faltering at a crucial juncture of his 'school career'.

The Education Market and School Success

In this section I focus on the role of financial resources or economic capital in determining the likelihood that children will succeed in school in
order to shed light on the increasing precariousness of education trajectories and the exacerbation of inequality. In an analysis of school achievement in Kenya, Buchmann (2002) underlines that in contexts with high
unemployment and where the education system is centred on national
school leaving examinations (that determine progress through the school
system), school enrolment in and of itself is not enough for the child to
succeed. Parents have to 'utilize various social and cultural resources',
including paying for tutoring and exam preparation classes, to ensure
that their children will 'get ahead' and progress to higher levels of education (Buchmann 2002: 136). Similarly, in Niamey, progressing through
school is often dependent on the opportunity that pupils have to take part
in what can be qualified as a 'market' of education services which has
emerged with the liberalization of the education sector and in step with
the crisis of the public education system.

Private schools play an increasingly important role in the emerging
education market especially in urban areas. The first private schools in
Niger were run by Catholic and Protestant missions and were attended
mainly by Christians. However, the good results gradually attracted a
wider clientele of civil servants and merchants (Meunier 2000: 221–22).
Over the years, the private school sector in Niamey has expanded and
diversified. Private schools have emerged as an increasingly attractive
alternative to the public education system which is associated with frequent strikes and overcrowded classrooms. It should be noted that the
private education sector is extremely diverse, ranging from exclusive
establishments with high tuition fees (frequented by the children of the
middle and upper class) to more modest private schools with only the
most basic facilities. Importantly private schools also play an important role in recuperating pupils that have been excluded from the public
school system. Many pupils' education trajectories thus move between
public and private schools in the quest for a diploma. This is exemplified
in the education trajectory of Mamadou.

In 2008, eighteen-year-old Mamadou had spent all of his education in public school. However, he had been excluded from public school after having repeated the eighth grade (*la cinquième*) twice. Mamadou lived with his mother, who made a living in trade. Mamadou's father, a policeman, was posted in the town of Zinder. When he was excluded from public school, Mamadou's mother had paid the tuition fee of 52,000 FCFA for him to enrol in the local private secondary school. The school was made up of two buildings meant to house the lower secondary school (*collège*) and the upper secondary school (*lycée*) respectively. According to the principal, the school operated at a loss, and only the building for the lower secondary school was used while the other was left half finished. Tellingly, this private school was dependent on pupils like Mamadou. In 2006 almost half of the total number of pupils enrolled in the school had been excluded from the public school system. For instance, of a total of seventy pupils enrolled in lower secondary school (*collège*), fifty pupils were in the final year and were, like Mamadou, hoping to pass the final exam to receive the *brevet* (marking the end of ten years of schooling). In the end, Mamadou failed the final exam for the *brevet*. Instead of trying a second time, Mamadou, who during his time in school had also worked as an apprentice in a bicycle repair shop in the evenings after school and on weekends, started a training course in welding at the National Museum in the city centre, reasoning that 'It's better than doing nothing'. Mamadou hoped to find a job as a welder in one of the big mining companies, a factory, or a workshop and to eventually open up his own welding shop. After investing himself in education in public and private school without success, welding promised a more easily accessible and financially secure future.

The crisis and selectivity of the public education system has also contributed to the emergence of other forms of privatization or marketization. For instance, private tutoring has become almost ubiquitous in Niamey where both parents and pupils see it as an essential supplement to the teaching received during school hours. Private tutoring takes different forms such as repeat sessions (*cours de rattrapage*), evening and weekend classes, and private home tutoring. After school classes and private tutoring represented an important additional income for teachers especially for contract teachers[5] faced with low salaries and little job security. However, in the peri-urban neighbourhood where Ibrahim lived, teachers complained about the weak local demand for private tutoring which was the most expensive option.

Another phenomenon which is indicative of the struggle to stay in the public school system is that of 'parallel recruitment' (or fraudulent recruitment), which meant that members of the school administration let excluded pupils re-enter the public school system in exchange for an informal fee or bribe. Taking recourse to parallel recruitment provided an alternative to paying tuition fees in private school, parents and pupils preferring to negotiate reentry into the public school system with the school administration. According to an official at the school inspectorate interviewed in 2007, parallel recruitment had initially been a strategy on the part of cash-strapped public schools to augment their budget by accepting a small number of unofficially 'paying' students, but the practice had spun out of control, turning some public schools into unofficial semi-private schools and providing school directors with a source of extra income. Ibrahim's mother recounted that she had been offered the opportunity to have her daughter Djamila reintegrated into another public school for a fee of 50,000 FCFA after she had repeated a class and failed the final exam (*brevet*). She referred to this offer as 'playing the tombola' and in the end decided not to pay for her daughter to be readmitted to the school.

Ibrahim's mother's comment about the tombola can be interpreted as a more general comment on the public education system, and the uncertain outcome of investments in education especially for families with limited economic resources. The increasing presence of the education market in educational trajectories shows the important role that economic and social capital play in determining chances of 'success' or 'survival' in school, indicating a clear stratification of education strategies as families with financial means can enrol their children in private schools, hire private tutors or pay for re-inscription in public school, in the drive to attain a school leaving diploma.

Educational Strategies and Social Aspirations

The vibrancy of the education market – and the effort that parents and pupils made to invest in education – is evidence of the continued importance accorded to formal education despite the saturation of the job market. In this section I will discuss education and the sometimes divergent social aspirations of parents and pupils in order to unpack the changing and sometimes contradictory relation between education, social climbing and cultural capital.

Education remains an important means of social reproduction for parents with formal employment. Investing in the education of their children, by for instance sending them to prestigious private schools, was a means of maintaining a socio-economic position and the associated cultural capital. Education also continued to represent a possibility for social ascent for parents who had never gone to school, like Ibrahim's parents, through the opportunity that it offered their children to access a new sphere of opportunities and a more economically secure future. At the same time, their expectations were tempered. This is illustrated in the case of Ibrahim's parents. Building on past experiences, they had quite a pragmatic approach in measuring up the potential benefits of formal education. Ibrahim's mother underlined the fact that if children have the chance to succeed in school they can help their parents, but even if they did not succeed they still had an advantage in comparison to people who have never been to school. Ibrahim's father, after pointing to a lack of employment prospects for school leavers, noted that children at least learn to read and write in school.

In order to increase the chances of securing a future income, Ibrahim's mother had at one point encouraged him to sign up for a police recruitment test when he had finished lower secondary school. She justified this by stating that studying 'for too long' ('*les longues études*') is not for the children of the poor, who need to double their chances in order to succeed. This was a common remark among both pupils and parents and led many to direct their efforts to more accessible professions like nursing or teaching that only required a *brevet* and two to three more years of study in a technical school. For Ibrahim's mother the important thing was that he would find work. The police force – like nursing and teaching – represented a steady source of income in contrast to the uncertainty of higher education. Joining the police or gendarmerie was also a favoured option for many pupils. In his work on education itineraries in Abidjan, Proteau points out that the army, customs agency and the police became increasingly desirable for pupils from lower and middle class families as high expectations were revised downwards. Such professions seemed to provide a route to economic security combined with the symbolic power represented by the uniform (Proteau 1995: 643). However, access to these professions hinged on passing entrance examinations (*concours*) which were often accompanied by scandals of corruption and favouritism. Despite Ibrahim's performing well, his mother claimed that all of the places had gone to the children of the rich (*fils des riches*) and well connected. This stayed in the memory of his parents, both of whom saw it as an example of the small chances 'the children of the poor' have of succeeding in a system replete with clientelism.

In thinking about the future, parents were mainly concerned with how their children would make a living. Ibrahim's mother's insistence that he enter the test (*concours*) for the police force reflects an anxiety about the future given the small chances of success both in school and after in a difficult economic conjuncture. For Ibrahim's mother, joining the police force seemed like the best option for securing a decent livelihood building on the social capital gained through education. However, pupils themselves often had much higher ambitions. Ibrahim, who was set on pursuing higher education, argued that the children of the poor were better motivated and thus more likely to succeed than the children of the rich in the city centre, who he said did not want to study and instead spent all of their time and energy on hip hop and leisure activities, noting that the most important authorities (political leaders) are 'villagers' (*'toutes les grandes autorités sont des villageois'*).

For many pupils, especially for pupils who had progressed to secondary school, the hope of social ascent through education was a central driving force and source of motivation and identification. One pupil in lower secondary school explained why he had invested himself in school, referring to material symbols of success, and contrasting this with occupations like agriculture and small-scale commerce:

> Me, I hung around singing for a while but eventually I left all of that. I was the only one among my friends who did not have the BEPC (*brevet*). All the others were preparing the Bac (*baccalauréat*). We all started school the same day. That's what encouraged me to stay in school. All the civil servants who have luxury cars and all that, it's because they have gone to school, isn't that right? Can someone who is unemployed have a luxury car or put his mother in a luxury car? He's only going to trade or cultivate the land.

At the same time, pupils were aware of the uncertainty of their future. One pupil who was active in the student union, after having enumerated the many dysfunctions of the public education system, remarked with sarcasm that the government does not invest in education because it does not want more graduates because they will end up being unemployed: 'There are no offices for graduates, no air-conditioned offices'. Such comments reflect the fact that pupils were well aware of the slim chances that education would in fact lead to formal employment and social advancement and that this was a state of affairs that caused much resentment.

The hopes that continued to be tied up with education are also evident in the deep disappointment that pupils expressed when they found themselves 'stuck' following failed exams or when faced with unemployment after graduation. Dropping out of school was often felt by pupils to be a failure. Yacouba, Ibrahim's brother who had dropped out of primary school and made a living fishing in the river and helping out in the gardens and rice fields, was considering joining a relative in Cotonou to try his luck in trade, as fishing had not proved to be very lucrative. Yacouba saw few other alternatives open to him, asking rhetorically, 'Now that you haven't studied, what can you become?' This comment is revelatory

of the close association between education and young people's imaginations of the future and the subsequent disappointment that follows an
interrupted 'school career'. As one girl commented when recounting that
she had had to drop out of school to take care of a sick aunt: 'School is
important, I regret having quit. When you succeed you can have a good
job. You can have everything if God is willing. You can have a beautiful
car. You can become a teacher, a doctor.'

Hassane, a young man who had dropped out of school in the last year
of primary school after having failed the final exam, deeply regretted that
he did not have a school leaving certificate. He made a decent living gardening on family-owned land and had plans to install a motor pump to
increase production and supplement gardening with animal husbandry;
however, he emphasized the fact that without a school leaving certificate
his job options were limited. Even when school 'drop outs' managed to
get by financially through other means than formal employment there
still seemed to be a lingering sense of disappointment. Hassane pointed
out that many of his former classmates who had successfully finished
school (with a *brevet* or the *baccalauréat*) were now economically better off
than he was.

From the parents' perspective – especially in these peri-urban neighbourhoods where agriculture continued to be an means of getting by – the
potential benefits of education were offset by the risk that their children
would neither succeed in school nor pick up another skill such as agriculture or trade and would thus be left empty-handed and susceptible to
finding an 'easy' way out (*chercher la facilité*) like petty crime. This worry
was voiced by Ibrahim's father:

> When a child attends school for all these years and in the end does not succeed,
> it is really a heavy loss. Because he will have wasted his time in school without
> learning any trade at home… you have never learned to work in the fields, so
> when you leave school… it will be difficult for you to cope with the pain (*souf-
> france*) of work [manual labour].

This echoes similar perceptions about schooling as described by
Hagberg in rural Burkina Faso where whether or not children 'learn to
live' (improve basic capabilities) or 'learn to leave' (leave the traditional
way of life, cultivation) through formal education was a central concern
(2006: 169). This – the break with the home environment and with tradition (traditional education) and agriculture – has also been identified as
one of the reasons why parents in rural Niger do not send their children
to school, especially in a precarious economic context when education
does not seem to lead anywhere (Meunier 2000: 226–27, Wynd 1999).
Such considerations have also been shown to have an important effect on

gender disparities, with some parents preferring to simply not send girls to school (Wynd 1999). In my peri-urban fieldwork context, although negative comments abounded about 'drop-outs' and school-leavers as well as university graduates who 'did nothing', the break that schooling caused was not necessarily cast as a break with the home environment but as the source of a refusal to do manual labour in the rice fields or gardens. This criticism comes through in one of Hassane's comments about educated youth:

> For them if you have the baccalaureate and people see you watering [working in the garden], it's shameful, but shame is stealing, you see someone with a cellphone, you steal it and they catch you, that's shameful... they sit in the *fada* and as soon as they see someone passing by they say, 'older brother, give us 25 f so that we can buy sugar'.

Criticism of youth often centred on the *fada* (conversation groups made up of mainly young men), as a place where youth are idle, opting to sit, drink tea and listen to music, instead of looking for work. While the older generation generally have a negative view of *fadas*, for jobless urban male youth *fadas* provide a space for sociality and support and a means of passing (excess) time in a meaningful way (Masquelier 2013). Faced with an uncertain economic future and with sometimes trenchant criticism from the surrounding society and community, pupils and school leavers were quick to emphasize the non-material benefits of education:

> Those who drop out in lower secondary or primary school are those who do not think about their future. Otherwise, even if you don't succeed in becoming what you want to become, you can have a different mentality than the others. You cannot compare someone who has the *Brevet* or the *Bac* to someone who has only reached the level of fifth grade [CM1].

In the absence of any significant economic difference, education could still be used as a ground for social or cultural distinction from peers who had not been to school or who had dropped out early. However, this distinction would only last for so long, as evidenced by the negative views of jobless school leavers. Although education represents both a route to material benefits (employment) and to gaining symbolic capital (Proteau 1995: 651), I would argue that among my young informants, the symbolic capital associated with education was still inexorably tied up with economic capital and social mobility. The failure to achieve economic stability and thus also social advancement made the symbolic capital gained through education volatile and uncertain. Mazzochetti found a similar phenomenon, namely the discordance felt by university students in Ouagadougou who had associated education with the symbolic social mobility of becoming 'intellectuals' but who were faced with a loss of social and economic status as university studies were no longer a source of employment or prestige (Mazzocchetti 2014: 73). The increasingly ten-uous link between education and social advancement led many youth to search for alternative paths to social status and economic stability.

Finding a Path of Social Recognition

In the face of unemployment, secondary school and university graduates attempted to make a place for themselves through involvement in vari-ous associations, thus drawing on and at the same time valorizing their acquired skills. This strategy is evident in the case of the youth associa-tion for former pupils of the local secondary school that Ibrahim attended. The association had been created in 2000 by a group of friends who had attended the upper secondary school Lycée Issa Korombé (formerly the Lycée National) in the city centre and had been inspired by the school's association of former pupils, which they said had been created by former president Ibrahim Baré Maïnassara. After having graduated from upper secondary school, some of them had found themselves unemployed and with little to do. Others who had started university also had a lot of spare time on their hands as the university semesters were frequently delayed and interrupted due to social unrest. They thus decided to create an association together with other youth who had attended the local lower secondary school. From the beginning the association was focused on helping pupils in the local secondary school by giving them extra classes and providing courses during the summer. The association was also involved in development funded activities directed towards youth, such as the creation of a community library by the French Development Cooperation and sensitization sessions about HIV/AIDS.

Interestingly, the members of the youth association seemed to model their engagement on an older local home town association that had been very visible in the locality. Many of the members of this home town asso-ciation had been the first pupils to be enrolled in the local public primary school in the 1960s, when enrolment rates were still limited, and were almost five decades later still referred to as 'the first class' (*la première promotion*). The generation of their parents, who had not gone to school, still referred to them as 'the pupils' (*les élèves*, or *lokolizey* in Zarma) or 'the intellectuals' (*les intellectuels*), a group which from the beginning was relatively small in the locality despite its proximity to Niamey. They were also often referred to as *ressortissants*, a French term which denotes a national or a citizen but which in this Nigerien context refers to someone who comes from or is born in a specific village or region, has moved out, usually to the capital or abroad, but still maintain links to the locality. The status of *ressortissant* is usually given to someone who has become influential or successful (civil servants, professionals, traders) and who takes an active part in local affairs. In a context of decentralization, *ressortissants* have also become important political actors, for instance as local benefactors contributing financial support to the construction of village infrastructure such as mosques, health centres and wells, and as emerging politicians (Olivier de Sardan and Tidjani Alou 2009: 5). In contrast to today's school leavers, for the members of the home town association, their advancement through the school system in the 1970s had opened the way to many different opportunities. Some had joined the army and others were sent abroad on state scholarships to continue their studies in Europe or in other African countries, returning to pursue careers in the public and private sectors. They clearly fit the image of the 'intellectual' as a 'figure of success' (Banégas and Warnier 2001: 5) as they held key positions in well paid jobs, drove cars and had built some of the few villas and two-storey houses in the neighbourhood. Although the association was no longer active, its presence still lingered, not least through the visibility and actions of its former members who continued to play a central role in the locality.

In contrast to the members of the home town association, the members of the youth association had not achieved an elevated socio-economic status and it seemed unlikely that they would manage to do so. In the context of an uncertain future, the creation of the youth association represented a means of seeking social status and social recognition through an active participation in the local political arena. Fokwang, studying youth and voluntary associations in Cameroon, has pointed to the role of youth associations as a means for youth to position themselves as important social actors – 'through associations, young people position themselves and claim adult status by participating as part of a collective in a range of social and moral projects' (Fokwang 2008: 159). Similarly, Diouf cites the emergence of youth organizations in Dakar that are active in the neighbourhoods, organizing clean-up sessions, opening public libraries, offering education classes and security, as one form of response to marginalization and a loss of status in the context of a sustained economic crisis (Diouf 2003: 8). The youth association also opened up opportunities for involvement in other associations, development initiatives and community committees in which the educated youth could make use of the skills gained through education, for instance by helping to write and type up the statutes of local association or putting together demands for financing. Participating in local development initiatives provided a potential platform for entry into the youth section of political parties who were dependent on members' capacity to mobilize supporters. In a rural Nigerien context Hahonou has also pointed to the importance of associations and NGOs as a political trampoline for youth (Hahonou 2010: 232). Building political contacts was also a potential means of accessing employment in the administration or the private sector.

While the above activities all conform to the expectations that pupils might have about future employment in an office and 'behind a desk', when faced with the risk of unemployment and of not being able to reach adulthood, other alternative paths have also become increasingly important. These include learning a trade (as in the case of Mamadou described above), migrating, or pursuing a religious education. Mazzocchetti (2014) and Masquelier (2013) have both highlighted the importance of migration for educated youth. Mazzocchetti argues that dreams of (international) migration can be seen as the extension of a life project centred on education as a path to success, with migration offering a continuation of this project in the face of diminishing opportunities at home (Mazzocchetti 2014). Migration can also provide a means of getting by on low status (menial) jobs (petty trade, manual labour) that educated youth might be reluctant to do at home out of fear of a lack of prestige (Masquelier 2013: 471). Other researchers have pointed to the increasing importance of Islam for youth as a mode of social engagement (Masquelier 2007; Sounaye 2015). For many youth, religion and religious education also provided a means of filling the void left after a failed school career. Most pupils had on their parents' insistence attended Qur'anic lessons at the same time as they attended school. For youth who had dropped out of school, Qur'anic schools and other kinds of Islamic education provided a means of continuing one's education with a focus on religion and religious learning. Nafissa, a young married women in her twenties, had dreamt of becoming a teacher or a doctor. However, she had dropped out of primary school. She was now attending Qur'anic school and underlined the satisfaction she felt in learning more about Islam, envisioning a future in which she would teach others. Religious learning thus provided her with an alternative path to social recognition.

Conclusion

Several years after he had failed the final exam for the *baccalauréat*, Ibrahim finally made it into the police force. The fact that he had a job and a stable income then made it possible for him to get married and he was now living in the family compound with his young wife and their new-born son. However, Ibrahim had still not given up on getting the *baccalauréat* and was planning to prepare the examination as an external candidate. Aware of his responsibilities as family provider, he said that he would remain in the police force even if he managed to get the *baccalauréat*. In one sense Ibrahim, who despite his parents' reluctance had wanted to go to university, had been forced to revise his ambitions downwards. At the same time joining the police force had allowed him to reach social adulthood by marrying and it also represented a significant move in the social space as it provided a steady salary. Yet, after investing so much time and energy in education, the *baccalauréat* was still on Ibrahim's mind, illustrating its symbolic importance as the crowning achievement of a successful education career.

At the beginning of this chapter I pointed to the centrality of social advancement in people's representations of school. Education has historically played an important role as a path to social advancement, mainly through entry into the state apparatus and to economic privilege symbolized by formal employment. However, this link was challenged by the economic crisis of the 1980s, which curtailed employment opportunities, and by the ensuing 'education crises' marked by protest, annulled school years, reforms and cutbacks, the repercussions of which are still being dealt with today. However, despite the increasingly tenuous link between education and social advancement and the emergence of alternative models of success, peri-urban residents – parents and, not least, pupils themselves – continued to invest themselves in education. The representation of education as a source of social and cultural capital continues to be reproduced despite structural conditions that challenge such links. Among my informants, pupils from disadvantaged urban backgrounds in particular faced difficulties progressing through public school as succeeding in school was increasingly dependent on the possibility of taking part in the education market (which required economic capital). However, despite the uncertainty that characterized education trajectories, education was central to young people's imaginations of the future and to their identity as education still represented a chance of social mobility. School thus continues to be an important site for understanding young people's aspirations as well as their experiences of inequality and of social immobility when school careers end early or when the successful attainment of a diploma does not automatically translate into social advancement and hopes for the futures are transformed into the disappointment that accompanied the failure to successfully finish school or land a job. However, in the face of a failed school career and bleak employment prospects youth also sought alternative ways to seek social recognition or status through for instance migration or religious education. The analysis of different trajectories also reveals how different dead ends are transformed into new beginnings as youth search for alternative paths to independence and social status.

Gabriella Körling is a researcher at the Department of Social Anthropology, Stockholm University. She holds a PhD in cultural anthropology from Uppsala University. Her PhD dissertation, 'In Search of the State: An Ethnography of Public Service Provision in Urban Niger' (2011), was awarded the Westin Prize for the best thesis in the humanities at Uppsala University. Her research interests include the state, infrastructure, urban anthropology, politics and decentralization in Niger. Körling's current research project focuses on the construction of Niger's first railway and explores expectations and urban transformations in a town situated alongside the future railway tracks.

Notes

1. Parts of this chapter have previously appeared in my PhD thesis (2011) in Uppsala Studies in Cultural Anthropology, Acta Universitatis Upsaliensis. The chapter is based on fourteen months of fieldwork carried out between 2006 and 2008 in Niamey complemented by shorter fieldwork periods and revisits in the period between 2012 and 2016.
2. Enrolment rates at primary level stagnated at around 30 per cent during much of the 1990s (Meunier 2009: 24).
3. http://www.uis.unesco.org/DataCentre/Pages/country-profile.aspx?code=NER. Last consulted 16 November 2016.
4. http://www.uis.unesco.org/DataCentre/Pages/country-profile.aspx?code=NER. Last consulted 16 November 2016.
5. The 'contract' was introduced in 2004. Contract teachers are hired on temporary contracts instead of being integrated into the civil service. The salary of contract teachers is lower than the salary of 'permanent' teachers. Contract teachers now make up the majority of teachers in Niger.

References

Abbink, J., and I. van Kessel (eds). 2005. *Vanguard or Vandals: Youth, Politics and Conflict in Africa*. Leiden: Brill.
Banégas, R., and J.-P. Warnier. 2001. 'Nouvelles Figures de la Réussite et du Pouvoir', *Politique Africaine* 82: 5–23.
Bourdieu, P. 1985. 'The Social Space and the Genesis of Groups', *Theory and Society* 14(6): 723–44.
Buchmann, C. 2002. 'Getting ahead in Kenya: Social Capital, Shadow Education, and Achievement', in B. Fuller and E. Hannum (eds), *Schooling and Social Capital in Diverse Cultures*. Bingley: Emerald, pp. 133–59.

Camfield, L. 2011. '"From School to Adulthood"? Young People's Pathways through Schooling in Urban Ethiopia', *European Journal of Development Research* 23(5): 679–94.

Cruise O'Brien, D. 1996. 'A Lost Generation: Youth Identity and State Decay in West Africa', in R. Werbner and T. Ranger (eds), *Postcolonial Identities in Africa*. London: Zed Books, pp. 55–74.

Diouf, M. 2003. 'Engaging Postcolonial Cultures: African Youth and Public Space', *African Studies Review* 46(2): 1–12.

Fokwang, J. 2008. 'Youth Subjectivities and Associational Life in Bamenda, Cameroon', *Africa Development* Vol. XXXIII(3): 157–62.

Hagberg, S. 2006. '"Why Do the Bench?": Education as Modernity and Estrangement', *Mande Studies* 8: 169–182.

Hahonou, E.K. 2010. *Démocratie et Culture Politique en Afrique: En Attendant la Décentralisaiton au Niger*. Saarbrucken: Éditions Universitaires Européennes.

Hansen, K.T. 2005. 'Getting Stuck in the Compound: Some Odds against Social Adulthood in Lusaka, Zambia', *Africa Today* 51(4): 2–16.

Institut National de la Statistique. 2015. *Monographie sur les Adolescents: Région de Niamey*. Niamey: Institut National de la Statistique.

Jeffrey, C. 2008. '"Generation Nowhere": Rethinking Youth through the Lens of Unemployed Young Men', *Progress in Human Geography* 32(6): 739–58.

Körling, G. 2011. *In Search of the State: An Ethnography of Public Service Provision in Urban Niger*, Uppsala Studies in Cultural Anthropology 51. Uppsala: Acta Universitatis Upsaliensis.

Lange, M.-F., and O. Diarra. 1999. 'Ecole et Démocratie: L'Explosion Scolaire sous la IIIe République au Mali', *Politique Africaine* 76: 164–72.

Masquelier, A. 2007. 'Negotiation Futures: Islam, Youth, and the State in Niger', in B.F. Soares and R. Otayek (eds), *Islam and Muslim Politics in Africa*. New York: Palgrave, pp. 243–62.

_____. 2013. 'Teatime: Boredom and the Temporalities of Young Men in Niger', *Africa* 38(3): 470–91.

Mazzocchetti, J. 2014. '"Le Diplôme-Visa". Entre Mythe et Mobilité: Imaginaires et Migrations des Etudiants et Diplômés Burkinabè', *Cahiers d'Etudes Africaines* 213–214: 49–80.

Meunier, O. 2000. *Bilan d'un Siècle de Politique Educative au Niger*. Paris: L'Harmattan.

_____. 2009. *Variations et Diversités Educatives au Niger*. Paris: L'Harmattan.

Ministère de l'Education Nationale. 2007. *Statistiques de l'Education de Base Annuaire 2006–2007*. Niamey: Ministère de l'Education Nationale.

Olivier de Sardan, J.-P., and M. Tidjani Alou. 2009. 'Introduction: Le Local comme Enjeu Politique et Enjeu Scientifique', in J.-P. Olivier de Sardan and M. Tidjani Alou (eds), *Les Pouvoirs Locaux au Niger. Tome 1 : A la Veille de la Décentralisation*. Paris: Karthala, pp. 1–11.

Proteau, L. 1995. 'Le Champ Scolaire Abidjanais: Stratégies Educatives des Familles et Itinéraires Probables', *Cahiers des Sciences Humaines* 31(3): 635–53.

Pype, K. 2015. 'Becoming a Diplômé in Kinshasa: Education at the Intersection of Politics and Urban Livelihoods', *Diversité Urbaine* 15(1): 5–26.

Robinson, P. 1994. 'The National Conference Phenomenon in Francophone Africa', *Comparative Studies in Society and History* 36: 575–610.

Sounaye, A. 2015. 'Irwo Sunnance yan-no! Youth Claiming, Contesting and Transforming Salafism', *Islamic Africa* 6(1–2): 82–108.

Tidjani Alou, M. 1992. 'Les Politiques de Formation en Afrique Francophone: Ecole, Etat et Sociétés au Niger', PhD Dissertation. Bordeaux: Université de Bordeaux.

UNESCO Institute for Statistics (UIS). 2014. 'Niger: Participation in Education'. Retrieved 16 November 2016 from http://uis.unesco.org/country/NE.

United Nations Data. 2015. 'Social Indicators: Education, Primary Gross Enrolment Ratio'. Retrieved 1 May 2018 from http://data.un.org/en/iso/ne.html.

Welmond, M. 2002. 'Globalization Viewed from the Periphery: The Dynamics of Teacher Identity in the Republic of Benin', *Comparative Education Review* 46(1): 37–65.

Wynd, S. 1999. 'Education, Schooling and Fertility in Niger', in C. Heward and S. Bunwaree (eds), *Gender, Education and Development: Beyond Access to Empowerment*. London and New York: Zed Books, pp. 101–16.

Chapter 4

'Precarious Prosperity'?
Social Im/mobilities among Young Entrepreneurs in Kampala

Laura Camfield and William Monteith

Introduction

Bourdieu's concept of 'social space', which brings together the chapters within this volume, has particular salience for the entrepreneurs discussed in this chapter. Their economic positions and hence social and political interests are too varied for it to be meaningful to talk of them as a single group, even though this is often done in writing on entrepreneurship.[1] In understanding their current positions, we need to look vertically at their relationships with parents, aunts and uncles, and horizontally at those with neighbours and fellow traders. The social networks they are embedded in shape their lives, including ones that connect rural and urban and span other East African countries (a quarter of the sample are East African migrants). We need to take advantage of the longitudinal nature of the data used in this chapter to look backwards and forwards in time, disrupting any sense of a singular, linear trajectory. Here, as in Bourdieu's world, the game is not 'snakes and ladders' where one moves along a single, unidimensional scale from lower lower to upper upper class (Bourdieu 1979: 137). It is closer to 'three-dimensional chess' where it is possible to move sideways, for example, into a field with a different structure of capitals, rather than simply up and down.

In understanding social mobility, or the lack of it, we need to see how actors occupy positions in 'social space' relative to each other and

---

Notes for this chapter begin on page 106.

to various types of capital (resources). These are economic (money and assets), cultural (socially or culturally relevant knowledge and skills, synonymous with formal education in the global North, but less so in other contexts), social (who we know), and symbolic (any form of capital that is recognized as legitimate and therefore increases social recognition)[2] (Hilgers and Mangez 2015). For example, Agnes describes how when she moved from Rwanda to Kampala she changed from selling clothes to selling vegetables, which is more lucrative because it is less highly taxed. While this has improved her economic position, she feels it may have reduced her status – 'some people minimize it as a cheap job and say "that woman sells tomatoes", yet I gained much more from it than selling clothes'. Similarly, Eria, who trained as a welder, started running a salon 'because it gives me more money to look after my family and baby' but despite this '[my wife's] relatives were saying my job of the salon is fit for useless people'. Even though his previous experiences suggested welding was less well paid, 'in welding people respect you more'.

We also need to understand entrepreneurs' aspirations, or rather their subjective sense of themselves as entrepreneurs, recognizing that for women in particular this is unlikely to be articulated in the language of a business school (Basu and Werbner 2009). Female respondents talk instead about the pleasure they gain from increasing their skills (Aida says that 'I am no longer at the stage I started from and this encourages me a lot in whatever I do'). They are able to meet their own and their children's needs, often in the absence of spousal support (Mbazi says that 'I like my job because it has enabled me to survive, though it is not a big business').

Finally, we need to look at the other social properties active in African 'social spaces' today – in urban Uganda gender, age, ethnicity and religion are important, although ethnicity is rarely mentioned here.[3] For example, in our third interview with him, one of the respondents told us a long story about converting to Islam and changing his name on reuniting with his father's family. However, his wife separately explained that he had always been a Muslim, but had chosen to use someone else's name to get identity documents, recognizing that in the sector in which he worked a Muslim name would be a disadvantage. We need to explore how these social properties relate to class, or rather, the way in which relative status and economic positions intersect to produce unequal life chances (Bourdieu 1979: 113–21). This insight is often framed as an attention to intersectionality (Collins 2015) where the structural entwinement of, for example, gender and class, produces more than a simple addition of variables (Bourdieu 1979: 119–20).

As Noret argues in the introduction to this volume, the broad depictions of people's lives common in studies of urban Africa are only possible through a neglect of people's social positionality. Their positionality is expressed through the detail of their lives and the way these lives intersect with those of the people around them. In understanding people's social positionality, we draw on Hübinger's (1996) concept of 'precarious prosperity', which identifies a 'structural break' or 'prosperity threshold'. Beyond this threshold, prosperity is 'secure' and life contingencies are not usually followed by impoverishment. Precarious prosperity seems to be a more specific and grounded notion than becoming middle class and thus analytically more helpful in this context.[4] It also implicitly critiques the 'stretching' of the notion of the middle class to apply to individuals in circumstances not only much poorer, but also much less secure than the ones in which it was originally developed. Nonetheless, the analysis of the entrepreneurs presented in this chapter shows that few have reached even precarious prosperity, as also found by Budowski et al. (2010) in Europe and Chile. While Hübinger developed the concept in Western Germany where the welfare regime and levels of income are very different, and perhaps more prosperous than precarious when put in a global perspective, it captures the experience of living substantially below the median income. This does not provide security and in some contexts may not be enough to function in society. The combination of relative and actual deprivation has been shown to reduce people's wellbeing across a range of contexts.

In the second part of the chapter, we briefly describe the place of entrepreneurship in Uganda and in the third we present the theoretical framework. We then describe the context in which the research took place and the methodology. In the fourth section, we present the findings, structured primarily around the story of two entrepreneurs, who are partners and initially appeared to be the most successful of the cohort. This illustrates the precarious nature of people's situations and the strategies they use to manage this. Finally, we conclude by looking at how Bourdieu's understanding of 'social space' helps us understand how precarious prosperity operates in particular contexts.

Entrepreneurship in Uganda

The most authoritative data source on entrepreneurship in Uganda is the Global Entrepreneurship Monitor or GEM survey, collected in 2014. According to the GEM country profile, Uganda has shown consistently high levels of entrepreneurial activity since 2003, particularly amongst young people and more recently women (this reflects high levels of youth unemployment [Bbaale 2014]). The average entrepreneur in Uganda is female,[5] aged between eighteen and thirty-four, with at least secondary education, and working in the consumer service sector, something borne out by our sample (Appendix 1). The attitudinal surveys administered by GEM suggest that Ugandans have high aspirations and positive attitudes towards entrepreneurship. They have low levels of fear of failure and see good opportunities to start a business. Despite this, lack of capital is a major constraint, as discussed in relation to specific entrepreneurs later in the chapter and shown in Appendix 1. For women in particular, being able to draw on capital from spouses or family members was very important, as there were no cases where people unrelated to them lent women money. Although a third of the entrepreneurs had taken loans once they were established, commercial interest rates are high and this was raised by all the entrepreneurs sampled (for example, Regina complained that even the INGO BRAC's rates were too high). Jimmy explained:

> we should be getting money from banks or loans, but those people want a lot of profit… they will give you a loan of 3 million shillings for one year and maybe they want you to pay 300,000/= per month … the month you miss to pay back due to unavoidable circumstances, they will double it for the following month. So, for me, I fear that loaned money.

For these reasons businesses remain small – only 2 per cent of businesses expect to employ more than twenty people in the next five years – and the business discontinuation rate is 21 per cent (GEM 2014).

In order to understand these figures, Langevang et al. (2012: 444) propose a model of 'social embeddedness' which looks at entrepreneurs' multiple embedding in their 'socio-economic context,[6] social networks, family relations[7] and the life course'. They emphasize the constraints of their institutional environment and lack of capital rather than their motivations, for example, the intense competition between businesses in a context where the youth unemployment rate is 78 per cent (Ugandan Bureau of Statistics 2016: 4) and few people without connections can get salaried employment[8] (Wiegratz 2016). Langevang et al.'s (2012) qualitative study of thirty-four young entrepreneurs unpicks the necessity–opportunity dichotomy, which is so important in entrepreneurship research and practice. They argue that the motivational differences between so-called survival and opportunity entrepreneurs are overstated. They also show how people's motivations change over time because they are 'socially embedded and inextricably interwoven with the socio-economic environment, social networks, family circumstances and life events', underlining the value of a longitudinal approach (ibid.: 455). To secure their prosperity, as discussed in the next section, nearly a quarter of the entrepreneurs engage in activities characteristic of the emerging middle classes in Sub-Saharan Africa, such as building 'rentals' (self-contained rooms for rent) (Page and Sunjo 2018, Cameroon). Nearly half of the sample aspire to build their own house (see also Mercer 2014, Tanzania) and some have done so already (e.g. Musa who plans to buy a bigger plot to expand it). In her third interview, Joan, who has left her partner, says 'I am looking at getting someone who … has already built a house', indicating the value of this marker in 'concretizing a new middle class identity' (Page and Sunjo 2018: 75).

Theoretical Framework

The intention of the chapter is to explore Bourdieu's concept of 'social space' more directly by looking at 'precarious prosperity',[9] an idea originally put forward by Hübinger in 1996 following a quantitative study on poverty and social inequality in Western Germany. Hübinger identifies five positions within 'social space', only two of which could be seen as prosperous. He identifies a 'structural break' or 'prosperity threshold', between the third and fourth quintile above the poverty line where prosperity can be described as 'secure' and life contingencies are not usually followed by impoverishment (Hübinger 1996: 207). His focus is on people in precarious prosperity, i.e. receiving 60–80 per cent of median equivalized household income and adjacent to or just above the poverty line. This depicts a dynamic position in between secure prosperity and poverty, rather than precariousness: 'the paradox of a certain level of material wellbeing, allowing for a certain scope of agency and planning, on the one hand, and by an inherent insecurity and perceived threat of downward-mobility, on the other hand' (Budowski et al. 2010: 16). Crossing from poverty to precarious prosperity is more common than upward mobility to secure prosperity. This segment of the population between rich and poor is increasing in size in most countries due to economic deregulation and structural adjustment.

The work of Budowski in Europe and Chile, and by others not using this theoretical framework,[10] suggest that in the global North and South few households pass above or below the prosperity threshold, whereas a large part of households in precarious prosperity are threatened by moving into poverty. Quotations from interviewees in Budowski et al.'s study (2010: 29) illustrate their daily struggle to maintain their social position and not move into poverty. This can also be seen in the interviews from this sample where the realities of rising input prices, increased competition, rising taxes and levies from the Kampala Capital City Authority (KCCA) are set against aspirations for new income streams (three respondents wanted to build properties to rent) and children to attend university and even attain doctorates (six respondents). This experience is equally common in urban Africa; while the African Development Bank (2011) famously claimed that 34 per cent of Africans are middle class, they drew a distinction between the 'floating middle class' who hover just above the poverty line in the $2–4 a day bracket and the 'true middle class' (these can be considered as equivalent to Hübinger's category of the securely prosperous).

Taking an historical perspective, and particularly one supported by longitudinal data, is invaluable in understanding what makes individuals and households vulnerable (Baulch 2011). The changes in the lives of the entrepreneurs tracked over the past four years challenge the notion of a linear life course and show the value of anthropological concepts such as subjunctivity (Whyte 2002), discussed in di Nunzio (2017). This captures what people as subjects are trying to do – what they are hoping for, how they deal with their life conditions, and how things unfold for them over time. Vigh's (2009, 2010) notion of social navigation,[11] developed through work with young men in Guinea-Bissau, also captures the interplay between people's choices and the social bonds in which they are embedded in a volatile and interactive environment. Their perpetual motion does not mean that they are moving in the sense of social mobility – they can also be experiencing how 'societal movement becomes motion without progress' (Vigh 2009: 422). The sense of moving without moving – or running to keep still – and the importance of relationships can be seen in the lives of the female entrepreneurs from this sample. While their social embedding enables them to flourish (for example, Joan drawing on her father-in-law's experience with citrus fruit wholesale to start her new business), it also constrains the individual agency supposedly so characteristic of entrepreneurs (Monteith and Camfield 2019).

A greater attention to relationality (Lamb 1997, Locke et al. 2017) reveals the ways in which this is not a constraint, as is sometimes argued in relation to entrepreneurs' kin networks (Khavul, Bruton and Wood 2009, Khayesi, George and Antonakis 2014). For example, the majority of entrepreneurs in this sample say that they learned their skills by working alongside a family member. Many then took the enterprise over or started a new one with support from that person and other family members. Jimmy described how, having learned how to produce poultry and animal feed from his uncle, 'I was now being left to manage the store. Time came when he left the poultry feed business for good. I remained behind to run the store until today.'

We can even argue that entrepreneurs' lives are inherently relational, made up of networks of ties that they share with other people, places and things (Lamb 1997: 297, Elder's [1999] concept of 'linked lives'). In Bourdieu's terms, this understanding of relational is captured in the concept of social capital. However, he also understands relational in another sense, which involves treating social reality as a system of differences and understanding social practices primarily in relation to other social practices (Bourdieu 1998: 3). His theory of fields places the 'relationships' between the elements rather than the elements themselves at the heart of the analysis: 'space, whether social or physical, is relational' (Hilgers and Mangez 2015: 4–5). People's embedding in relationships can make them more able to manage chance (di Nunzio 2017, Cooper and Pratten 2015) as they can draw on support in emergencies (for example, a place to live or childcare). This may make them more willing to take risks in their economic activities. While social support offers the promise of reversing trajectories of marginalization and exclusion, di Nunzio (2017) suggests that this can be illusory, unless it also leads to social recognition.

The fluid and dynamic understandings of people's lives expressed in concepts such as relationality owe much to ideas about the life course that developed in the 1960s and crystallized with Glen Elder in the 1980s and 1990s.[12] Analytically Elder offered concepts such as 'linked lives' where, for example, the lives of children and parents evolve together. As an example of this, Rose's children look after her chickens and work in her feed store, which she feels is important for their future development. She structures her working day around sharing the care of her elderly mother with her brother, who also works in the store. Life course ideas highlight the importance of development across the life span and the influence of historical time[13] and geographic place (see, for example, Langevang et al.'s [2016] description of entrepreneurial activity in the low-income settlement of Bwaise in Kampala). Finally, they pay attention to agency and to the timing of decisions (see also Johnson-Hank's [2002] notion of 'vital conjunctures' where structure and agency collide). An example is how the death of Musa's friend (paternal uncle), and his friend's knowledge of how vulnerable his wife might be without a male provider, set him on the path to owning his own butcher's shop: 'he told me that even when he dies I should keep running his butcher's so that I get money to look after his children, which I am doing up to now'.

The notion of life course avoids the rigidity of 'life stage' approaches where people are seen as progressing along a single, linear pathway. Instead, it allows for a patterned indeterminacy that can be obscured by the language of pathways and trajectories. In the empirical section we use the examples of Jimmy, Rose and others to look at how young entrepreneurs are positioned within 'social space' in Uganda and the resources or capitals they draw on to achieve often fleeting social mobility.

Methodology

This chapter uses an opportunistic sample of sixteen male and female entrepreneurs (twelve female and four male), four of whom were partners. They were aged between twenty-three and forty at the start of the fieldwork in 2012 and operated a business in Kampala, Uganda. Five of them were market vendors (all fruit and vegetables, except one who sold fish), seven had retail or wholesale stores (two of them were husband and wife teams) and four offered services (tailoring and hair/beauty). The respondents were selected from a larger, random sample of entrepreneurs surveyed as part of the GIGA project Employment, Empowerment and Living Standards[14] as broadly representative of 'young entrepreneurs'. Three rounds of in-depth interviews were conducted in 2012, 2013 and 2015 with the assistance of a small team of Ugandan researchers.[15] These interviews focused on their life histories and career trajectories, including the resources, skills and networks they were able to draw upon at different stages in their lives. The characteristics of the sample are summarized in Appendix 1. In terms of their enterprises, they reported working between forty-five and ninety-one hours per week and earning between 5,000 and 300,000 Uganda Shillings per week (one respondent earned between 500,000 and 2 million; however, they were an outlier). Five of the premises had electricity, indicating their greater permanence. Seven entrepreneurs reported having a bank account and those who did not participated in either a SACCO (Savings and Credit Cooperative) or a ROSCA (Rotating savings and credit association).

Interviews were conducted in Luganda by the Ugandan research team and translated into English. The authors were present at the majority of the interviews and there were lengthy debriefing sessions at the end of each day where they talked through the interview content with the researchers.

Findings

In this section, we first look at the sample as a whole and review how their lives have changed personally and professionally over the four years of the research (summarized in Appendix 1 and Appendix 2). We then look at which of the sixteen could be considered to be in a state of 'precarious prosperity' and discuss their experiences in more detail. Finally, we return to Jimmy, the chicken feed entrepreneur described at the start of the chapter, and look at how his positioning within 'social space' affects the outcomes of the fire that destroyed his stock and machinery. We contrast his experience with that of his business partner and wife, who has kept some of her assets separate from his and is in a more fortunate position.

The Sample

While we have promised to step away from language implying that trajectories are linear, in understanding the nature of precarious prosperity it may be worth looking at the 'direction of travel' for the participating entrepreneurs. Of the sixteen entrepreneurs, nearly half could be described as being on a downwards course in relation to the performance of their business (Appendix 2). However, the picture is rarely as clear as in, say, Hadijia or Janat's case. Even where respondents have lost their previous businesses through marital breakdown (Joan, Agnes), this may have enabled them to form new relationships, or start businesses that, while currently in the early stages, have the potential to be more profitable than their previous endeavours. For example, according to the interviewer, '[Joan] is healthy, grew fatter and seems to have more peace of mind than before... Now she stays just 500 m from where she was before, in a house which is moderately good, spacious and is gated'. This shows the multiple nature of the drivers and outcomes of changes in the lives of entrepreneurs.

All the entrepreneurs, no matter how strained their situation, have concrete plans for the future, for themselves and their children. The interviewer of Agnes, who has recently remarried, notes that 'she boasts that her child will be a president of the country in future if he studies ... if she had not shifted from the slummy area and hadn't got the new husband she could probably have less expectations about her child's future goals and life attainments'. Typically, entrepreneurs have more than one plan, which like chess pieces can be moved in and out of play as different opportunities arise (see also the *bricoleurs* or *débrouillards* described in other African contexts). For example, in relation to her sons Aida says pragmatically, 'I want them to study up to university, but if I fail to get money to take them that far, they will join mechanic training after senior 4'.

In looking at the direction of travel, there are no clear determinants of success or failure. For example, marital breakdown can be a factor in a downwards course (Janat) or an upwards one (Agnes) or even, in the case of Regina, an irrelevance. Nonetheless, there are concrete material differences in their circumstances (Appendix 1) – where they got their capital from, whether they are able to save, their asset holdings (aside from household goods, equipment and stock), and whether they can support employees or apprentices. In relation to the source of their capital, the majority (ten) acquired this from an uncle, aunt or male sibling (these categories are often used loosely), six had support from a husband and four from a parent.[16] Six people held livestock or poultry, often with family in a rural area, four had land, three had 'rentals', and one person rented out a motorbike, car and lorry. Everybody saved to some extent, even if this was only in kind or in a cash-around (a way of earmarking smaller sums of money for stock purchases). However, there was a great difference between those saving bars of soap and sugar and others setting aside 50,000–85,000 UGX per week. Finally, although none of the market vendors had employees, the majority of those who owned shops or provided services did. These sorts of differences underpin the extent to which people's prosperity can be seen as precarious or not, as discussed in the next section.

Precarious Prosperity

In the second part of this section, we look at six entrepreneurs whom we propose are living in precarious prosperity. They all own established and profitable businesses (electronics, animal feed and butchery) and in one case supplement this with formal sector employment as a welder. In two cases, we were able to interview both partners, although in the second (Moses and Amina), the female partner takes a secondary role in the running of the business. Of the six, only Jimmy and Rose are experiencing a downwards course, as described in more detail in the final section. However, they retain sufficient resources and networks to run their business, suggesting they can be described as experiencing precarious prosperity.

Of the others, Amina and Moses are clearly on an upwards trajectory, professionally and personally. They are also the most educated couple; Moses uses both the subject of his degree and the connections he made through it in his work. While it is less clear what purpose Amina's degree serves, presumably it made her a more eligible partner and may provide employment opportunities once her children are older. Despite the death of their infant son in an accident at the shop, they have since had twin babies. They have also expanded the shop considerably – the floor space has increased by 400 or 500 per cent – allowing them to stock high-value items, which Moses owns outright. They sell mobile money and airtime and plan to develop a home-based poultry business. According to his wife, Moses has life insurance and has saved regularly in a bank account since 2008. While they are not (yet) what Hübinger would call the securely prosperous, they certainly have precarious prosperity.

Musa is also on an upwards trajectory. His butchery business has expanded and he runs rentals, owns livestock, and leases a lorry, motor-cycle and car. He has further plans for expansion, including moving to a kiosk on the main road, and investment. The extent of his assets means that he certainly has precarious prosperity and should be able to with-stand most shocks.

Finally, Eria is on an upwards trajectory as in addition to his salon, he has secured formal sector employment as a welder, which brings status and money, including a pension. To enhance his financial security further he saves 100,000 UGX per month,[17] which is impressive given that he is one of the youngest members of the sample. In the future, he plans to start his own construction company and has purchased a welding machine in preparation.

What resources have these entrepreneurs been able to draw on at the start of their business careers and subsequently to secure their prosperity? In the case of Moses, he began by borrowing 300,000 UGX from a friend who was working for Coca-Cola to buy a shop that sold switches and sockets. He then built the business up slowly, drawing on his previous experience repairing machinery in a neighbour's shop and selling elec-tronics in his uncle's shop, as well as post-secondary education in elec-tronics. When he had repaid the initial loan, his friend lent him another 100,000 UGX to expand his stock – 'I started slowly with switches, sockets and I started growing from there'. Musa came from a poorer family than Moses and went through a succession of jobs – casual labour, farm work, trading offal and even setting up a motorcycle taxi business. He describes how he slowly gathered together enough money to buy a motorcycle:

> My friend who used to sell meat would at times help me out; give me a kilo of meat and 1000 UGX to buy posho ... I had my black and white picture television which I had bought at 90,000 UGX and I sold it to my friend at 75,000 UGX, but he first paid me 35,000 UGX. ... I boarded a bus and went to my mother's ... I explained to her the situation I was in and she gave me 30,000 UGX ... So I came back to Kampala and went to the abattoir in Kalerwe and went with my friend to whom I had sold the television and bought a bicy-cle at 30,000 UGX. There after I joined the abattoir and started trading in offal from the 25,000 UGX that had remained... I kept on collecting money like that until I managed to buy my first motorcycle.

Finally, he set up a butcher's with his friend (paternal uncle) who died and left it to him, on the condition that he use some of the profit to support his friend's children. He saves 85,000 UGX every week in the Bukoto market SACCO and another group.

Both Moses and Musa were able to draw on family and other networks in starting their business, and have attempted to secure their prosperity by saving and investing, including in their children's education, as well as diversifying into other activities (e.g. rentals and sponsoring friends' micro businesses). The timescale of the research is too short to see whether this will be effective, especially given that entrepreneurs in the sample who have not been successful have also followed these strategies. However, they will provide some insurance against the contingencies discussed in the final section.

Managing Contingency: Rose and Jimmy

Rose and Jimmy are partners who manage a poultry and animal feed business and met through their business. Rose is older and more confident and while Jimmy initially seemed equally confident, significant discrepancies across three rounds of interviews (for example, around his use of credit) suggest that some of this was pretence. Talking to Rose and others, we gained the impression that when they met Jimmy was working as a daily labourer, and that this shaped the nature of their relationship. For example, although Rose says that now her mother is ill Jimmy is the first person she talks to about the business, she still talks about him as though he were an employee: 'on a bad day when sales are down I get him lunch and transport back home as a way of motivating him'. She says that as she has many activities to engage in (her shop, her poultry farm, caring for her mother and children), 'the good thing is, my husband is always here, except there are wiseacre customers who don't want to deal with him' (because she is seen as the boss). Conversely, Jimmy talks as though the business were his and she participates on an ad hoc basis, rewarded by treats such as a new hairstyle: 'you know women like to beautify their hair. Can you tell her that there is no money for her hair when she has worked for you? You give her money and she buys a handbag, makes a new hairstyle, and buys earrings'.

Both of them entered the business through family connections. Jimmy's mother sold poultry feed and so do two of his five siblings. His uncle trained him and he ran his uncle's store when he retired. He also inherited customers from his mother – 'she had many friends and customers when she was still selling feeds. So, it was very easy for me to deal with these people'. Rose grew up in a poor family and lived with many different family members. Her aunt funded her education until her aunt's marriage broke up and Rose regretted leaving school before completing her primary education: 'my entire life has been through struggle because we were not so much educated… I want to see my children excelling up to the university so that they get white-collar jobs. Because less educated children suffer a lot here in Uganda'.

Due in part to leaving school early and having no other support, she married an irresponsible man who did not provide for her or their three children. She supported them by selling bananas, then working in a salon and a restaurant, and finally working with her uncle's wife in poultry feeds. She says that when her aunt left the business, '[my friends] told me not to return the store to the landlady, but instead I should look for money to pay for its rent'. She took over her aunt's premises, machinery, and many of her customers and suppliers. In order to secure a flow of goods on credit, she also engaged in relationships that were more personal: 'one of these men who were advising me, got into an affair with me, and advised me to increase on the stock with his support'. She has already started to bring her children into the business (one works in the shop and the other on the poultry farm) and says 'I discuss a lot with my children especially the eldest three [from her first marriage] because the young ones only have childish thoughts'.

In December 2013 there was a fire in the wooden sheds in the old market, probably set deliberately to conceal a theft, which caused them to lose all their stock and three machines. Jimmy estimates the losses to be 15 million UGX ($4,200) and says they are now operating at a quarter of their previous capacity. They moved the business to a smaller and less central space with higher rent, which they share with three other feed retailers. As they are only running one machine, they need to exchange processing services with neighbours to provide the range of products that they used to offer. Unfortunately, many of their contacts are no longer in business, due to the fire. Jimmy says that 'all the business plans and personal and family improvements that I hoped to do by 2015 are now impossible; because of the fire we have now gone backwards'.

While Jimmy is slowly trying to rebuild the business, one transaction at a time, Rose was affected less because she has a second shop (Wakiso Poultry Feeds in Lubijii). They now use this to store customers' orders, as it is more secure. Her family supported her: 'I have a brother who sent me 2 million UGX but told me to refund him later as I work but according to my abilities. Though I haven't refunded since up to now … I am still struggling [Laughs].' This meant that while Jimmy had to sell his poultry business of over 1,500 'layers', she retained hers. While Jimmy's SACCO collapsed, as all the members were affected by the fire, hers continued. She also draws support from membership of her church, a burial society, and the ADA (a financial services programme run by Austrian

Development Agency) where she saves 10,000 UGX per week. This combination of factors partially accounts for how she remained resilient while she describes her husband as 'losing hope'. The two accounts show that even where two entrepreneurs are part of the same household and experiencing the same circumstances, they can have very different responses. These reflect their prior resources – including their positioning in 'social space' (for example, Rose is older than her partner Jimmy and part of a wealthy, close-knit family). It also reflects their current networks or social capital, the benefits of which are not always equally shared. Comparing the two accounts shows how some people's precarious prosperity can be more precarious than others.

Conclusions

The empirical analyses in the preceding section suggest that the concept of precarious prosperity adds substance to the idea of a 'floating middle class' who are growing in number (see also Darbon and Toulabor 2014). But within this group there is considerable heterogeneity – the stories of Jimmy and Rose show how differences in social positionality and access to different types of capital, which mediate access to economic resources, are reflected in different degrees of bouncing back after a major shock. Of the sixteen entrepreneurs, nearly half could be described as being on a downwards course in relation to the performance of their business; however, there are only two cases where the picture is bleak (Hadijia, Janat). While it is not always clear what role education plays in entrepreneurs' success, the fact that the most educated in this sample are the most successful and the least educated, the least successful (neither Hadija or Janat completed primary school) suggests it captures something that is important in entrepreneurs' success (for example, stable and financially secure families). For others, business failure – typically through marital breakdown – has created opportunities in other areas.

Heterogeneity in outcomes is not arbitrary and Bourdieu's concept of 'social space' enables us to look at how this indeterminacy is patterned. Specifically, it enables us to understand how precarious prosperity is experienced and reproduced by looking at the multiple positionalities of entrepreneurs within this sample. These can explain why marital breakdown can be a factor in a downwards course, an upwards one, or an irrelevance, which undermines the false certainty of variable based approaches to social mobility. 'Social space' enables us to look at trade-offs between cultural and economic capital, as exemplified by Eria and Agnes. Eria, who is one of the youngest entrepreneurs within the sample, as well as one of the best educated, combines comparatively prestigious formal employment with running a salon. He perceives the latter as time limited ('I have never seen a grey-haired man doing this kind of job') but necessary to establish his financial security and expand his networks. Agnes similarly had taken on a less prestigious activity on returning to Uganda ('some people minimize it as a cheap job'), but had made it profitable, in part through her ability to speak multiple languages fluently as an educated migrant. Her education may not have been why she was able to marry again to a wealthy man who has promised to support 'a better business of retail shop or selling clothes'. However, the fact that the most educated woman in the sample (Amina) has also married a wealthy man suggests that in this context education represents symbolic as well as human capital. 'Social space' highlights the importance of social capital through family connections (translated into financial capital to start businesses) and more widely, as entrepreneurs such as Rose and Moses use skills in social navigation to form relationships that support their businesses. There is also an element of reciprocity and mutual insurance, for example, the embracing of SACCO and ROSCA or Musa's investing in friends' micro businesses once he had become established.

Entrepreneurs' life courses are rarely linear and instead involve a series of sideways moves (for example, Agnes's move from successful trader to wealthy housewife). These can then shift people's aspirations and sense of themselves as entrepreneurs. In understanding these moves, we need to keep our focus on Langevang et al.'s (2012) socio-economic context, manifested in legal and institutional structures (e.g. KCCA rules, fishing legislation), theft, fire and fraud. These combine with the destabilizing effects of ill health (e.g. Rose, Aida) and marital breakdown (e.g. Janat, Joan), even if the latter is ultimately positive. What is added to understandings of these vital conjunctures by the life course and the anthropological concepts we discussed earlier?

Life course approaches provide a better understanding of the relational through concepts such as linked lives, which highlight the crucial importance of family in the narratives of male and female entrepreneurs. They provide a greater attention to subjunctivity, for example, how aspirations changed in the case of Agnes' plans for her son. They foreground the agency of entrepreneurs, for example, the creative bricolage of Musa's gathering together of resources for his butcher's shop. Finally, they show that while Kampala is a dynamic and unpredictable context, what is striking is the extent to which people do plan and the agility with which they move between plans as different opportunities arise. This is facilitated by the way they are positioned within 'social space', which gives them different levels of resources with which to plan and 'play' with. As Jimmy says of the future, 'I am trying to plan, but our plans can't go through because they depend on the money you have... All our programs are off'.

Laura Camfield is a Professor in Development Research and Evaluation at the University of East Anglia. She trained as an anthropologist, but now works collaboratively using qualitative and quantitative methods, most recently with the DFID-funded Gender and Adolescence: Global Evidence longitudinal evaluation (2016–2025). She works predominantly in East Africa and Bangladesh in relation to socially differentiated experiences of poverty and changes in livelihoods over time. She has published widely on methodology, specifically in relation to mixing methods to improve the quality of surveys and measures.

William Monteith is a Lecturer in the School of Geography at Queen Mary University of London. He obtained his PhD from the School of International Development at the University of East Anglia in 2016. Will's research examines lived experiences of 'work' at the margins of formal economies, the relationships and places produced through these experiences, and the ways in which they challenge theories of development based on the historical experiences of wage labourers in the global North.

Notes

Appendices for this chapter begin on page 213.
1. See Gartner (1985) for an early critique of this practice.
2. For example, having a large social network in a society where this is considered important provides both social and symbolic capital.
3. Two respondents mentioned this, Agnes and Kiyingi, in relation to attracting customers. Kiyingi said that 'if a Munyankole comes you speak in Runyankole, a Mukiga comes to you speak in Rukiga... this will ensure that you get their trust and they buy from you'.
4. See also Dominique Darbon's proposal that the new African middle class can be considered as living in a form of 'moderate prosperity' or *petite prospérité* (Darbon and Toulabor 2014).
5. The current ratio of male to female entrepreneurs is 0.92:1 (GEM 2014).
6. The socio-economic context is summarized in Namatovu et al. (2016: 18–19) which chronicles the dominance of Asian businesses pre-independence, their forced departure in 1972, the subsequent collapse of these businesses which triggered civil unrest, periods of hyperinflation and budgetary deficit. Structural adjustment and public sector unemployment followed, causing a rise in the number of small businesses, few of which thrived. While there has been a marked improvement in key economic indicators since the late 1990s and growth has averaged 7 per cent a year, inflation is high and the benefits of growth are unequally distributed.

7. Or 'family embeddedness' (Aldrich and Cliff 2003, in Langevang et al. 2012).
8. Moses, one of the entrepreneurs discussed later, described how 'I would do [job] interviews, but find that people had already booked the positions for the people they know'.
9. 'Precarious prosperity' is different from precarity or precariousness, which focus on economic deregulation and insecure forms of labour (Gallie and Paugam 2000: xvi). As in Sub-Saharan Africa, most labour is precarious, precarious prosperity offers greater analytical traction.
10. Portes and Hoffman (2003), for example, identify the 'informal proletariat' and the 'informal petty bourgeoisie' and confirm its growth following neoliberal adjustment and deregulation in the 1990s and early 2000s.
11. See also 'bricolage', and 'débrouillardise' (Vigh 2009), or what Langevang (2008) calls 'managing' in her description of the strategies of urban youth moving towards 'respectable adulthoods' in Accra.
12. See for example Elder's (1999) seminal work, *Children of the Great Depression*.
13. See Holland's (2011) distinction between biographical, historical and generational time in longitudinal research.
14. Approximately 5,000 enterprises were listed across the city in 2012, of which 1,000 were randomly sampled for household and enterprise surveys.
15. We would like to give thanks to our fantastic research team in Uganda: John Ssendagire, Douglas Nsibambi, Hilda Rukundo and Maxima Tibwita. Thanks also to the Centre for Basic Research (CBR) in Kampala and the Employment, Empowerment and Living Standard project team at GIGA.
16. A further six had taken out loans, but usually once the business was established, and three were supported by friends.
17. To put this in context, one study calculated the median net hourly wage as 1121 Ugandan Shilling (UGX), ranging from 443 (agricultural workers) to 1,600 (managers) per hour (Besamusca and Tijdens 2012).

References

African Development Bank. 2011. *The Middle of the Pyramid: Dynamics of the Middle Class in Africa*. Retrieved 20 April 2018 from https://www.afdb.org/fileadmin/uploads/afdb/Documents/Publications/The%20Middle%20of%20the%20Pyramid_The%20Middle%20of%20the%20Pyramid.pdf.

Basu, D., and P. Werbner. 2009. 'Who Wants to Be a Millionaire? Gendered Entrepreneurship and British South Asian Women in the Culture Industries', *Revue Européenne des Migrations Internationales* 25(3): 53–77.

Baulch, B. 2011. *Why Poverty Persists: Poverty Dynamics in Asia and Africa*. Camberley: Edward Elgar.

Bbaale, E. 2014. 'Where Are the Ugandan Youth? Socioeconomic Characteristics and Implications for Youth Employment in Uganda', *Journal of Politics and Law* 7(1): 37–63.

Besamusca, J., and K.G. Tijdens. 2012. *Wages in Uganda: Wage Indicator Survey 2012*. Wage Indicator Data Report October 2012. Amsterdam: Wage Indicator Foundation.

Bourdieu, P. 1984 [1979]. *Distinction: A Social Critique of the Judgement of Taste*, trans. R. Nice. London: Routledge & Kegan Paul.

Bourdieu, P. 1998. *Practical Reason: On the Theory of Action.* Stanford: Stanford University Press.

Budowski, M., et al. 2010. 'Conceptualising "Precarious Prosperity": Empirical and Theoretical Elements for Debate', *International Journal of Comparative Sociology* 51(4): 268–88.

Collins, P.H. 2015. 'Intersectionality's Definitional Dilemmas', *Annual Review of Sociology* 41(1): 1–20.

Cooper, E. and D. Pratten (eds). 2015. *Ethnographies of Uncertainty in Africa.* New York: Palgrave.

Darbon, D., and C. Toulabor. 2014. *L'Invention des Classes Moyennes Africaines: Enjeux Politiques d'une Catégorie Incertaine.* Paris: Karthala.

di Nunzio, M. 2017. 'Marginality as a Politics of Limited Entitlements: Street Life and the Dilemma of Inclusion in Urban Ethiopia', *American Ethnologist* 44(1): 91–103.

Elder, G.H. 1999. *Children of the Great Depression: Social Change in Life Experience.* Boulder, CO: Westview Press.

Gallie, D. and S. Paugam (eds). 2000. *Welfare Regimes and the Experience of Unemployment in Europe.* Oxford: Oxford University Press.

Gartner, W.B. 1985. 'A Framework for Describing the Phenomenon of New Venture Creation', *Academy of New Management Review* 10: 696–706.

GEM. 2014. Global Entrepreneurship Monitor Country Profile, Uganda. Retrieved 4 April 2018 from http://www.gemconsortium.org/country-profile/117.

Hilgers, M., and E. Mangez (eds). 2015. *Bourdieu's Theory of Social Fields: Concepts and Applications.* London: Routledge.

Holland, J. 2011. 'Timescapes: Living a Qualitative Longitudinal Study', *Forum: Qualitative Social Research* 12(3), Art.9.

Hübinger, W. 1996. *Prekärer Wohlstand: Neue Befunde zu Armut und Sozialer Ungleichheit.* Freiburg im Breisgau: Lambertus.

Johnson-Hanks, J. 2002. 'On the Limits of Life Stages in Ethnography: Toward a Theory of Vital Conjunctures', *American Anthropologist* 104(3): 865–80.

Khavul, S., G.D. Bruton and E. Wood. 2009. 'Informal Family Business in Africa', *Entrepreneurship: Theory and Practice* 33(6): 1219–38.

Khayesi, J.N.O., G. George and J. Antonakis. 2014. 'Kinship in Entrepreneur Networks: Performance Effects of Resource Assembly in Africa', *Entrepreneurship: Theory and Practice* 38(6): 1323–42.

Lamb, M.E. 1997. 'Fathers and Child Development: An Introductory Overview and Guide', in M.E. Lamb (ed.), *The Role of the Father in Child Development.* New York: Wiley, pp. 1–18.

Langevang, T. 2008. '"We Are Managing!" Uncertain Paths to Respectable Adulthoods in Accra, Ghana', *Geoforum* 39: 2039–47.

Langevang, T., K.V. Gough and R. Namatovu. 2016. 'Youth Entrepreneurship in Kampala. Managing Scarce Resources in a Challenging Environment', in K. Gough and T. Langevang (eds), *Young Entrepreneurs in Sub-Saharan Africa.* London: Routledge, pp. 80–93.

Langevang, T., R. Namatovu and S. Dawa. 2012. 'Beyond Necessity and Opportunity Entrepreneurship: Motivations and Aspirations of Young

Entrepreneurs in Uganda', *International Development Planning Review* 34(4): 439–60.

Locke, C., et al. 2017. 'Innovation and Gendered Negotiations: Insights from Six Small-Scale Fishing Communities', *Fish and Fisheries* 18(5): 943–57.

Mercer, C. 2014. 'Middle Class Construction: Domestic Architecture, Aesthetics and Anxieties in Tanzania', *The Journal of Modern African Studies* 52(2): 227–50.

Monteith, W., and L. Camfield. 2019. 'Business as Family, Family as Business: The Socioeconomic Journeys of Female Entrepreneurs in Kampala, Uganda', *Geoforum* (under review).

Namatovu, R., et al. 2016. 'Youth Entrepreneurship Trends and Policies in Uganda', in K.V. Gough and T. Langevang (eds), *Youth Entrepreneurs in Sub-Saharan Africa*. London: Routledge, pp. 18–31.

Page, B., and E. Sunjo. 2018. 'Africa's Middle Class: Building Houses and Constructing Identities in the Small Town of Buea, Cameroon', *Urban Geography* 39(1): 75–103.

Portes, A., and K. Hoffman. 2003. 'Latin American Class Structures: Their Composition and Change during the Neoliberal Era', *Latin American Research Review* 38(1): 41–82.

Ugandan Bureau of Statistics. 2016. *Labour Market Transition of Young People in Uganda: Highlights of the School-to-Work Transition Survey 2015*. Retrieved 4 April 2018 from http://www.ubos.org/onlinefiles/uploads/ubos/pdf%20 documents/Labour%20Market%20Transition%20of%20Young%20People%20 in%20Uganda_SWTS%202015.pdf.

Vigh, H. 2009. 'Motion Squared: A Second Look at the Concept of Social Navigation', *Anthropological Theory* 9(4): 419–38.

_____. 2010. 'Youth Mobilisation as Social Navigation: Reflections on the Concept of Dubriagem', *Cadernos de Estudos Africanos* 18/19: 139–64.

Wiegratz, J. 2016. *Neoliberal Moral Economy: Capitalism, Socio-cultural Change and Fraud in Uganda*. London and New York: Rowman & Littlefield International Limited.

Whyte, S.R. 2002. 'Subjectivity and Subjunctivity: Hoping for Health in Eastern Uganda', in R. Werbner (ed.), *Postcolonial Subjectivities in Africa*. London and New York: Zed Books, pp. 171–90.

Chapter 5

'Here Men Are Becoming Women and Women Men'

Gender, Class and Space in Maputo, Mozambique

Inge Tvedten, Arlindo Uate and Lizete Mangueleze

Introduction

Several classic anthropological urban studies in Southern Africa have focused on the different positions of men and women in social space, presenting women as integral and male-dependent members of permanently settled or migrant households (Hellmann 1948, Mitchell 1969, see also Bank 2011).[1] In the feminist literature of the 1980s, 1990s and early 2000s, urban women were seen as oppressed by society at large as well as within households, leading to a 'feminization of poverty' paradigm[2] (Tinker 1990, Jackson and Pearson 1998, see also Chant 2008). As pointed out by Eriksen, Ødegaard and Fagertun (2007), more recent anthropology – including that of gender – has tended to emphasize individual identity and subjectivity, often losing sight of the interrelation between structural constraints and opportunities, on one hand, and human agency, on the other (see also Ortner 2016).

This chapter analyses the positions of urban men and women as subjects in social spaces vital for their wellbeing and examines the ways in which women challenge the boundaries of those spaces. Grounded in Bourdieu's theory of practice (Bourdieu 1990, see also Ortner 2006, Wacquant 2013), it emphasizes the role of historically situated political, economic and socio-cultural structures as having a powerful impact upon human action. The kinds of activities people perform are effected by their social positions within these structures, as determined by unequal social relations and dominant cultural discourses, including those based on class and gender.

This approach also allows for an exploration of human agency, resistance and social change. Actors are, in the words of Henrietta Moore with reference to Bourdieu, 'continually involved... in the strategic interpretation and reinterpretation of the cultural meanings that inform the organization of their world' (1994: 76). While there is a set of structuring principles and common schemes for perception and action that generate practices and representations of gender in urban space (Bourdieu 1990), there is also room for creativity and change because actions themselves can be a type of critical reflection. In fact, Bourdieu (1977: 214) states that social space has no meaning apart from practice: the system of generating and structuring dispositions (i.e. habitus) constitutes and is constituted by actors' movements through space.

In contrast to recent analyses emphasizing gender performance and women's scope for individual creative improvization (Pellow 2008, Osirim 2009, see also Clark 2003), the practice theory framework gives greater emphasis to social mobility through 'structured strategizing'. Social change, we postulate, occurs through what we will call 'structural conjunctures', or changes in the structural environment, which may provide restrictions as well as opportunities for change in the social positions of men and women (see also Miranne and Young 1999). These structural changes arise from the very process of urbanization and the ensuing alterations in central political, economic and socio-cultural spaces.

This chapter focuses on Mozambique's capital city, Maputo. There are significant differences in poverty and wellbeing between the city's spatial formations (Bertelsen, Roque and Tvedten 2014, INE 2015). The *cidade* is the central, affluent city of formal employment, considered largely unattainable by all but a very few from Maputo's poor neighbourhoods or *bairros*. Beyond the central city are the *subúrbios*, the informal city, seen as dense and perilous but also associated with economic opportunities. Finally, an outer tier of peri-urban settlements has a mixture of long-term residents, poor and recent migrants, and better-off households that have moved away from the increasingly congested *cidade* and *subúrbios*.

All these formations are dominated by a masculine socio-cultural order, both in terms of skewed power relations between men and women and in terms of explicit or implicit gendered structures of local governance, employment, education, etc. (Paulo, Rosário and Tvedten 2011). But there have also – historically as well as more recently – been moments of disorder or resistance that have led to slippages in structural constraints and opened up opportunities for alternative practices and strategies that have challenged these gendered asymmetries.

In contemporary Maputo women who achieve basic economic and social independence from men – by being de jure or de facto heads of households that account for about one third of the city's domestic units, and by building female-focused networks – seem to be in the best position to take advantage of the city's spaces of opportunity. In fact, official statistics on poverty and wellbeing in Mozambique show that urban female-headed households have consistently reduced the poverty gap vis-à-vis urban male-headed households over the past couple of decades, with data from Maputo showing that since 2010 poverty is less prevalent among female- than among male-headed households (INE 2010, Jones 2013).

This study uses a combination of quantitative data on gendered poverty (to show variations over space and time in the city as a whole) and qualitative data to assess the dynamics of poverty and gender (Jones and Tvedten 2019). We make use of official gendered data on poverty and wellbeing in Maputo's urban spaces (INE 2010 and 2015), along with a survey covering four of the city's suburban/peri-urban *bairros* (Paulo, Rosário and Tvedten 2011). We analyse spatial perceptions and strategies – that is, agency – on the basis of longitudinal fieldwork/participant observation in the two *bairros* of 25 de Junho and Inhagóia as well as by following twenty-five households from different social classes or positions identified through a Wealth Ranking exercise (Mikkelsen 2005) – analysing their life histories, recording their spatial moves, and accompanying selected household members in their daily routines.

Historical Trajectories

Lourenço Marques (now Maputo) was established as the capital of Mozambique at the end of the nineteenth century. The colonial occupation, based on economic exploitation and racial discrimination, classified the vast majority of Africans as subject to a separate legal regime known as the *indigenato*. This distinction was given spatial expression through the establishment of a formal city (*cidade de cimento*) or 'city of cement' for the colonial white population, with informal city spaces (*cidade de caniço*) or 'city of reeds' for the black indigenous majority (Newitt 1995).

The city's formation represented a convergence of two male-centred, patriarchal cultures: the Tsonga and the Portuguese (Newitt 1995, see also Stoler 1995). Indigenous black women were initially banned from urban space through a combination of pass laws and labour market exclusion. Under the pass laws, women needed signatures both from the colonial administration and from a male member of their family to enter the city

(Sheldon 2003). Women were also effectively excluded from the urban labour market; exceptions were made for women working as small-scale farmers, cleaners and prostitutes (Penvenne 1995). The white colonial population was also overwhelmingly male, with women representing only 3.5 per cent in 1912. As late as 1940, women of both races made up only 9 per cent of the total population of 74,000 in Lourenço Marques (Zamporini 1998: 271).

In the first half of the twentieth century, male dominance of urban space was further strengthened by two parallel and mutually reinforcing structural changes (Rita-Ferreira 1968). One was the increase in male employment opportunities in Lourenço Marques in the early years of the century, linked primarily to the port and the railway to Johannesburg. Beginning later in the 1930s, with nationalist economic policies under the Estado Novo, Portugal increased its investments in the colonial capital, expanding local industrialization. The other factor was the reinforcement of the system of forced labour (*shibalo*) in rural areas, with men escaping to Lourenço Marques in search of employment that would exempt them from the danger and drudgery of the *shibalo* (Penvenne 1981, Sheldon 2002).

With the male exodus, women left behind in the rural areas saw their support systems collapsing. More and more particularly young African women who were not yet married began moving to Lourenço Marques in order to create new lives for themselves (Penvenne 1995). From the late 1930s the colonial Portuguese lifted their formal ban on, and control of, movements to the city, making these moves legal. As with indigenous men, however, indigenous women's movements within the city were strictly controlled.

The African population lived in sprawling neighbourhoods or *bairros de caniço*. Those *bairro* women who were married typically lived in domestic units where men had considerable power, based on patrilineal, male-dominated tradition as well as the widespread use of bride-wealth (*lobolo*) (Penvenne 1995, Granjo 2005). In a transitional period of partial restrictions on urban migration and increased industrialization in Lourenço Marques, most married men were, despite low wages, able to support their households in accordance with socio-cultural expectations of men as breadwinners (Zamporini 1998).[3] Many of them maintained their wife or wives in their rural area of origin to take care of extended family and farming.

With young unmarried women continuing to dominate the rural-urban migration, the majority of African women in Lourenço Marques were single heads of household supporting minor children by the 1960s (Sheldon 2002). Black women who were not married implicitly challenged the patriarchal social order by establishing their own domestic units, thereby violating hegemonic socio-cultural rules and expectations. Such independent women were seen as a 'social evil' by the Portuguese colonists, who thought they would ruin the social order (Zamporini 1998). Facing considerable economic and social constraints, these women were compelled to seek their own sources of income and expand their spatial outreach in order to survive (Rita-Ferreira 1968). With children, their options for marrying later were significantly reduced.

Employment opportunities for women were restricted: they could work in agriculture in the vicinity of the *bairros* or as domestic servants (*empregadas*) in the formal *cimento* part of the city (Sheldon 2003).[4] Many also turned to illegal activities such as beer-brewing and prostitution. Otherwise, women were largely restricted to the African neighbourhoods. 'We did not have places of recreation, everyone stayed at home. We were not at ease in the centre of the city', said one woman, Augusta Artiel, revealing both material barriers and an internalization of the colonial order (Frates 2002: 187).

With the end of the Estado Novo in the early 1960s, an influx of Portuguese settlers arrived to compete with Africans for jobs. This coincided with increasing migration from the rural hinterland, so that Lourenço Marques quadrupled its population from 93,000 to 395,000 between 1950 and 1970 (Jenkins 2012). Formal employment was no longer readily available for adult men in the indigenous population. This structural conjuncture enhanced the importance of the informal sector as a source of employment as well as a means of access to cheap goods and services. The informal sector was initially largely confined to the *cidade de caniço*. However, larger markets soon developed in what came to be a 'transitional zone' of suburbs (including Alto Maé and Chamanculo) between the formal city and the shantytowns, serving both population groups (Monteiro 2002).

Men were initially reluctant to take part in the informal sector, as this was not seen as proper 'work' (*emprego*). Instead, they were mainly involved in semi-formal productive activities as labourers, carpenters, mechanics and the like, often for smaller Portuguese enterprises. Women, meanwhile, became involved in a broad range of activities including petty trade and sale of agricultural products and cooked food, in effect taking their domestic responsibilities into public spaces (Monteiro 2002).

A distinction soon emerged between informal traders with access to the larger markets and superior purchasing power in the new *subúrbios*, and those who – for economic or family reasons – were not in a position to leave their *bairros*. Alice Chivinze, quoted by Frates (2002: 182), stated that during colonial times, 'I did not know many things because I did not often go to the centre of the city because from here it is very far. We did not have many markets like we do today… We had to walk everywhere because no buses came to this area.' The quote exemplifies both physical and internalized barriers to crossing urban spaces for many women.

With new employment opportunities and an informal sector accessible to women, the informal *bairros de caniço* changed from primarily being sites for domestic activities and social relations with family, neighbours and friends to becoming communities with a broad range of economic activities (Sheldon 2003). These included not only small-scale agriculture, food markets and beer-brewing as before, but also trade in a range of commodities and new services such as child care, hairdressing and healing. For some women, these represented new opportunities for cooperation with other women and for combining their domestic responsibilities with income-generating activities within the same urban space. This in turn brought increasing options for independence from men and subsequent spatial expansion.

With independence in 1975 and the coming to power of the Mozambique Liberation Front (Frelimo), a great deal of political attention was directed toward the urban environment in Maputo and especially the popular *bairros*. Except for the takeover of formerly white areas by a new African ruling and middle class, however, little changed at the structural level (Morton 2013). In addition, while Frelimo emphasized the importance of women in the construction of an independent Mozambique, this was limited to the public sphere in the form of political representation. It did not include policies for social transformation through gender equality (Urdang 1989, Tvedten, Paulo and Montserrat 2008).

The war in the rural areas that began in the early 1980s initiated a series of structural conjunctures. One the one hand, the population of what had by then become the city of Maputo increased dramatically, reaching 950,000 in 1990 (Jenkins 2012). At the same time, the informal sector grew with the de facto failure of the centrally planned economy, mass unemployment following 'structural adjustment', and the emergence of a parallel (*candonga*) market for practically all goods and services. These developments all contributed to opening up new urban spaces (Lundin 2007).

In the mid-1990s, only 30 per cent of Maputo's adult population had formal employment, with the rest depending on the informal economy. Among women, the proportion of formally employed was considerably lower, at 5 per cent. The large majority of women were self-employed in the informal sector (INE 1998). Espling (1999: 150) shows how women dominated major marketplaces like Xipamanine, Mercado Central and Estrela Vermelha as well as smaller local markets in the *bairros* and sales on the street by *vendedores ambulantes*. 'The most frequent activity that the women do here in the *bairro* is on the informal market. All women from here are selling some kind of product, in the yard, in front of the entrance, in the street, in the market... Some are going to work, [but] at night they are selling in the street' (separated woman, age sixty, Mafalala).

Central to women's increasing spatial outreach were the religious communities to which the large majority of women adhered, primarily the Catholic Church, the Presbyterian Church (Swiss Mission) and Islam. Most of these places of worship were located in the formal parts of the city and hence served women who could afford the trip out of their local *bairros* (Schuetze 2010). Women also came together through informal saving societies (*xitique*), meeting either at the marketplace or in their local community or neighbourhood, which gave them additional resources and flexibility (Espling 1999: 165). '*Xitique* is done by women who are selling, the ones doing business. There is a lot of *xitique*, involving a lot of money. The system of *xitique* is old; it was always like that, it hasn't changed. Only the amounts have increased' (widow, age sixty-nine, Mafalala).

The enhanced spatial outreach of women demanded a certain independence from men, as well as access to their own income. Many married and poor women continued to be constrained by structural limitations: that is, by men who wanted them to stay home and care for the family, and by poverty, which tied the poorest women to their *bairros* where economic opportunities were more limited (Espling 1999). For others, towards the end of the 1990s the dense and tense city and suburbs were still associated with fears, although different ones than during colonial times: 'Today I go to places that I did not before, but not often, as I am afraid. But the fear is not the same as that I had before. Today we have ninjas [thieves]. They are not under control, and thus I do not like to move around very much' (Ferdina Mveavele, quoted in Frates 2002: 236).

Toward the end of the twentieth century, then, the spatial layout of postcolonial Maputo consisted of a formal and affluent city centre (*cidade*), still largely out of reach for the poor *bairro* population; transitional suburbs (*subúrbios*), seen as congested and volatile but also as representing economic opportunities; and peri-urban *bairros* where most people lived. The three sectors no longer carried the colonial racial connotations and had more socio-economic diversity and complexity than during colonial times. Class and gender had largely taken over from race and gender as the key factors distinguishing segments of the population in Maputo (Sumich 2011, Morton 2013).

Spatial and Gender Inequalities

Since the turn of the century, Maputo's urban spaces have continued to undergo political and economic transformations, with implications for the distribution of scarce material resources and social positions (CMM 2013, Barros, Chivangue and Samagoia 2014). However, there is still a spatial trichotomy between the central, affluent *cidade*; the dense, tense, and volatile *subúrbios*; and the peri-urban areas with a mixture of poor and better-off households (Bertelsen, Roque and Tvedten 2014).

Such differences are immediately evident when one moves across these spaces, from the well-organized streets and plots of land in the *cidade* to the apparent disorganization and chaos of narrow back alleys (*becos*) and small houses and shacks (*palhotas*) in the suburban and peri-urban settlements. This section combines an assessment of structural economic limitations with excerpts from conversations with people from the two peri-urban *bairros* of 25 de Junho and Inhagóia, showing how male and female residents relate to and internalize these constraints.

Since the mid-1980s, Mozambique has followed neoliberal economic policies, and the last two decades have seen rapid macroeconomic growth (Orre and Rønning 2017). In Maputo the growth is most evident in hectic building activities, with shopping centres, high-rise towers, restaurants and private homes going up, particularly in the central parts of the *cidade*. However, this economic growth has been accompanied by sharply rising costs for food and basic commodities – most recently in the form of a devastating hyper-inflation (Cunguara 2012).

Moreover, except for temporary employment for men in construction, growth has not led to improvements in formal employment opportunities (Paulo, Rosário and Tvedten 2011, Jones and Tarp 2013). Work is difficult to get and often comes with only the minimum wage of 2,500 meticais ($86) per month, which is hardly enough to feed a family in Maputo. At the same time, competition in the informal sector is fierce, with profits for informal traders reduced by high transportation costs and a heavy taxation regime on petty trade (Vletter 2001, Monteiro 2002, Paulo, Rosário and Tvedten 2011).

Maria, a young woman living in 25 de Junho bairro, had to drop out of university because of the costs and start working in the informal sector: 'Even when I'm working, it's difficult to make ends meet for me and my child, as I have no one who can support me.' Ricardo, living in Inhagóia, has lost several jobs as a construction worker in the past year because he could not afford transport and often came to work too late: 'Now I always stay here in the *bairro*. There is nothing for me in the *cidade*.'

Sharp spatial disparities are also evident in poverty rates (INE 2010, Jones 2013). The consumption-based poverty rate[5] is highest in the district of Nlhamankulu (36.4 per cent), in the suburban zone; lowest in the district of KaMpfumu (2.3 per cent), in the *cidade*; and intermediate in the peri-urban district of KaMavota (27.4 per cent). Moreover, inequality as measured by the Gini coefficient has increased for Maputo as a whole, from 0.420 to 0.502 in the past decade (Jones 2013; INE 2015).[6]

These economic inequalities are increasingly evident to people who cross the city's spatial boundaries in their daily lives. Carlos travels from 25 de Junho to work as a cleaner in the Municipality in the *baixa* area of the central city every day. He says: 'I used to live in Alto Maé, but I had to move because rents were too high. One day I hope to be able to move back. This [25 de Junho] is not the real city.' Mwnaiba, who works as a domestic servant (*empregada*) in Sommerschield, an upscale central neighbourhood, talks about her daily encounters with the *cidade* as a completely different world than her own in Inhagóia, as if they have nothing to do with each other at all.

Maputo's urban spaces are also highly gendered. Still with reference to data from the National Household Survey (INE 2010, see also INE 2015), among adult men 71 per cent are fully employed, 12 per cent are under-employed, and almost 11 per cent are unemployed. Moreover, 67 per cent of all men have employment in the public or private sector, mainly in formal urban space, while 22 per cent are self-employed, primarily in the informal city. Among women, by contrast, only 42 per cent are fully employed, while 29 per cent are underemployed and 24 per cent are unemployed. Fifty-one per cent of women are self-employed and only 21 per cent work in the public or private sector (see also Jones 2013).

Women's work and income, whether in the informal or formal sector, is affected by patriarchal gender norms. Selma is in her late thirties and goes to the Xipamanine market to sell vegetables three days a week. 'When I come home I give my earnings to my husband [who is unemployed], and he decides how to spend it. I only put aside a little for my children's school.' At the other end of the employment scale, Roberta has a senior position in a ministry. When she obtained the position, which is higher and better paid than her husband's, he demanded that she either stop working or leave the home. 'I divorced him', she said.

Gendered inequalities in Maputo are also reflected in the high rate of female-headed households, at 29 per cent. These are made up of single women, most often with children, along with widows and divorced women (INE 2010, see also INE 2015).[7] Being a female head of household and a single mother still carries negative stigmas in a context where women are still expected to marry and men are expected to head households and be 'breadwinners' (Membawase 2005, see also Kabeer 2007). Still, the proportion of female-headed households is about the same in Maputo's most affluent district of KaMpfumu, at 27.8 per cent, as in the peri-urban district of KaMubukwana, at 29.2 per cent; it is highest in the suburban district of Nlhamankulu, at 33.4 per cent (INE 2010, Jones 2013).

Alma became pregnant when she was sixteen years old, has not married since and describes herself as a 'community worker': 'I have a male friend (*amante*), who is married, and takes good care of me.' Teresa sells tomatoes and other vegetables from a stand outside her dwelling, lives with one of her daughters and three grandchildren and has not heard from her husband for many years: 'One day he just left, and never came back.' Clara claims she does not want to marry, even though she has a daughter: 'I manage well as it is [working as a trader in the central *Mercado do Povo*], and cooperate well with my sister and neighbours.'

Over the past two decades, urban female-headed households in Mozambique, while still generally poorer than urban male-headed households, have seen a more consistent drop in their poverty rate based on income and a broad range of expenditures for consumption items and services (INE 2010, see also INE 2015). In Maputo, where the general poverty rate is lower than in the rest of urban Mozambique, female-headed households have seen a dramatic drop in poverty, from 47.5 per cent in 1996–1997 to 34.6 per cent in 2008–2009. Their poverty rate was lower than the rate for male-headed households in Maputo, which was 35.6 per cent in 2008–2009 (INE 2010, Jones 2013).[8]

In sum, notwithstanding the multiple structural, political, economic and socio-cultural constraints discussed above, many women heading households have been in a position to exploit changes in the structural environment to improve their situation through their own agency. These changes are, as we have seen, primarily related to an economic context of high formal unemployment and low incomes that undercuts the basis for male domination; and the increasing importance of the informal economy for survival among the poor. In the next section, women's social positions and strategies will be analysed with reference to their relations to men and urban spaces in the two peri-urban *bairros* of 25 de Junho and Inhagóia.

Social Position and Spatial Strategies

Men and women in the *bairros* of 25 de Junho and Inhagóia hold perceptions of Maputo's urban space that match the structural distinctions outlined above. But there are also inherent contradictions and fluidities.

The accessibility and relevance of different urban spaces combine with people's social position and gender to shape their spatial strategies and options for social mobility. This section will explore the intersection of gender, social position and space by analysing how men and women from different economic categories relate to the spatial constraints and opportunities discussed above.[9]

Social position or 'class' (Ortner 2006 and Wacquant 2013) will be defined with respect to people's own emic categorization of poverty and wellbeing. In the current context this is primarily based on a combination of material poverty and social relationships – the latter with reference to the importance of social relations in a volatile urban setting with limited extended family or other 'traditional' networks (Costa 2007).[10] In the local vernacular, the general term for being poor (*xisiwana*) refers to 'somebody who has nothing' or 'people who are afraid to talk to other people', while the general term for being rich (*aganhile*) means 'to win'. Within the first category, people distinguish between the 'very poor' (destitute) and the 'normal poor', who may be 'chronically' or 'transient' poor (Paulo, Rosário and Tvedten 2011).

Destitute men, known by the local euphemism *xangamo*, are seen as violating the essence of urban manhood. They are often found strolling the narrow *becos* of their *bairro* looking for places to sit down, talk and perhaps get something to eat and drink. Among such men there is a strong sense of having given up and of seeing urban spaces beyond their immediate *bairro* or even *quarteirão* as being unattainable. Many of these men are single, often divorced, or are part of a de facto female-headed household where they have an inferior position because they are unemployed, do not contribute to the household economy, and (often) do not own the dwelling in which they reside. According to Armando (age fifty, caretaker at the *bairro* administration, 25 de Junho), women are to blame: 'Here men are becoming women and women men. The work which was done by men is now being done by women. This is the time of women. Everything has changed. For this reason there are many unemployed men: we are here without work because women occupy our space.'

Destitute women (known by the euphemism *nfelacase*) are also largely confined to their *bairros*, perceiving other spaces as unattainable. Compared to men, however, they spend more of their time with neighbours, friends and other women in female-focused meeting places, such as around the water post, in community markets and in playgrounds. There are, moreover, economic activities accessible to women in the *bairro* with very low barriers to entry, such as selling leaves (*folhas*) on the street outside informal markets where no taxes are claimed and doing small chores (*ganho-ganho*) in the houses or garden plots of other people. The poorest women are hence in a better position to cope within the confines of their immediate community space than are poor men.

We met Antonietta in Inhagóia. She is forty-two years old and sells lettuce on a large plastic sheet outside the informal market, but acknowledges that she earns very little as 'only the poor buy here'. Her husband does odd jobs within the *bairro*, transporting goods for mainly female traders – which in itself carries a stigma – and he hardly ever leaves the *bairro*. Antonietta concedes that she cannot afford to buy 'good products' and transport them to the city, which would have been most lucrative, and she needs to stay close to home in order to combine making money and taking care of her husband and their children (indicating that she is the actual head of the household).[11]

Men who are 'normal poor', categorized as *xakwiantxahana*, tend to leave their *bairros* on a regular basis, usually because they have menial employment or seek work in such positions. Most of the lower-paid formal employment opportunities, as guards, construction workers or handymen, for example, are located in the *cidade* or suburban parts of Maputo. Getting such jobs requires making contact directly with the company, often through middlemen who charge a bribe (*refresco*) equal to the first two months' salary (Tvedten and Picardo 2019). Employment is considered so important that some men who are unable to afford transport walk long distances to the city centre with the pretence, rather than a realistic chance, of finding work. Formal employment is vital for a man's status as household head. According to Marcos, age thirty, who is a builder and lives in Inhagóia: 'When a woman has a level above the man ("um nível em cima do homem"), he loses respect. For the man to dominate the woman, he needs to have a level above her.'

Women who are 'normal poor', categorized as *nkansakaia*, leave their *bairros* on a regular basis for informal trade and depend on wide horizontal social networks. Goods have to be collected at one of the major wholesale markets (such as Zimpeto) and then transported to the markets in the city or suburbs that have the most customers and best prices (such as Xipamanine and Mercado do Povo). Cooperation with other women enables female traders to ensure that their responsibilities at home, in 25 de Junho or Inhagóia, are taken care of while they are away. Among our female interlocutors, such relationships are primarily with other women in their immediate neighbourhood doing the same type of business, 'because we must work with women we trust' (Anabela, trader at the Mercado Municipal, age thirty, Inhagóia).

The different strategies for employment and income pursued by poor men and women also reflect different perceptions about what constitutes 'work'. Men tend to refer to employment with a salary and regular hours as more dignified (*digno*) than working in markets or on the street. Street peddlers (*dumba nengues*, literally 'trust your feet') are considered to be at the lowest end of the occupational scale. In fact, men consistently disparage the informal livelihoods of women by maintaining that they do not have work (*emprego*) but do 'activities' (*actividades*), as if to insist on male superiority in a situation where men find their role as household heads and breadwinners threatened (see also Silberschmidt 2001, Milani and Shaikjee 2013, Clark 1994).

The better-off (*aganhile*) category in 25 de Junho and Inhagóia is defined as people who have prospered through their own hard work.[12] Men in this position usually have higher education and formal employment in the city. They have been able to invest in a good brick house. They have a wife (though many maintain a mistress on the side; see Manuel 2008) and have children whom they put through school. All this is in accordance with socio-cultural expectations for the successful urban man. A man in this category is in a position to provide for his family, and his spouse often stays at home. 'Men want to be in charge, and they feel good when their wives ask them for money. When wives do not ask for anything, it feels strange' (Armando, former teacher, age fifty, 25 de Junho).

Many of the more successful *aganhile* women also actively transgress spatial boundaries. Since they usually earn lower wages than men,[13] they tend to have several activities going on at the same time to increase their chances of success and reduce risk. Women with formal employment often run informal businesses on the side, such as market stalls, hairdressing, sale of second-hand clothes, or traditional medicine, either in the city or in their own *bairro*. They may also have small urban-based agricultural fields (*machambinhas*) with hired labour (Cairns, Tschirley and Cachomba 2013, Tvedten 2018, Tvedten et al. 2018).

Pursuing multiple livelihood activities requires maintaining relations of trust with others, usually through local churches or saving societies (*xitique*) where women dominate (Kamp 2010) or with immediate family members, extended family or young people from the woman's rural area of origin. In fact, many women bring new members into their households for the purpose of forming stronger economic units. This may be one reason why in *bairros* like 25 de Junho and Inhagóia, female-headed households are as large as male-headed households despite the absence of a husband, with 7.2 and 7.1 members respectively (Paulo, Rosário and Tvedten 2011).[14]

Catarina is an unmarried mother with three children; she lives with her older unmarried sister, who has two children. A third younger sister has a dwelling of her own close by, but she is effectively part of the same household unit as they share income and 'eat from the same pot'.

Catarina has a job as a cleaner at the local primary school, and she is active in her community as one of the few female *chefes de quarteirão*. Her older sister is an active trader (*comerciante*) at the main municipal market in the city centre. The younger sister has a small market stall outside her two sisters' dwelling, where she sells foodstuffs while looking after all the children. This way, the three sisters share domestic and income-generating work, and free time. They say they have no plans to include men in their extended household arrangement ('at least not on a permanent basis', according to Catarina).

While many women manage to surmount spatial constraints in order to engage in activities outside their *bairros*, some also manage to overcome positional as well as spatial barriers and enter male-dominated occupations. Given the strongly gendered labour market, entering such occupations requires women to contend with direct opposition from many men. Women in higher positions report resistance from their own husbands, forcing them to make a choice between their careers and their partners. There are also accounts of local male community leaders refusing to verify residency, which is necessary in order to access resources such as permits and loans. In some cases, women trying to enter male-dominated occupations, such as female managers, taxi drivers and construction workers, have been physically assaulted on the grounds that 'this is no place for women'.

Felizmina was one of the first women taxi drivers in Maputo. In the beginning, she experienced resistance not only from her boyfriend and from other drivers, but also from passengers who refused to enter her car. Explaining why she chose such an unusual occupation, she said that growing up in a poor family with a single mother meant that she had to take initiatives and contribute from a very young age. Later, driving a taxi gave her the necessary flexibility to take care of her children, with the help of her mother: 'In the beginning my daughter was embarrassed and didn't want to tell her friends what I do, but now she brags about it in class.'

The ongoing 'structural conjunctures' in Maputo provide an important basis for understanding spatial outreach strategies among poor households in *bairros* such as 25 de Junho and Inhagóia. Low wages and high costs make it increasingly difficult to make ends meet. This has led to the growing influence of women as breadwinners. The inability to pay bride-wealth (*lobolo*) and marry among poor men is reflected in the high proportion of single women and women in consensual unions. In Inhagóia, 36 per cent of households are based on formal civil or traditional marriages, while 24 per cent involve consensual unions; fully 39 per cent are single-headed households, in many cases headed by single mothers, divorced women or widows (Paulo, Rosário and Tvedten 2011).

In an urban context of structural conjunctures, then, people's spatial strategies are influenced by their economic position as well as gender – which again has implications for domestic relations. Many poor men are losing the economic basis for their authority in households, and their position as household head is often threatened. Better-off men have been able to fulfil their obligations as 'breadwinners' and maintain their customary rights in patriarchal society. The continued power of such men is reflected in a comment by Lucía (age thirty-eight, petty trader selling in front of her house, 25 de Junho): 'It's the children and I who take care of everything in the house, and normally [during the day] we stay outside in order not to make it dirty. It is only at night when *papá* comes home that we stay inside.'

While being unmarried is still associated with negative sanctions from the community at large, many women see it as offering a better opportunity than marriage for improving their situation and taking care of their children. In 25 de Junho and Inhagóia we met employed 'career' women who have made a conscious choice to live alone, either by leaving their husbands or by not marrying at all. 'If my husband asked me to choose between work and him, I would prefer to work, because I need my independence. I need to have weight in my family and be respected' (Susana, hairdresser, age twenty-three, Inhagóia). Among poorer women, who often work long days with low pay in the informal sector, alternative relationships with neighbours, friends or the family of origin are considered more helpful than the additional responsibilities involved in taking care of a husband.

Instead of being married to a man who may spend more than he earns ('or says he earns,' to quote one single mother in Inhagóia) and who may restrict his wife's spatial movements and thus her income-earning potential, many women thus opt for an alternative strategy of forming their own households or becoming de facto heads in consensual unions. As noted above, as many as 29 per cent of all households in Maputo are currently female-headed and the poverty rate among such households is lower than among male-headed households. As Teresa in 25 de Junho puts it: women 'move around more' (*andam mais*) in search of ways to secure a better life for themselves and their children. Many men, on the other hand, 'wait for employment' (*esperam pelo emprego*), ostensibly to maintain their customary positions as urban men and heads of households in a structural context where this is becoming increasingly difficult.

Conclusions

In line with the general trend in anthropology toward a focus on human agency and subjectivity (Robbins 2013, Ortner 2016), recent urban anthropology has tended to emphasize innovation and the ability to cope among people in Africa's peri-urban shantytowns (Diouf and Fredericks 2014). At the same time, data from a number of countries on the continent shows that urban poverty and urban inequality are on the rise, indicating continued strong forces of structural oppression (Fox 2018).

In this chapter, we have argued for the need to combine an analysis of structural economic, political and socio-cultural constraints with a focus on social positions and human agency. Our fieldwork in two of Maputo's *bairros* found men and women continuously involved in the strategic interpretation of the constraints and opportunities emanating from urban transformations.

We have shown how urban space, originally largely closed to women migrants from the hinterland, has slowly opened up through a set of 'structural conjunctures' in the history of the city of Maputo. The colonial regime gradually gave up political control and thus the capacity to maintain separation between a formal city space (predominantly white) and an informal city space (almost entirely African) – and effectively also between men and women as colonial subjects. At independence, the exodus of the overwhelming majority of settlers made the formal economy largely collapse and be replaced by informal economic relationships.

In post-independence Maputo, the racially based dichotomy has largely been replaced by a spatial trichotomy between the central, the suburban and the peri-urban city. With rising inequality and a limited formal employment market, poor men in the *bairros* find themselves in a social position where they have increasing problems living up to the socio-cultural expectations of being breadwinners. Most respond to the situation by continuing to seek formal employment opportunities in low-paid workplaces outside their own neighbourhoods or resort to unemployment, while the informal sector in the *bairros* is increasingly occupied by women.

Most women, for their part, pursue new structural openings and opportunities for social mobility through social relationships. They purposively include other women and subordinate men in their households, enhancing their spatial outreach and their ability to pursue livelihood activities while also meeting domestic responsibilities. They make active use of horizontal women-focused networks in informal trade and social arenas such as churches and saving societies. And a few women have been able to enter traditional male social spaces such as community leadership, construction work and taxi driving, often through the support of other women.

With the continued stronghold of most men over domestic and public spaces, those women in the best position to exploit new structural and spatial opportunities are those who head households. They can invest in a better life for themselves and their children, even though they pay a social cost due to the continuing stigma attached to unmarried women in society at large. Female-headed households in Maputo have seen their rate of poverty decline over the past ten years. Given that their poverty rate is now lower than the rate for male-headed households, there is a need to reassess the notion of a widespread 'feminization' of urban poverty in Africa.

Inge Tvedten is a social anthropologist/senior researcher at the Chr. Michelsen Institute in Bergen, Norway. He has a PhD from the University of Cape Town, and has a long career combining basic and applied research primarily on urban poverty and gender in Mozambique, Angola and Namibia. He has published extensively in books, peer reviewed journals and applied reports for poverty reduction policies and interventions. Tvedten headed the research project 'The Ethnography in a Divided City: Socio-politics, Poverty and Gender in Maputo, Mozambique' funded by the Norwegian Research Council and upon which his contribution to this volume is based.

Arlindo Uate is an anthropologist, researcher and lecturer at the Pedagogical University (UP) in Maputo, Mozambique. He has a master's degree from Eduardo Mondlane University, and his professional interests include social conflicts, gender and development. Uate has taken part in a number of research projects, including 'Pedagogical Practises' at UP and 'The Ethnography in a Divided City: Socio-politics, Poverty and Gender in Maputo, Mozambique' funded by the Norwegian Research Council and upon which his contribution to this volume is based.

Lizete Mangueleze has an Honours Degree in Anthropology from Eduardo Mondlane University, and is an independent media and communication consultant for think tanks and civil society organizations in Mozambique. Her main professional interests include gender, culture, identity, transnational culture and urban studies. Mangueleze has taken part in a number of academic and applied research projects, including 'The Ethnography in a Divided City: Socio-politics, Poverty and Gender in Maputo, Mozambique' funded by the Norwegian Research Council and upon which her contribution to this volume is based.

Notes

1. This chapter is part of the project 'The Ethnography of a Divided City: Socio-politics, Poverty and Gender in Maputo, Mozambique', funded by the Norwegian Research Council (2012–2015).
2. The 'feminization of poverty' pardigm postulates that i) women are poorer than men, ii) the incidence of poverty among women is increasing relative to men over time, and iii) growing poverty among women is linkd to the feminization of headship (Chant 2008).
3. Married Portuguese women were even more firmly confined to their domestic space, as indicated by a statement in the local paper *O Brado Africano* in 1921: 'A morada do homem é o mundo, e o mundo da mulher é o lar doméstico' [The home of the man is the world, the world of the woman is the home] (Zamporini 1998: 276).
4. The majority of domestic servants continued to be men throughout the colonial period, reflecting the strong male dominance of formal urban space and employment (Zamporini 1998).
5. In a consumption-based poverty measure, the levels of consumption of households are assessed and compared to poverty lines constructed from a basket of basic foodstuffs conforming to a basic caloric minimum.
6. Where 0 corresponds to perfect equality and 1 to perfect inequality. The last figure is taken from INE (2015).
7. The formal definition of a female-headed household covers both de jure and de facto units (single mothers, widows, divorcees and polygamous wives not living with their husbands, INE 2010). However, domestic units where a man and a woman both 'eat from the same pot' and 'live under the same roof' are counted as male-headed. While rare, as both men and women will prefer to split households in such cases, it is still likely to account for a small under-estimate of de facto female-headed households.
8. The most recent Household Survey (2014/2015) had a number of technical problems, and does not give a basis for a similar comparison of poverty rates between male- and female-headed households (INE 2015; Sam Jones pers.comm.).
9. These spatial strategies are 'visualized' through a film eminating from the research project upon which this chapter is based, called 'Maputo: Ethnography of a Divided City' available through Tvedten et al. 2018.
10. See Paulo, Rosário and Tvedten 2011 for a more detailed discussion.
11. See note 7 for how such a situation relates to the statistical representation of female-headed households.
12. In other contexts in Maputo, the second subcategory of the better off (*xigogo*) is made up of people who have become rich by luck or by exploiting others (Paulo, Rosário and Tvedten 2011).
13. The average formal wage is 1.5 times higher for men than for women (Jones and Tarp 2013).
14. The survey shows that female-headed households 'compensate' for the lack of a husband by having a larger number of extended- or non-family members than male-headed households do.

References

Bank, L. 2011. *Home Spaces, Street Styles: Contesting Power and Identity in a South African City*. London: Pluto Press.

Barros, C.P., A. Chivangue and A. Samagoia. 2014. 'Urban Dynamics in Maputo, Mozambique', *Cities* 36: 74–82.

Bertelsen, B.E., S. Roque and I. Tvedten. 2014. 'Engaging, Transcending and Subverting Dichotomies: Discursive Dynamics of Maputo's Urban Space', *Urban Studies* 51(13): 1–18.

Bourdieu, P. 1977. *Outline of a Theory of Practice*. Cambridge: Cambridge University Press.

_____. 1990. *The Logic of Practice*. Stanford, CA: Stanford University Press.

Cairns, J., D. Tschirley and I.S. Cachomba. 2013. *Typology of Horticultural Producers Supplying Maputo*. Flash no. 70E. Maputo: Directorate of Economics, Ministry of Agriculture.

Caldeira, T.P.R. 2010. *City of Walls: Crime, Segregation, and Citizenship in São Paulo*. Berkeley: University of California Press.

Chant, S. 2008. 'The "Feminisation of Poverty" and the "Feminisation" of Anti-Poverty Programmes: Room for Revision?', *Journal of Development Studies* 44(2): 165–97.

Clark, G. 1994. *Onions are My Husband: Survival and Accumulation by West African Market Women*. Chicago: University of Chicago Press.

_____ (ed.). 2003. *Gender at Work in Economic Life*. Walnut Creek, CA: AltaMira Press.

CMM. 2013. *Report Card sobre a Satisfacão dos Municipes: 2012*. Maputo: Conselho Municipal.

Costa, A.B.d. 2007. *O Preço da Sombra: Sobrevivência e Reprodução Social entre Famílias de Maputo*. Lisbon: Livros Horizonte.

Cunguara, B. 2012. 'An Exposition of Development Failures in Mozambique', *Review of African Political Economy* 39(131): 161–70.

Diouf, M., and R. Fredericks, eds. 2014. *The Arts of Citizenship in African Cities: Infrastructures and Spaces of Belonging*. New York: Palgrave Macmillan.

Eriksen, A., C. Ødegaard and A. Fagertun. 2007. 'Introduksjon: om Kjønn og Antropologi', *Norsk antropologisk tidsskrift* 2: 76–89.

Espling, M. 1999. *Women's Livelihood Strategies in Processes of Change: Cases from Urban Mozambique*. Göteborg: Department of Human and Economic Geography, School of Economics and Commercial Law, University of Göteborg.

Fox, S. 2018. 'The Political Economy of Slums: Theory and Evidence from Sub-Saharan Africa'. *World Development* 54:191–203.

Frates, L.L. 2002. *Memory of Place, the Place of Memory: Women's Narrations of Late Colonial Lourenço Marques, Mozambique*. PhD Dissertation. Los Angeles: University of California.

Granjo, P. 2005. *Lobolo em Maputo: um Velho Idioma para Novas Vivências Conjugais*. Porto: Campo das Letras.

Hellmann, E. 1948. *Rooiyard: A Sociological Survey of an Urban Native Slum Yard*. Manchester: Manchester University Press.

INE. 1998. *Inquérito Nacional aos Agregados Familiares sobre Condicões da Vida 1996/97: Relatório Final*. Maputo: Instituto Nacional de Estatística.

_____. 2010. *Inquérito sobre Orçamento Familiar 2008/09: Quadros Básicos*. Maputo: Instituto Nacional de Estatística.

_____. 2015. *Relatório Final do Inquérito ao Orçamento Familiar*. Maputo: Instituto Nacional de Estatística.

Jackson, C., and R. Pearson. 1998. *Feminist Visions of Development: Gender Analysis and Policy*. London: Routledge.

Jenkins, P. 2012. 'Maputo and Luanda', in S. Bekker and G. Therborn (eds), *Capital Cities in Africa: Power and Powerlessness*. Cape Town: HSRC Press, pp. 141–66.

Jones, S. 2013. 'Gender Data from the 2008/09 National Household Expenditure Survey and the 2007 Population Census in Mozambique', unpublished paper. Copenhagen: University of Copenhagen.

Jones, S., and F. Tarp. 2013. *Jobs and Welfare in Mozambique*. WIDER Working Paper, 2013/045. Helsinki: United Nations University World Institute for Development Economics Research.

Jones, S., and I. Tvedten. 2019. 'What Does It Mean to Be Poor? Investigating the Qualitative-Quantitative Divide in Mozambique', *World Development* 117: 153–66.

Kabeer, N. 2007. *Marriage, Motherhood and Masculinity in the Global Economy: Reconfigurations of Personal and Economic Life*. IDS Working Paper, 290. Brighton, UK: Institute of Development Studies.

Kamp, L.v.d. 2010. 'Burying Life: Pentecostal Religion and Development in Urban Mozambique', in B. Bompani and M. Frahm-Arp (eds), *Development and Politics from Below: Exploring Religious Spaces in the African State*. London: Palgrave Macmillan, pp. 152–68.

Lundin, I.B. 2007. *Negotiating Transformation: Urban Livelihoods in Maputo Adapting to Thirty Years of Political and Economic Changes*. Göteborg: Department of Human and Economic Geography, School of Business, Economics and Law, University of Göteborg.

Manuel, S. 2008. *Love and Desire: Concepts, Narratives and Practices of Sex amongst Youths in Maputo City*. Maputo: CODESRIA.

Membawase, R.N. 2005. *Mulheres Chefes de Agregado Familiar: Viúvas, Divorciadas, Casadas e Solteiras - Suas Características Sociais e Suas Estratégias de Sobrevivência*. PhD Dissertation. Maputo: Universidade Eduardo Mondlane.

Mikkelsen, B. 2005. *Methods for Development Work and Research: A New Guide for Practitioners*. London: Sage Publications.

Milani, T. and M. Shaikjee. 2013. 'A New South African Man? Beer, Masculinity and Social Change', in L.M. Atanga and D.E. Ellece (eds), *Gender and Language in Sub-Saharan Africa: Tradition, Struggle, Change*. Amsterdam: John Benjamins Publishing Company, pp. 131–48.

Miranne, K.B., and A.H. Young (eds). 1999. *Gendering the City: Women, Boundaries and Visions of Urban Life*. Lanham, MD: Rowman & Littlefield.

Mitchell, J.C. 1969. *Social Networks in Urban Situations: Analysis of Personal Relationships in Central African Towns*. Manchester: Manchester University Press.

Monteiro, N.T. 2002. *The Political Economy of Informal Markets: Restructuring Economies, Gender and Women's Lives in Maputo, Mozambique*. PhD Dissertation. Flagstaff: Northern Arizona University.

Moore, H. 1994. *A Passion for Difference: Essays in Anthropology and Gender.* Cambridge: Polity Press.

Morton, D. 2013. 'From Racial Discrimination to Class Segregation in Postcolonial Urban Mozambique', in F.W. Twine and B. Gardener (eds), *Geographies of Privilege*. New York: Routledge, pp. 231–62.

Newitt, M.D.D. 1995. *A History of Mozambique*. London: Hurst.

Orre, A., and H. Rønning. 2017. *Mozambique: A Political Economy Analysis*. Oslo: Norwegian Institute of International Affairs.

Ortner, S.B. 2006. *Anthropology and Social Theory: Culture, Power, and the Acting Subject*. Durham, NC: Duke University Press.

_____. 2016. 'Dark Anthropology and its Others: Theory since the Eighties', *HAU: Journal of Ethnographic Theory* 6(1): 47–73.

Osirim, M.J. 2009. *Enterprising Women in Urban Zimbabwe: Gender, Microbusiness and Globalization*. Washington, DC: Woodrow Wilson Center Press.

Paulo, M., C. Rosário and I. Tvedten. 2011. *'Xiculungo' Revisited: Assessing the Implications of PARPA II in Maputo, 2007–2010*. CMI Report, R 2011:1. Bergen: Chr. Michelsen Institute.

Pellow, D. 2008. *Landlords and Lodgers: Socio-Spatial Organization in an Accra Community*. Chicago: University of Chicago Press.

Penvenne, J.M. 1981. 'Chibalo and the Working Class: Lourenco Marques 1870–1962', *Mozambican Studies* 2: 9–25.

_____. 1995. *African Workers and Colonial Racism: Mozambican Strategies and Struggles in Lourenço Marques, 1877–1962*. London: James Currey.

Rita-Ferreira, A. 1968. *Os Africanos de Lourenço Marques*. Lourenço Marques: Instituto de Investigação Científica de Moçambique.

Robbins, J. 2013. 'Beyond the Suffering Subject: Towards an Anthropology of the Good'. *Journal of the Royal Anthropological Institute* 19(3): 447–62.

Schuetze, C.K. 2010. *'The World Upside Down': Women's Participation in Religious Movements in Mozambique*. PhD Dissertation. Pennsylvania: University of Pennsylvania.

Sheldon, K.E. 2002. *Pounders of Grain: A History of Women, Work, and Politics in Mozambique*. Portsmouth, NH: Heinemann.

_____. 2003. 'Markets and Gardens: Placing Women in the History of Urban Mozambique', *Canadian Journal of African Studies* 37(2/3): 358–95.

Silberschmidt, M. 2001. 'Disempowerment of Men in Rural and Urban East Africa: Implications for Male Identity and Sexual Behavior', *World Development* 29(4): 657–71.

Stoler, A.L. 1995. *Race and the Education of Desire: Foucault's History of Sexuality and the Colonial Order of Things*. Durham, NC: Duke University Press.

Sumich, J. 2011. 'The Party and the State: Frelimo and Social Stratification in Post-socialist Mozambique', in T. Hagmann and D. Péclard (eds), *Negotiating Statehood: Dynamics of Power and Domination in Africa*. London: Wiley Blackwell, pp. 679–98.

Tinker, I. 1990. *Persistent Inequalities: Women and World Development*. Oxford: Oxford University Press.

Tvedten, I. 2018. '"It's All About Money": Urban-Rural Spaces and Relations in Maputo, Mozambique', *Canadian Journal of African Studies* 52(1): 37–52.

Tvedten, I., M. Paulo and G. Montserrat. 2008. *Gender Policies and Feminisation of Poverty in Mozambique*. CMI Report 2008:13. Bergen: Chr. Michelsen Institute.

Tvedten, I., and A. Orre. 2016. *Country Evaluation Brief Mozambique*. Norad Report 8/2016. Oslo: Norwegian Agency of Development Cooperation.

Tvedten, I., F. Ribeiro, J. Graça and B.E. Bertelsen. 2018. 'Maputo: Ethnography of a Divided City', *Journal of Anthropological Film* 2(2). DOI: 10.15845/jaf. v2i2.1571.

Tvedten, I., and R. Picardo. 2019. 'Goats Eat Where They Are Tied up: Illicit and Habitual Corruption in Mozambique', *Review of African Political Economy*, early view, DOI: 10.1080/03056244.2018.1546686.

Urdang, S. 1989. *And Still They Dance: Women, War and Struggle for Change in Mozambique*. London: Earthscan.

Vletter, F. 2001. *Mozambique's Urban Informal Sector: A Neglected Majority*. Maputo: Ministério do Trabalho.

Wacquant, L. 2013. 'Symbolic Power and Group-Making: On Pierre Bourdieu's Reframing of Class', *Journal of Classical Sociology* 13(2): 274–91.

Zamporini, V.D. 1998. 'Entre Narros e Mulungos: Colonialismo e Paisagem Social em Lourenço Marques c. 1890–c. 1940'. PhD dissertation. São Paulo: Universidade de São Paulo.

Chapter 6

The Dynamics of Inequality in the Congolese Copperbelt
A Discussion of Bourdieu's Theory of Social Space

Benjamin Rubbers

Few Congolese people would acknowledge the existence of social classes in their own country. The categories that they use in everyday life (the 'unemployed', 'intellectuals', 'villagers' or 'whites', to give but a few examples) are based on different criteria of classification, ambiguous and ill-defined; for that reason, they cannot easily be matched with social classes. All would however acknowledge the existence of strong inequalities in Congolese society. So how can we account for these inequalities and their evolution since Congo's independence in 1960? In order to do so, a vast literature suggests starting from an a priori definition of class-in-itself (the political class, the working class, or more recently, the middle class), and then to study its formation, its interests, its conflicts and the forms of consciousness associated with it. This line of enquiry, however, is confronted by two longstanding issues in class analysis: to determine the boundaries of social classes (who belong to the class under study?), and to think the relationship between class-in-itself and class-for-itself (what is the relevance of class from people's point of view?).

This chapter argues that to account for the evolution of inequalities in Congo since independence, the theoretical framework developed by Bourdieu in *Distinction* (1979) offers a better starting point. It allows one not only to overcome the two above-mentioned difficulties faced by traditional class analysis, but also to study the dynamics of class in a broader perspective – beyond the usual emphasis on the formation of a particular class. In a nutshell, Bourdieu sees 'social classes' as emic categories that

Notes for this chapter begin on page 151.

result from the re-presentation work of cultural entrepreneurs and people's acts of classification in everyday life. Such categories are not purely
arbitrary: they are based on perceived discrepancies in lifestyles – that is,
ways of talking, eating, dressing, and so on; and these lifestyles, just like
the practical schemas through which they are perceived, are the product
of certain living conditions. In a society like France, living conditions
show deep inequalities that Bourdieu proposes to objectify (and measure)
under the form of three species of power, or capital: economic, cultural
and social capital. French society is thus represented not as a single hierarchy of socio-economic classes, but as a continuous and multidimensional space – what he calls the 'social space', or 'space of social positions'.

For Bourdieu, in other words, there is no class in itself that people
would become conscious of, and/or that the social scientist could take as
a research subject a priori. It is people and institutions that draw symbolic boundaries between social categories. At most, it is possible, on
the basis of the distribution of the different forms of capital, to delineate
some 'theoretical regions', or 'classes on paper', in order to account for
probable symbolic associations and divisions between people.[1] However,
Bourdieu (1984: 4) reminds us, the symbolic association of those who
are close in the social space (that is, in terms of economic, cultural and
social capital) is never necessary, and the symbolic association of those
distant never impossible. Indeed, the social space can be perceived and
represented according to other principles of division than class, such as
regional or national identity for instance.

Since its publication, *Distinction* (1979) has given rise to intense debate
among sociologists, and stimulated further research, to the point that it
has rapidly become the most cited book in the social sciences. The discussion, however, has to a large extent been limited to France and the United
States (see especially Lamont and Lareau 1988, Lamont 1992, Lamont
2000, Lahire 2004, Coulangeon 2004, 2011). With few exceptions (Hilgers
2009), Bourdieu's theoretical framework has not sparked much interest in
African studies. In addition, it is the prominent role that Bourdieu attributes to culture that has attracted the greatest attention. Most researchers
have focused on the social distribution of cultural practices, and their
implication in processes of boundary formation. By contrast, this chapter
pays more attention to the theory of social classes found in *Distinction*
(1979: chap. 2; see also Bourdieu 1984, 1993), which constitutes the foundation of Bourdieu's sociology of cultural practices. The discussion below
will be limited to this first step of analysis – the mapping of the social
space, and of the trajectories of socio-professional groups; for reasons of
space, it will not go further into the details of consumption and boundary-
marking practices.[2]

Bourdieu's theory of social space shows two main limitations. Built on the analogy of the economy, it reduces things, knowledge and relationships to forms of 'capital', in which people 'invest' to make 'profits' on different 'markets' (Graeber 2001: chap.1). Since it conceptualizes the social space as structured by only three forms of capital, it fails to account for variations between individuals, including within the same family (Lahire 1995, 2004). In my view, these limitations, although important, do not invalidate Bourdieu's theory to solve the problem of class analysis. As Passeron (1982, see also 1991) argues, the sociological mode of analysis is to a large extent founded on analogical reasoning, and the analogy of the economy is – within certain limits – analytically productive for studying non-economic processes like the so-called 'inflation' of educational titles. Bourdieu acknowledges that, to draw a detailed map of social positions and account for variations between individual trajectories, the analysis should take into consideration other factors, including gender, age, health, religion, ethnicity, place of residence, etc. In his view, however, these social characteristics are related, and secondary, to the volume and distribution of economic, cultural and social capital – the most determining factors of living conditions. It is therefore legitimate (and productive) to take these three key variables as a basis for studying the transformations of the social space, and the trajectories of socio-professional groups within it.

This chapter takes Bourdieu's theory of social space as a basis for reconstructing the dynamics of inequality in a society very different from France – namely the industrial and urban region of Katanga, in the Democratic Republic of Congo.[3] After having discussed the relevance of thinking of this region as a social space structured by the three main forms of capital identified by Bourdieu, I will focus on the trajectories of two categories of people within this particular social space: white businessmen, whom I interviewed during my doctoral research in 2002–2004 (Rubbers 2009), and Gécamines workers, with whom I lived in the course of several fieldtrips between 2006 and 2011 (Rubbers 2013). These case studies will provide the opportunity to compare their strategies of social mobility in the face of the powerful changes that have affected Katanga in the postcolonial period, and to reflect more broadly on the changing significance of economic, cultural and social capital in the structuring of inequalities in Africa.[4]

The Congolese Copperbelt as a Social Space

The choice to limit the analysis to the industrial and urban region of Katanga (or Congolese copperbelt) can be justified by its main character- istic features: (a) It has been dominated throughout the twentieth century by a single mining company, the Union Minière du Haut-Katanga, subse- quently nationalized and renamed as Générale des Carrières et des Mines (Gécamines); (b) a large number of its inhabitants have lived in town for several generations, and have to a large extent broken their rural ties; and (c) wage work has been historically important in the region; even today, it remains the main source of income for a significant proportion of the population.[5] One last feature could be added to the list: the presence of a powerful white minority, who has played a key role in the emergence of regional identity politics in the colonial period. As many observers have noted, all this tends to make Katanga a distinctive place, closer to south- ern Africa than the rest of Congo.

Several authors have sought to identify the classes that divide Congolese society on the basis of their position in the national politi- cal economy (Nzongola 1970, Schatzberg 1980, Callaghy 1984, Young and Turner 1985, MacGaffey 1987). They did not necessarily agree on the number of classes, their boundaries, and the criteria to be taken into account in order to distinguish them but all assumed that Congolese soci- ety was composed of classes, and that their relationship reflected the dynamics of an economy in the periphery of the capitalist system. The theory of social space, I think, provides analytical tools for developing a more complex understanding of the dynamics of inequalities in that soci- ety: as mentioned above, it invites us to study these dynamics as resulting not from relations of production, but from the volume and distribution of three forms of capital among different socio-professional groups. Before retracing the trajectories of two such groups, I would like to briefly study variations in the relative weight of economic, cultural and social capital in the Congolese copperbelt since 1960.

In his theoretical statements, Bourdieu argues that building a theory of social classes implies breaking with the narrow economic approach of Marxism, which tends to reduce class to a position in relations of pro- duction. In his study of France, however, economic capital is given the greatest importance: in the last instance, cultural practices are understood as reflecting distance/proximity with the experience of material neces- sity. The problem is that the concept of economic capital is itself largely under-theorized. As Burawoy and Von Holdt argue (2012: chap. 2), the sociology of Bourdieu lacks a theory of capitalism that would account for the accumulation of economic capital, changes in material living conditions, and dynamics of inequality.[6] The neo-Marxist approach advocated in studies on Congolese classes in the 1970s and 1980s was more satisfactory in that respect (see MacGaffey 1987: chap.1).

In line with this latter approach, one can retrace the dynamics of inequality in Katanga since 1960 by taking as a point of departure the main forces shaping this region's political economy. In the first place, this economy is strongly dependent on the mining industry and the fluctuations of the copper price on the world market. The slow decrease of the copper price from 1974 to 2004 led to the bankruptcy of Gécamines, the decline of most industrial and commercial activities, and the general impoverishment of the population. During the last decade, the mining boom was followed by a rise in living standards, albeit quite unevenly across society. Secondly, the state faced an informal privatization process that made 'corruption' in the broad sense of the word into a major instrument of economic capital accumulation. In such a context, opportunities for enrichment are closely associated with the occupation of a strategic position in the state apparatus and/or the possibility to benefit from the support of people in such a position – what Bourdieu (1994: 33–34) called, in a conference on the social space of soviet countries, 'political capital', or 'social capital of a political type'. Finally, due to economic decline and state predation, Congolese people experienced an exponential rise in inflation that gradually eroded real wages, especially in the public sector. This process contributed to an unprecedented growth of informal activities in urban areas. Most people in Katanga came to participate in this economy, but only a few managed to make sufficient profits to develop their business and accumulate economic capital.

In comparison to economic capital, the concept of cultural capital, grounded in Bourdieu's theory of habitus and cultural legitimacy, is more explicit. The theory of cultural legitimacy has been principally criticized for overestimating bourgeois culture's symbolic domination over the whole society, and therefore ignoring the multiplicity of social identifications, and the heterogeneity of cultural tastes (Lamont and Lareau 1988, Grignon and Passeron 1989, Hall 1992, Lahire 2004). This critique, made for France and the United States, is justified for Katanga as well. Since the late nineteenth century, this industrial and urban region has attracted migrants of different backgrounds, and been subjected to various cultural influences. Appropriated in original ways, these influences have given birth to cultural practices (habits, lifestyles and forms of artistic expression) that cannot be reduced to mimicry of the whites.

I would nevertheless argue that Bourdieu's broad argument is relevant for studying Katanga, where the cultural influence of colonial institutions has been particularly strong and lasting. In this region, the state, large companies and Christian missions have successfully imposed Western 'modernity' as a dominant cultural repertoire that Congolese people came to view as a major source of symbolic power. As Ferguson (1999: 108) puts it, 'it should not be obscured that, *de facto*, cosmopolitan styles in urban Africa are dominated by Western and Western-derived cultural forms; and that such cultural domination is hardly an accident'. Since independence, the cultural influence of colonization has been challenged by the cultural policy of the Mobutu regime; the collapse of the economy; the multiplication of schools, churches and media; and, more recently, the establishment of new mining investors. Even though the colonial version of 'modernity' has been continuously challenged, it has remained a privileged reference order in the local economy of distinction. As the case studies show, symbolic struggles in this urban society can hardly be understood without going back to the Belgian colonial legacy and to the cultural influence of the 'West' in general.

A good indication of this is of course school education, which continues to be viewed as crucial despite the very limited number of job opportunities. In the 1960s, the education system was an important channel of upward social mobility. However, the rise of demand for education that followed rapidly caused a devaluation of the values of school degrees on the market, an increase in the duration of studies, and the creation of numerous private schools, ranked according to their location, the amount of registration fees, and their reputation. This is a process very similar to that described by Bourdieu (1979) and Passeron (1982) for France. The main difference lies in the fact that, in Congo, the growing dependence of public schools on the fees paid by parents and the concomitant multiplication of private schools have completely altered the relative importance of cultural and economic capital in the access to recognized institutions: it is above all necessary to have money and/or support to get a (good) school education. Despite adverse conditions, the demand for school and university education has not declined since the 1970s (Rubbers 2003, De Herdt et al. 2010). The main reason for this is that to obtain an academic degree continues to be conceived by the majority of Congolese people as a source of prestige, the best means of getting a (good) job, and the most secure form of investment for the future of children.

Social capital is not more theorized than economic capital in the work of Bourdieu. Although it is mentioned in *Distinction* (1979), it is not used for mapping the French social space; the latter is only represented by a two-dimensional graphic. Later, Bourdieu (1980, 1986, 1994) discussed social capital in brief notes or passages, but only to treat it as a secondary variable, that allows for turning other forms of capital to good account. In his view, social capital is of lesser importance in 'advanced' societies – an unsubstantiated view that ignores variations between countries and sectors of social life.

It is unclear whether Bourdieu would have regarded contemporary Katanga – an industrial and urban area for a century – as a fully-fledged 'advanced' society or not.[7] Nevertheless, as my earlier discussion of the role of economic and cultural capital suggests, social capital is certainly key to understand the dynamics of inequality in that society. If, as Bourdieu (1980: 2) claims, the concept of social capital is above all intended to account for cases where individuals earn a different return on an equivalent economic or cultural capital, then it is necessary to use it in most circumstances. Whether for getting a job, developing economic activities, or getting access to public services, personal relationships play a crucial role – albeit in different ways – in Katanga.

This allegedly strong influence of social capital in Katanga raises both methodological and theoretical difficulties. This form of power is of course more difficult to measure than economic or cultural capital. The successive household surveys carried out in Lubumbashi (the capital city of Katanga) since 1958 provide information on levels of income and education, but not on the size and composition of social networks (Benoît 1958, Houyoux and Lecoanet 1975, Bruneau and Pain 1990, Petit 2003, Nkuku Khonde and Remon 2006). It is consequently impossible to precisely assess the relative weight of social capital in the (re-)production of inequalities in this city since 1960. Yet, if social capital is important (and I believe it is), then the theoretical representation of social space that Bourdieu proposed on the basis of the French case – a space divided in classes and class fractions, each developing a specific habitus and cultural lifestyle – needs to be made more complex. On the one hand, social capital blurs the probable effects of the economic and cultural capital inherited from parents on children's dispositions, practices and trajectories. On the other, it is not in any simple way determined by proximity in the social space or, to put it differently, correlated to the volume and distribution of economic and cultural capital. To study the dynamics of inequality in Katanga, we need therefore to pay more attention to the interplay of social capital with economic and cultural capital. This is what the two following case studies illustrate.

White Businessmen

In my doctoral research, I studied the trajectory of white businessmen who were dominating the most important economic sectors (mining, import trade and construction) in the early 2000s (see Rubbers 2009). Even though some had migrated to central Africa after 1960, most were born in families of Belgian, Greek or Italian origins established in the area for two or three generations. They were part of a white population that sharply declined from 14,000 in 1960 to less than 1,500 in 2001 – these figures are for Katanga province alone.[8]

White businessmen have been directly touched by the events that marked the postcolonial history of Congo-Zaire: the rebellions and wars that followed Congo's independence, and Katanga's secession, from 1960 to 1963; the nationalization of foreign companies in 1973; and the looting of factories and shops by the army and the population in 1991. They were also, at a more general level, affected by the bankruptcy of Gécamines, the extension of the informal economy, and the growing poverty of the population. These changes nonetheless offered to some new opportunities in return: some small building contractors could get public contracts previously granted to major construction companies; some retail traders formerly established in rural areas could move into wholesale trade and industrial transformation in town; and some earthworks companies working for Gécamines managed to become the latter's partner in joint venture projects and enter in the mining business. From 1960 to now, an ever decreasing number of European entrepreneurs succeeded to develop their activities on the ruins of the industrial and commercial base inherited from the past.

This can be briefly illustrated by the trajectories of the two most important businessmen in Katanga, George Forrest and Georges Psaromatis. In 1986, soon after he became the managing director of the Entreprise Générale Malta Forrest (EGMF), a family company with a long experience in the construction of buildings and roads, Forrest managed to obtain subcontracting contracts with Gécamines for earthworks. After the collapse of the state mining company in the early 1990s, however, he started to invest in other sectors and countries. This extraversion strategy later allowed him to come back in the Congolese mining sector with a stronger negotiation position. From 1994 onwards, Forrest succeeded in attracting major companies to sign partnership agreements with both Gécamines and EGMF, and develop together several mining projects. In the early 2000s – before the arrival of more important investors – EGMF had replaced Gécamines as the leading company in the Congolese mining sector. Through other companies, Forrest had also managed to develop operations in a dozen other sectors in Africa, Europe and the Middle East. The family business of the 1980s had turned into a multinational group.

Psaromatis began his career as a retailer in the small town of Kalemie. After the nationalization of foreign companies in 1973, he moved to

Lubumbashi and followed other Greek merchants in the food import trade. During the lootings of 1991, all of them lost the bulk of their goods. To face the situation, Psaromatis managed to obtain new goods on credit from suppliers in Southern Africa – many of them traders of Greek origins, with long-lasting connections to the Greek diaspora in Central and South Africa. Thanks to this support, he gained a position of virtual monopoly, and made very high profits. In the years that followed, he strengthened this comparative advantage by opening a purchasing office in South Africa, developing his political connections, and granting goods on credit to local retailers. In the late 1990s and early 2000s, he also increased the number of cold-storage rooms and shops, built small processing units, and took over an oil distribution company. Up to the present day, this strategy has allowed the Greek businessman to face the growing competition of Indian, Chinese and South African importers.

The economic upward mobility of businessmen such as Forrest or Psaromatis in the postcolonial period came with a redrawing of hierarchies within the white minority and of the boundary demarcating it from Congolese society. In the colonial period, most non-Belgian settlers in Katanga were Italians from Piedmont, Greeks and Jews from the Dodecanese, or Portuguese. Generally poor with little school education, they were regarded with contempt by the Belgian establishment, as they could undermine white prestige and blur the racial order on which colonial rule was founded. Inside their own communities, since they came from the same social milieu, migrated to Congo to make a fortune, and often operated in the same sector, these settlers were competing on essentially economic grounds. It was not until the 1950s that the most successful among them began to learn French, to put their children in Belgian schools, to give their daughters in marriage to Belgians, and to apply for Belgian citizenship.

After independence, the situation progressively reversed. With the departure of colonial administrators, company managers and employees, businessmen came to hold a dominant position in the white minority. At the time of my fieldwork in the early 2000s, they were not only the principal employer for Europeans living in Katanga, but also the main source of funding for social institutions catering to the latter (schools, hospitals, recreational clubs, etc.). In these circumstances, it is no surprise that cultural capital has to a large extent given way to economic capital as the main principle of symbolic distinction among whites: it turns around houses, cars, mobile phones, holiday destinations, dinner invitations, parties and the size of domestic staff. Whereas the signals marking distinctions among whites were principally culturally acquired ones in the colonial period, they have become increasingly purchasable ones since the 1970s.

Access to goods and services is now deemed more important than education or connoisseurship. In these circumstances, it is not the non-Belgian trader with a poor school education that is marginalized from the white community, but anyone unable to afford a certain living standard. Here is for instance the story of a Belgian university graduate, who saw his children progressively ostracized after the family moved into a flat:

> Parents don't want their kids to come and play with ours anymore because we live in a flat: 'they don't have a garden', 'they don't have a swimming pool', 'they don't want a nanny', and so, 'what are my kids going to do at their place, in a flat?' There are not many kids who come and spend the afternoon playing with my daughter or my son.

This growing importance of economic capital must be understood in the light of white businessmen's social background: they grew up in migrant communities entirely dedicated to business that gave limited value to schooling. It must also be understood in the light of the evolution of race relations. Since school and university education is now accessible to many Congolese people, it has lost much of its symbolic power from Europeans' point of view – unless it is provided by expensive and exclusive institutions abroad. At the same time, regardless of the sector, white businessmen continue to be in a dominant position, and white workers continue to earn much higher wages than nationals with the same qualification. Only money now allows the Europeans to preserve their relative social rarity. Practices of social distinction are now primarily based on economic capital (money), not on cultural capital (school education), and put the great majority of Congolese people at some distance: obviously most Congolese people cannot afford to buy a villa, to put children in a consular school, to join expatriate social clubs, and to take holidays in Europe. This redefinition of the racial boundary has involved a tighter social control over whites' own standard of living. To adopt practices accessible to most Congolese people is quickly subjected to disapproving comments and derogatory comments that have the effect of making expatriates hold their position as whites: 'when I bought my bike here', a woman who arrived from Greece in the 1990s told me, 'the entire Greek community was shocked: a Greek woman cannot cycle here; she must move around by car because bikes are for the Blacks'.[9]

Whether based on economic or cultural capital, the symbolic distinction of the white community is not completely alien or illegitimate to Congolese people for they use similar signals to make distinctions among themselves, and closely associate them with whiteness. The tautology used in local Swahili for modernity – *'kizungu bazungu'*, literally the 'Europeans' European way of life' – is a clear indication of this. In accordance with this symbolic proximity between race and class, whites tend to be seen a priori as rich, educated and high-status. In the same way, Congolese people with a 'modern' lifestyle (rich, educated and high-status) can be referred to as whites (or *'bazungu'*) by the poor. Having said this, race is not entirely synonymous with class for it is also based on moral boundaries: whites are usually seen by both European and Congolese people as better organized and more trustworthy. In addition, it is not all white/Western culture that is regarded as more legitimate or high-status. In relation to food, music, religion or family life, for example, Congolese people tend to have relatively autonomous cultural preferences. As explained above, Western culture's symbolic domination should not be overestimated.

Since independence, the fall in the number of expatriates, their aggregation around a limited number of institutions, and their concern to reproduce the colour bar contributed to their integration in a very dense social network. Clearly this social capital provides them with economic advantages: those entering active life can mobilize it to find employment, to take over a business, or to get goods in credit; as for those already in business, it gives them the opportunity to make deals with a relatively trustworthy partners, provided that they know their partners personally, and that they can exert social pressure on them. This form of trust is not to be neglected in a context marked by the weakness of formal institutions (see Rubbers 2009). It is nevertheless a factor of secondary importance to account for white businessmen' relative success in comparison to Congolese competitors. Independently of their business acumen, their success derives to a large extent from their privileged access to capital abroad: it is above all their contacts with traders or mining companies abroad that allowed businessmen like Forrest or Psaromatis to gain a dominant position in the Congolese market. In comparison, for lack of credibility and/or connections, Congolese businessmen have much more difficulties in attracting capital, or to obtaining goods on credit, from foreign partners.

Gécamines Workers

From 2006 to 2011, I conducted ethnographic research in Likasi with Gécamines workers who were made redundant from the company in 2003–2004 within the framework of a voluntary departure programme (VDP) designed by the World Bank (Rubbers 2013).[10] This generation of workers started their career at the company in the late 1950s and early 1960s. At that time, the social policy that Union Minière had put in place from the late 1920s onwards offered significant benefits to them. Provided that they agreed to live under the disciplinary regime in the company's camps, they could take advantage of its comprehensive social infrastructure, and provide a certain material security to their wife and children (food, health, education, etc.). For this reason, they represented a relatively protected category in Congolese society.

This generation of workers has experienced a long and progressive decline of its living conditions in the postcolonial period. From the 1970s onwards, following the decrease of copper prices, Gécamines let their real wages devaluate because of inflation. In the early 1990s, the company fell into bankruptcy, abandoned its social infrastructure, and ceased to distribute benefits to its personnel. Finally, in the context of the war between 1998 and 2003, workers began to receive their wages irregularly. In 2002, just before the VDP, they had on average thirty-six months of wage arrears. According to a survey conducted at that time (University of Lubumbashi 2005: 8–20), their standard of living was then lower than the rest of Katanga's urban population. Retrospectively, the only advantage that they obtained from their employer to face the deterioration of their living conditions was the opportunity to buy back the company houses they occupied in the late 1980s. This property subsequently protected them against an even more dramatic fall.

This collective downward spiral conceals disparities between different categories of employees, particularly managers and workers (see Rubbers 2017). It is therefore useful to come back in more detail to the economic, cultural and social strategies that they developed to face the decline of their living conditions. In the aftermath of independence, the company began to nationalize its staff.[11] During a brief period, this policy was of most benefit to skilled workers, who could obtain a promotion in the company hierarchy. Subsequently Gécamines gave preference to university and college graduates recruited externally instead. Those who could get access to a managerial position lived in another neighbourhood, and enjoyed a much higher living standard: a garden villa, a car, domestic workers, and so on. In a sense Gécamines did not bridge the economic, cultural and social gap that existed between European managers and Congolese workers in the colonial period. The Africanization of personnel simply consisted in granting to the new Congolese managers the benefits formerly reserved for whites.

Following the decline of Gécamines, the social distance between managers and workers was put into question. The living standard of employees came to depend less and less on their position in the company hierarchy, and more and more on the informal activities that they developed on the side with their wife and children (agriculture, petty trade, poultry farming, etc.). Managers often found it harder to engage in such activities because they were less accustomed to manual work, and had a social status to uphold. In the 1990s, their total income could be, for that reason, lower than that of workers. Managers nevertheless found themselves in a better position after the VDP in 2003–2004. They received a severance payment (between US$8,000 and 15,000), significantly higher than that of workers (between US$2,000 and 4,000), that allowed them to invest in real estate. They could also move into the cottage for domestic workers in their garden, and rent their own house to an expatriate family – an opportunity inaccessible to workers, who lived in small houses in a former work camp on the outskirts of the city.

This is the decision that Kalombo, a former Gécamines manager in his seventies, took after having invested in a cooperative, a bread oven, a small shop in front of his house, and the cultivation of a plot of land. Although some of these activities keep going, the income that they generate is not sufficient for Kalombo to make a living. Part of the money that Kalombo received as severance payment was also shared with his adult children to give them the opportunity to complete their studies and move abroad: one now practices as a doctor in Canada, and four are employed by private companies in South Africa. These children send him some money in case of emergencies, but not for ordinary expenditures. Consequently Kalombo and his wife decided to move in the cottage and to rent their house for US$700/month to an Indian family: 'I thought that I should be autonomous, and to be autonomous, I had to rent the house and put myself in here. As I only have two dependent children now, it's easier.'

As this case shows, another reason for which managers became better off than workers in the 2000s is that some of their children came to enjoy a more comfortable situation that allowed them to financially support their parents. Even though this support is generally small and/or irregular, it is critically important in difficult circumstances, whether it is for facing health problems, paying school fees, or recapitalizing a small business. The reasons that the children of managers came to enjoy a more comfortable situation in the 2000s are complex. Like the children of Kalombo, many received money from their father after the VDP to leave the country, and succeeded in getting a job or developing a business abroad. In addition, the children of managers were more likely than those of workers to continue their education in a graduate school or at university, and accordingly found themselves in a more favourable position to get a job when new opportunities opened up in the context of the mining boom. To study in a higher education institution gave them access not only to a degree, but also to a social capital independent from the one that they acquired in Gécamines' townships. Both are of crucial importance to get a job in Congo (Rubbers 2003, 2004).

The children of workers did not have the same opportunities. Take the example of Makumbi's children. After having repaid his debts and bought a field, this seventy-year-old former trainer gathered his eleven adult children to share the remainder of his severance payment (US$3000) among them. Needless to say, the amount of money that they received (approximatively US$100) could only be used for ordinary expenses, not for investing in a business or financing a trip abroad. In return, Makumbi asked them to assist him in the payment of school fees for the three remaining dependent children. Since then, however, he has not received anything: 'Not even a pen or a notebook. If I had not bought this field, where would I be today? I have been disappointed by my children; I'm disappointed up to the present day.' In their defence, it must be pointed out that none of his children had the opportunity to study beyond secondary school and get a stable job. All struggle to make a living in farming, small businesses or artisanal mining.

To understand this broad contrast between managers' and workers' children, it is necessary to come back to their unequal access to the educational system in the heyday of Gécamines. Until the 1980s, both Gécamines managers and workers prepared their children to pursue a career in the company and, if possible, to rise in the occupational hierarchy. The opportunities to advance to managerial positions, however, were profoundly unequal. Managers' children were prepared to become managers too, and benefited from various advantages in order to do so: they had guaranteed access to the company's secondary schools and technical colleges; they could study in their own bedroom, and did not have to participate to the housekeeping; and they regularly spoke French at home. Workers' children did not enjoy such favourable conditions. As they grew up in crowded houses, they were expected to assist their parents from an early age, and to start working at the end of primary school, or at the end of training school[12] (three years). In addition, the spoken language at home was usually Swahili. As a result, only a minority continued their secondary and post-secondary studies, usually thanks to the support of some teachers.

From the 1980s onwards, however, the decline of Gécamines gradually pushed workers to encourage their children to continue their school education and to find employment elsewhere. This was made possible by the creation of numerous private schools in the same period. Although more expensive, these schools offered worker households the opportunity to circumvent the company's discriminatory school system. Generally speaking, workers came to give increasing importance to school education. Today, they consider it as the only form of 'capital' that they can pass on to their children, and the only 'bargaining chip' that they have to ask for their assistance later. Much more than that, they expect that school education will teach a sense of discipline, arouse children's desire to progress in life, and open their mind to the modern world. This latter discourse on the school's moral mission became more and more widespread in the 1990s and 2000s, when Gécamines workers began to experience growing difficulties in paying school fees. The growing number of school drop-outs in that period caused what my informants consider as a profound moral crisis. Tommy, a young man who worked as an artisanal miner before returning to school, explains that a 'wall of incomprehension' has emerged between some school drop-outs and those who continue to study like him:

> In the past, we could study normally, we could eat normally. If we had to eat, we could eat. If we had to do something for the benefit of human kind, we did it. But since then, with the collapse of Gécamines, all has changed really. As people don't study normally, one can see young children not wanting to study: they prefer to look for money. Girls don't want to resume their studies. They prostitute themselves. ... For boys, it is bizarre too. They don't want to hear about the studies. They don't want anymore. For them, it is only about having money, getting drunk, that's all. Most don't even have a vision about becoming better-off in the future. They became narrow-minded: they only look for something to eat, dress, and that's all. Yet a human being must normally have a project so that one day, he may become someone in society. But these guys, what society forbids is what they do. .... They call university graduates 'fools': 'No, they can even make three months without getting anything'. They often say: 'Many people have studied here but up to now, they have nothing, no house, nothing'. So it's better for us to be wary. Instead of being together with them, it's better to make a break. We really split. They can do what they want, and we also, we do what we want.

This moral crisis calls into question the norms and values inherited from the company since the colonial period. Within the framework of its stabilization policy from the 1920s onwards, the Union Minière attempted to instil in workers, their wives and children a whole series of norms and values related to the body (nutrition, conduct, dress, etc.), work (time, productivity, progress, etc.), and the family (monogamy, domesticity, savings, etc.). This cultural policy led in company townships to the emergence of an economy of distinction based on the mastery of 'modernity', allowing the most educated employees to consider themselves as '*évolués*' (civilized), and to look down on the '*basses classes*' – the lowest categories of workers. Following the decline of Gécamines, it became increasingly difficult for employees to participate in this economy of distinction:

everyone, including managers, was forced to reduce his/her living standard. The upward symbolic competition of the past even changed direction, to give place to a levelling down process through which managers began to imitate workers – to farm, to speak local Swahili, to wear second-hand clothes, and so on. In the 1990s, the 'trickle-down effect' of social distinction was working in reverse. Still, 'modernity' as a symbolic system continued to be struggled for, and remained a key repertoire of social distinction. A striking instance of this is provided by the great efforts that Gécamines households make during the holiday season to buy new clothes, decorate their homes and serve 'European' dishes to guests.

At the same time children dropping out from school began to elaborate a lifestyle which challenged the norms and values once promoted by the company, the Catholic Church and the school. For many, the '*voyou*' among artisanal miners is this counter-culture personified: he speaks a popular slang; he dresses like musicians; he spends his money on alcohol, drugs and prostitutes; and he overtly make fun of school graduates, church goers and even elders. This oppositional culture shows many similarities with that of British working-class children described by Willis (1978), including the rejection of school education, the importance of money, conspicuous consumption, the centrality of the peer group, an active and open sexuality, and opposition to any form of authority. Unlike the culture of the 'lads' in Britain, however, the counter-culture of Congolese artisanal miners does not derive from that of their fathers in the workplace; it has been largely developed in opposition to the norms and values inherited from – and embodied by – their father. It is better understood as a youth culture than as a working-class culture.

As such, the lifestyle of these young miners is best interpreted relationally as resulting from a 'dominated search for distinction', that consists in openly claiming for oneself what is stigmatized by dominant culture (Bourdieu 2001: 140). In doing so, they express their deep ambivalence towards the 'modernity' to which their parents aspired – a culture that they have been taught since childhood, but to which they do not have access anymore. It is this ambivalence that gives their cultural practices a 'postmodern' dimension – by which I mean here altogether posterior, alternative and apparently opposite to the modernity promoted by the company and embodied by their parents.

Secondly, contrary to the culture of British working-class children, the youth culture of artisanal miners does not lead them to get working-class jobs, and reproduce the social position of their father, but to live from a precarious informal activity, and experience a downward economic trajectory. They not only have a lower income than their parents, but as they are progressively chased from the most accessible mines by foreign companies, they are also condemned to give up artisanal mining sooner or later, and find other, less profitable, sources of income.

Thirdly, since this youth culture gives more symbolic weight to economic than to cultural capital, it points at a progressive change in the legitimate forms of distinction in Gécamines townships. In these townships, economic disparities have historically been low so that more importance was given to cultural capital. Today, most inhabitants live from informal activities, and new economic inequalities have emerged among them. Economic capital has accordingly become more salient in their everyday practices of distinction than in the past.

Although it is not limited to Gécamines townships, this youth culture is of special significance in these areas not only because it opposes the norms and values previously promoted by the company, but also because opportunities of social mobility through school education and formal employment have become particularly limited for Gécamines employees and their children. The main reason for this is that their social capital is to a large extent confined to the company's social world: the Union Minière, and then the Gécamines, gave priority to its employees' children and relatives for recruitments, built townships equipped with all the necessary infrastructure to take charge of all the aspects of their existence, and took measures to limit, and control, their contacts with relatives and friends outside. This paternalistic policy led to make its employees' social network limited, dense and multiplex. All my informants in Likasi had spent most of their life in the company's townships. Most of their parents, parents-in-law, friends, neighbours, brothers and sisters in Christ, and so on, were also (former) Gécamines employees. And their contacts with more distant relatives were generally weak or even broken.

Up to the 1980s Gécamines employees could use these relations to obtain occasional assistance, or develop informal economic activities together. However, they turned out to be of limited use once all of them saw their means of existence decline and were left without resources. Later, after the VDP in 2003–2004, few Gécamines workers found new employment in the new companies that established in Katanga in the context of the mining boom. Unless the joint venture agreement stipulates that they must rehire the Gécamines employees working on the site, foreign investors prefer to recruit young graduates from technical colleges and universities. As a result, it is principally through these graduates' social networks that people get jobs in new mining companies. At most some ex-Gécamines employees in Likasi could get an unskilled and low paying job in small Asian companies thanks to the support of neighbours, former colleagues, or brothers in Christ.

Conclusion

This chapter has argued that, although Bourdieu's theory of social space has limitations, it provides a fruitful starting point for studying the dynamics of inequality in the Congolese copperbelt over the postcolonial period. It needs to be adapted in order to take into consideration: (a) the macro processes shaping the local political economy; (b) how 'modernity' as a dominant culture form has been imposed, used and contested; and (c) the decisive role of social capital in individual strategies of mobility. Once the specific conditions that have presided over the formation of Katanga's social space have been established, Bourdieu's theoretical framework sheds new light on the trajectories of different social groups. It provides conceptual tools to understand how they faced the economic and political changes that have marked Katanga's postcolonial history, and came to (re-)position themselves in relation to each other as a result of these changes.

This is what the two case studies on white businessmen and Gécamines workers aimed to illustrate. At the eve of independence in 1960, both groups had in common the fact that they lived in relatively closed social worlds and participated in an economy of symbolic distinction principally founded on 'modern' culture. They have however responded to the turmoil of the postcolonial period in different ways. Gécamines workers were directly affected by the fall in copper prices and the plunder of the company by state authorities. To face this situation, they principally invested in informal economic activities and their children's school education. By contrast, the European businessmen I met in the early 2000s – that is, businessmen who had decided to stay in Congo after the Zairianization of foreign companies in 1973, and the looting of plants and shops by the army and the population in 1991 – managed to take advantage of their competitors' departure from the country, the decline of public companies, and the informal privatization of the state apparatus. To do so they built on their relationships with economic partners abroad. It is principally these relationships that allowed them to adapt to changes, and to provide jobs and contracts to the white minority as a whole.

Besides their respective economic capitals, the main difference between the trajectories of white entrepreneurs and Gécamines workers, I would argue, has depended on their social capital. Gécamines workers' social capital has remained very much confined to the Gécamines community, which has been collectively confronted with a dramatic decline of its living conditions. It has accordingly tended to limit their investments' profitability in economic and/or cultural capital, unless they had the opportunity to send their children abroad. In contrast, white businessmen's transnational network gave them the opportunity to gain market shares in the most profitable sectors of the local economy, and in so doing, allowed the white community to reproduce itself as a profitable social capital for its members. The importance of this form of capital should not be a surprise to students of Africa. However, the challenge is to understand how it works for various social groups within the same social space, and what effects it tends to produce on the structure of social inequalities. These are issues that researchers have rarely addressed since the pioneering work of the Rhodes Livingstone Institute.

From a more general perspective, although the trajectories of white businessmen and Gécamines workers in the postcolonial period took different directions – upward for the former, downward for the latter – in both groups economic capital has tended to gain in symbolic significance while cultural capital was increasingly put into question. This tendency must be understood in the light of the profound changes that have affected the educational system, the job market and the economy in Congo since independence. Since a similar change may be observed in other places around the world (see Piketty 2013), however, it may viewed as part of a more global transformation, to be associated with the rise of neoliberalism in a labour-surplus economy (Ferguson 2015).

How economic, cultural and social capital interrelate with other factors of inequality, and how processes of identity formation are influenced by the distribution of these different factors, deserves more research. On the basis of research in the Congolese copperbelt, this chapter has attempted to show that Bourdieu's theory of social space could nevertheless provide a relevant framework for studying the dynamics of inequality in Africa from a new vantage point: it offers a solution to the old problem of defining class boundaries; it invites us to understand class inequalities relationally, in their broader social context, beyond a narrow focus on individual life courses, or the formation of a single social class; and it provides tools for understanding the social conditions of people's subjective experience, and the larger power dynamics underlying it, without making of this experience the simple reflection of class position. This is an important challenge for anthropological research in Africa, where numerous studies in the last two decades have tended to give a phenomenological account of a (very) limited number of people's experience, to emphasize fragmentation and movement, and to gloss over everyday life in entire cities, regions or countries (Rubbers 2017). Partly developed on the basis of a critique of phenomenology, Bourdieu's theory of social space provides a good place from which to start paying more attention to living conditions, differences in social trajectories, and broader dynamics of inequality again.

Benjamin Rubbers obtained his PhD degree from the Université Libre de Bruxelles and the Ecole des Hautes Etudes en Sciences Sociales in 2006. He is now full professor in social anthropology at the University of Liège, Belgium. Benjamin is the author of three monographs and more than twenty journal articles and book chapters on the Congolese copperbelt, where he has carried out frequent fieldtrips since 1999.

Notes

1. According to Lamont (1992), however, the three 'theoretical' classes – dominant, middle and popular – distinguished by Bourdieu are based on an a priori definition, not on inductive analysis. In support of this critique, they are presented in numerous passages of his work as classes-in-themselves. So, even though the theoretical framework developed by Bourdieu in *Distinction* offers a way to overcome the classical problems of class analysis, these problems are not entirely resolved in his empirical study of France.

2. This analytical choice is justified by the concern to not take the primacy of cultural capital over economic and social capital for granted. The work of M. Lamont (1992, 2000) suggests that cultural capital in the United States is less important than in France, and takes a different form. As Coulangeon (2004: 78; 2011) points out, the weight that Bourdieu himself gives to cultural capital in French society is the product of a given context: the 'thirty glorious years' that followed World War II, during which France experienced a reduction in income inequalities. Since the 1980s, this trend has reversed, and economic capital has become an increasingly salient factor of social stratification again. In a sense, these studies invite us to come back to Bourdieu's theory of social space (the first step of his analytical methodology) so as to better take into consideration the relative weight of different forms of capital in the (re-)production of inequalities and the trajectories of socio-professional groups.

3. In 2015, Katanga was divided in four smaller provinces. For reasons of convenience, however, I will continue to refer to Katanga below.

4. This chapter expands some of the theoretical directions behind the WORKINMINING research project 'Reinventing Paternalism: The Micropolitics of Work in the Mining Companies of Central Africa' (www.workinmining.ulg.ac.be). Led by the author, this project received funding from the European Research Council (ERC) under the European Union's Horizon 2020 research and innovation programme (grant agreement n° 646802). The ideas developed in this chapter reflect only the author's view. The ERC is not responsible for any use that may be made of the information it contains.

5. In a survey of 13,832 households in Lubumbashi in 2002, 42 per cent of respondents declared wage work as their main source of income (Nkuku Khonde and Remon 2006: 60). Today, this percentage is certainly much higher since the mining boom has caused a strong rise in employment and wages between 2004 and 2015.

6. To be more precise, Bourdieu (2000, 2003) proposes a culturalist theory of capitalism that associates it with a specific habitus founded on calculation. At no time does

he goes back on the historical conditions that would account for the emergence of the 'worldview' conveyed by this habitus; he assumes that in the economic field of 'advanced' societies, this habitus functions more or less in accordance with the logic of *homo economicus*. Hence his theory of capitalism supports the idea of a cultural divide between 'traditional' and 'modern' societies, and acknowledges the relevance of conventional economics for the latter. From an anthropological perspective, it is for that reason highly questionable.

7. As mentioned above, Bourdieu postulates a cultural divide between 'advanced' and 'traditional' societies. Perhaps he would have compared Katanga to colonial Algeria in the 1950s, and considered it as a society subjected to the devastating effects of colonialism? In his article 'La hantise du chômage chez l'ouvrier algérien' (1962), he stresses the role of personal contacts for Algerian urban workers in their search for employment. It is however impossible to draw from this a general argument about the relative weight of social capital in (post)colonial societies.

8. Since then, Katanga witnessed a mining boom, and the foreign population rose again. This recent development is not discussed here.

9. Interestingly, this social control is situational. When expatriates go back to Europe, it loses much of its significance. There, they have a much more relaxed lifestyle: they may walk, eat African food, and even mix with the Congolese.

10. This programme involved 10,000 employees out of a total of 24,000.

11. In 1965, the Union Minière employed 229 Congolese managers out of a total of 2,247 managers; in 1974, 1,135 out of 2,497; and in 1980, 2261 out of 3220 (Young and Turner 1985: 107). In 1990, there were only 247 expatriate managers remaining, mostly at retirement age.

12. 'Training school' is the translation of 'école préprofessionnelle', a school that provides basic technical training during three years after primary school.

References

Benoît, J. 1958. *La Population Africaine à Elisabethville*. Elisabethville: CEPSI.

Bourdieu, P. 1962. 'La Hantise du Chômage chez l'Ouvrier Algérien. Prolétariat et Système Colonial', *Sociologie du Travail* 4: 313–31.

_____. 1979 *La Distinction. Critique Sociale du Jugement*. Paris: Minuit.

_____. 1980. 'Le Capital Social', *Actes de la Recherche en Sciences Sociales* 31: 2–3.

_____. 1984. 'Espace Social et Genèse des "Classes"', *Actes de la Recherche en Sciences Sociales* 52–53: 3–14.

_____. 1986. 'The forms of Capital', in J. Richardson (ed.), *Handbook of Theory and Research for the Sociology of Education*. New York: Greenwood, pp. 241–58.

_____. (ed.). 1993. *La Misère du Monde*. Paris: Le Seuil.

_____. 1994. *Raisons Pratiques: Sur la Théorie de l'Action*. Paris: Minuit.

_____. 2000. *Les Structures Sociales de l'Economie*. Paris: Le Seuil.

_____. 2001. *Langage et Pouvoir Symbolique*. Paris: Le Seuil.

_____. 2003. 'La Fabrique de l'Habitus Economique', *Actes de la Recherche en Sciences Sociales* 150: 79–90.

Bruneau, J.-C., and M. Pain (eds). 1990. *Atlas de Lubumbashi*. Nanterre: Centre d'Etudes Géographiques sur l'Afrique Noire.

Burawoy, M., and K. Von Holdt. 2012. *Conversations with Bourdieu: The Johannesburg Moment*. Johannesburg: Wits University Press.

Callaghy, T.M. 1984. *The State-Society Struggle: Zaire in Comparative Perspective*. New York: Columbia University Press.

Coulangeon, P. 2004. 'Classes Sociales, Pratiques Culturelles et Styles de Vie: Le Modèle de la Distinction Est-Il (Vraiment) Obsolète?', *Sociologie et Sociétés* 36(1): 59–85.

_____. 2011. *Les Métamorphoses de la Distinction: Inégalités Culturelles dans la France d'Aujourd'hui*. Paris: Grasset.

De Herdt, T. et al. 2010. *Enjeux et Acteurs autour de la Réduction des Frais Scolaires en RDC*. DFID, Final Report.

Ferguson, J. 1999. *Expectations of Modernity: Myths and Meanings of Urban Life on the Zambian Copperbelt*. Berkeley: University of California Press.

_____. 2015. *Give a Man a Fish: Reflections on the New Politics of Distribution*. Durham, NC and London: Duke University Press.

Graeber, D. 2001. *Towards an Anthropological Theory of Value: The False Coin of our Dreams*. New York: Palgrave.

Grignon, C., and J.-C. Passeron. 1989. *Le Savant et le Populaire: Misérabilisme et Populisme en Sociologie et en Littérature*. Paris: Gallimard & Le Seuil.

Hall, J.R. 1992. 'The Capital(s) of Cultures: A Nonholistic Approach to Status Situation, Class, Gender, and Ethnicity', in M. Lamont and M. Fournier (eds), *Cultivating Differences, Symbolic Boundaries and the Making of Inequality*. Chicago: The University of Chicago Press.

Hilgers, M. 2009. *Une Ethnographie à l'Echelle de la Ville: Urbanité, Histoire et Reconnaissance à Koudougou (Burkina Faso)*. Paris: Karthala.

Houyoux, J., and Y. Lecoanet. 1975. *Lubumbashi: Démographie, Budgets Ménagers et Etude du Site*. Kinshasa: Bureau d'Etudes d'Aménagements Urbains.

Lahire, B. 1995. *Tableaux de Familles: Heurs et Malheurs Scolaires en Milieux Populaires*. Paris: Seuil/Gallimard.

_____. 2004. *La Culture des Individus: Dissonances Culturelles et Distinction de Soi*. Paris: La Découverte.

Lamont, M. 1992. *Money, Morals, and Manners: The Culture of the French and the American Upper-Middle Class*. Chicago: The University of Chicago Press.

_____. 2000. *The Dignity of Working Men: Morality and the Boundaries of Race, Class, and Immigration*. New York: Sage.

Lamont, M., and A. Lareau. 1988. 'Cultural Capital: Allusions, Gaps and Glissandos in Recent Theoretical Developments', *Sociological Theory* 6(2): 153–68.

MacGaffey, J. 1987. *Entrepreneurs and Parasites: The Struggle for Indigenous Capitalism in Zaire*. Cambridge: Cambridge University Press.

Nkuku Khonde, C., and M. Remon. 2006. *Stratégies de Survie à Lubumbashi (R.D.Congo): Enquête sur 14,000 Ménages*. Paris: L'Harmattan.

Nzongola, G.N. 1970. 'The Bourgeoisie and Revolution in the Congo', *The Journal of Modern African Studies* 8(4): 511–30.

Passeron, J.-C. 1982. 'L'Inflation des Diplômes: Remarques sur l'Usage de Quelques Concepts Analogiques en Sociologie', *Revue Française de Sociologie* 23(4): 551–84.

_____. 1991. *Le Raisonnement Sociologique: L'Espace Non-Poppérien du Raisonnement Naturel*. Paris: Nathan.

Petit, P. (ed.). 2003. *Ménages de Lubumbashi entre Précarité et Recomposition*. Paris: L'Harmattan.

Piketty, T. 2013. *Le Capital au XXIe Siècle*. Paris: Le Seuil.

Rubbers, B. 2003. *Devenir Médecin en République Démocratique du Congo: La Trajectoire Socioprofessionnelle des Diplômés en Médecine de l'Université de Lubumbashi*. Tervuren and Paris: MRAC & L'Harmattan.

_____. 2004. 'The University of Lubumbashi between the Local and the Global: The Dynamics, Management and Future of University Education in the DRC', *Canadian Journal of African Studies* 38(2): 318–43.

_____. 2009. *Faire Fortune en Afrique: Anthropologie des Derniers Colons du Katanga*. Paris: Karthala.

_____. 2013. *Le Paternalisme en Question: Les Anciens Ouvriers de la Gécamines face à la Libéralisation du Secteur Minier Katangais (R.D.Congo)*. Tervuren and Paris: MRAC & L'Harmattan.

_____. 2017. 'Towards a Life of Poverty and Uncertainty? The Livelihood Strategies of Gécamines Workers after Retrenchment (D.R. Congo)', *Review of African Political Economy* 44(152): 189–203.

Schatzberg, M. 1980. *Politics and Class in Zaire: Bureaucracy, Business and Beer in Lisala*. New York: Africana.

University of Lubumbashi. 2005. *La Restructuration de la Gécamines: Impacts sur la Pauvreté et le Social. Avenir des Services Sociaux et Stratégies de Réinsertion*. Lubumbashi, final report.

Willis, P. 1978. *Learning to Labour: How Working Class Kids Get Working Class Jobs*. New York: Columbia University Press.

Young, C., and T. Turner. 1985. *The Rise and Decline of the Zairian State*. Madison: University of Wisconsin Press.

Chapter 7

Crisis, Work and the Meanings of Mobility on the Zimbabwean-South African Border

Maxim Bolt

Introduction: A Visit Home

As personnel manager, Michael was among Grootplaas's most senior black employees. This meant acting as a key intermediary between the farm's white owners and managers and the black, mostly Zimbabwean, workforce. It was Easter 2007, and the border farms were about to begin picking fruit and cotton. Their populations would expand from tightly-knit core labour forces to include migrant pickers and packers. The residential labour compounds for black workers would change abruptly from quiet, village-like communities to sprawling, loud, overcrowded settlements full of strangers. At Grootplaas – an export farm producing oranges and grapefruits – it was Michael's job to regularize the new arrivals, taking them in groups to the border post to process their paperwork.

Before all this happened, there was just enough time for Grootplaas's permanent workers to visit kin back in Zimbabwe. And so, on a March morning, Michael and his neighbour tightened the straps on the canopy of my tiny pickup truck, while a small crowd looked on. The pickup truck sat low on its wheels under the weight of several sheets of corrugated metal, door and window frames, other building materials, and provisions including petrol for our trip and goods for remittance. It still had to accommodate Michael, his neighbour, their partners and me.

Notes for this chapter begin on page 175.

Michael and his neighbour were making a trip to their rural homes across the border. After months saving his wages, Michael had invested in housing materials, which he was stockpiling at home to build a house for his retirement. Like many members of Grootplaas's black workforce, who live in the farm's labour compound and visit rural homes in Zimbabwe on holidays, Michael was saving for his old age. Since Grootplaas is located right on the banks of the Limpopo River, its workers and their dependents often just climb through the border fence. But such a trip, laden with investments and remittances, meant going by road.

As one of the most senior black workers in the racially and class-divided world of a white-owned agricultural estate, Michael was paid well and unusually well placed to make such long-term investments. Others, positioned lower in the hierarchy, made similarly strenuous efforts. Gerald, who lived next to me in the labour compound, put some of his monthly earnings towards buying cattle to expand his herd, in a manner common to male labour migrants across the region. Others returned home to show their success and to maintain prestige and connections: Elton, another permanent employee, did so by spending lavishly on beer for his friends and relatives, despite serious debts to Grootplaas residents. His sharp leather cowboy hat and jacket augmented his reputation as conspicuous consumer.

For all of them, forms of physical mobility underpinned projects of social mobility. But how we understand this is not straightforward. The scene above is one that reflects the classic dynamics of southern African labour migration, in which black men from rural areas spend their working lives at hubs of capitalist production in order eventually to return home as esteemed elders. The compounds in which workers reside on the farms, and the sharp racial division between these and white spaces of residence and sociality, resemble those typical of the better-known case of the mines. For workers on border farms like Grootplaas, spending their wages on remittances draws money away from what they might expend on living life in the compound itself. Labour compounds, in addition to being places of accommodation for workers, become homes and closely-knit communities in their own right. As in mine compounds, workforces develop and uphold complex status hierarchies.

But the opening scene is also an indicator of Zimbabwe's recent political and economic crisis. A huge number of Zimbabweans now depend on work in South Africa to sustain themselves and their families. Michael's remittances included basic necessities that his relatives were unable to obtain in Zimbabwe because of supply shortages. He himself had sought employment at Grootplaas when opportunities in Zimbabwe began to shrink in the 1990s during the Economic Structural Adjustment

Programme (ESAP), before the country's decline accelerated. Formerly an administrator in the Zimbabwean army, he had attempted to capitalize on increased migration southwards by operating a taxi, then unsuccessfully sought work in Johannesburg as an undocumented migrant, before joining a relative on the farm.

Michael feels trapped in agricultural work, after expectations of a better future. But he has at least risen to the top of a hierarchy on the border farms. Few manage this. Gerald had been an activist for the Zimbabwean opposition party, the Movement for Democratic Change. He had left Zimbabwe in the early 2000s after having been imprisoned for his political activities. A high-school graduate with A-levels,[1] he had never expected to be a farm worker. His story of dislocation and personal disruption echoes those of others in Grootplaas's core workforce. Such stories are even more typical in the case of its harvest-time seasonal labourers. For them, moving to South Africa has been not only about finding alternative opportunities – new social ladders to climb – but about mitigating the effects of precipitous downward mobility. The terms 'labour migrant' on the one hand, and 'displaced' or 'refugee' or a context of 'crisis' on the other, evoke very different images, especially in this region of the world. But here they converge. The effects of various displacements and the legacies of southern Africa's racialized systems of labour migrancy profoundly inflect each other.

People's trajectories are far from uniform. For some, repetition has created well-worn routes. Norman's wife, Sarah, works in the packshed each year, and is a familiar face in the compound because of her regular visits. There is even an established arrangement to accommodate both her and Norman's 'farm wife': Sarah moves into his prestigious senior worker-house while he stays with Joyce and their son in her smaller room. For Norman and Sarah, the Easter 2007 trip held few surprises. Its purpose was to undertake a vital kinship ritual that involved ancestral spirits, and in which she was key as an important spirit medium. Travel upheld success and a degree of respectability, on the farm and back across the border.

For others, the visit was less predictable, illustrating the improvisatory nature of physical mobility between the border farms and Zimbabwe, as people make do and strive to keep hopes and aspirations in play. When Michael reached his mother's rural home,[2] near the site of his own future house, he found that an uncle had appropriated the pile of building materials from his last trip. The roofing, frames and ventilation blocks that we brought simply replaced the previous delivery. Other aspects of the visit were more successful, although equally makeshift. Michael persuaded his sister Pula and niece Lovely to come to the farm. Pula had cattle, but the hyperinflation of the Zimbabwean crisis meant that it was a bad time to sell, and she needed money to provide for herself and her young son. Lovely was in a rather different situation. Life at home was sustainable and her parents had recently renovated their house. But she needed money to pay for further education to supplement her existing four O-levels[3] – this education would now take place at home because Zimbabwe's school system had collapsed under the weight of hyperinflation.[4] Michael ensured that they were employed at the farm, and they undertook domestic tasks for him. At the farm, Pula would join countless other single mothers attempting to support their children, through formal and informal employment and by establishing domestic arrangements with influential and permanently employed men. And Lovely would join a similarly large number of Zimbabweans who required income for further advancement, but whose education left them with the sense of sharp downward mobility and exile on the farms.

Diverse forms of mobility intersect on the Zimbabwean-South African border and its farms. This chapter explores how physical mobility and its limits relate to social mobility and immobility. Border agriculture represents a bewildering kaleidoscope that cautions against any unidimensional view of social space. Former members of a middle class pick fruit alongside lifelong farm workers; transience jostles with settlement; wage labour is intertwined with informal trade; and living from one day to the next co-exists with attempts to plan for the longer term. People bring sharply contrasting backgrounds and class-inflected expectations to labour arrangements, and these different trajectories shape what forms of social mobility farm work represents to them. Moreover, as we will see, strategies are themselves unstable. Plans change. The terms on which farm residents recognize one another are fragile and multiple. Workforce diversity confronts farm-based social stratification, inflected by the immediate importance of access to employment and shelter. It is under these conditions that farm workers and dwellers attempt and sometimes fail to produce future possibilities through physical mobility as well as immobility.

Mobility on the Zimbabwean-South African Border

The border is a zone of startling mobility. This is unsurprising in the context of a wealth of scholarship that emphasizes porous national boundaries and the gatekeeping opportunities they afford (e.g. Heyman 1990, Flynn 1997, Donnan and Wilson 1999, Coplan 2001, Pelkmans 2006, Titeca and de Herdt 2010, Quirk and Vigneswaran 2015). But, as the opening vignette suggests, mobility on South Africa's northern edge raises questions about any single overdetermining narrative.

This requires understanding in a historical context of still greater diversity. When Boers began settling the region in the nineteenth century, it was characterized by shifting political authorities (including those of the overstretched Boers themselves), ethnic mixture and itinerancy (see Wagner 1980, Boeyens 1994; Bonner and Carruthers 2003). This was further augmented by the disruption of the South African Wars at the turn of the twentieth century (Braun 2013). Within a few years, migration to the new Messina Copper Mine drew workers to the border from as far afield as Malawi. Throughout the twentieth century, Zimbabweans responded to crises – from droughts to state violence – by crossing the Limpopo River to seek employment. Displacement and labour migration, therefore, have long been difficult to distinguish. People uprooted by a range of crises have become labour migrants once they have found work (Bolt 2015).

South Africa's boundary with Zimbabwe has equally been made through white mobility. The importance of the Limpopo Valley as a thoroughfare was gradually overlaid by kinship networks connecting the farms that developed on each side. Older white residents on the South African side can still plot the genealogies, and they remember regular journeys through what used to be a sleepy, barely guarded border post. Yet, until the late 1970s, the southern side of the Limpopo River remained largely uncultivated land for cattle and game. In the 1980s, South Africa's apartheid regime promoted more intensive agriculture as a buffer zone in the low-intensity border war with *Umkhonto we Sizwe*,[5] which operated from newly liberated Zimbabwe. A new soft loans scheme drew white Zimbabweans, among others, who had decided to abandon their country at majority rule. Their migratory projects, and the large commercial farms that developed, became new centres of gravity for mobility on the border. The growing estates led to the establishment of regular migratory routes from villages in the ecologically, economically and politically marginal area across the river in Zimbabwe. These are trodden by many of Grootplaas's work supervisors and other permanent employees, as well as their kin and acquaintances who enjoy privileged access to seasonal employment.

Structural adjustment in Zimbabwe coincided with the liberalization of agriculture in South Africa, and the shift of border farmers into export and larger-scale cultivation to weather the storm – overall, a shift from cotton to citrus. Greater demand for labour was matched by increasing numbers of migrants, as jobs and welfare support in Zimbabwe disappeared, and Grootplaas reached one million crates of oranges and grapefruits in 2007.

Many of the better established among the core workforces today, including Michael, arrived as this expansion gathered steam.

Southwards migration has increased exponentially since 2000. An increasingly weak Zimbabwean economy was battered from the 1990s by a series of interlinked troubles: spending crises and an unbudgeted 'pension' pay-out to liberation war veterans; increased opposition to the government, and increasingly authoritarian repression, following a failed constitutional referendum; and the expropriation of commercial farms as part of Fast-Track Land Reform (Dorman 2003, Muzondidya 2009, Raftopoulos 2009).[6] Many people were compelled to migrate by a complex combination of economic collapse, new forms of political exclusion and direct coercion in Zimbabwe. One aspect of migration is thus predictable on the border: the farmers are never short of labour.

If earlier eras of mobility were characterized by movement at different scales for different reasons, people now came from far afield, and from an ever-greater diversity of class and ethnic backgrounds. They included those such as Gerald, mentioned earlier, who had suffered political violence. And, during my fieldwork, I picked fruit alongside recent A-level graduates from Harare and Bulawayo (Zimbabwe's capital and second city respectively), as well as a former teacher with a postgraduate qualification (Jameson, see below). As part of the increase in number of Shona and Ndebele speakers, their presence was a challenge to the VhaVenda who dominate the border and the upper echelons of the farm workforces. Their mobility can be seen as 'mixed migration' in a further-reaching sense than the indistinguishability of refugees and non-refugees (the official definition used by UNHCR and the IOM). Rather, migration to South Africa has come to involve constant shifts in motives, patterns of movement, and use of official documentation (Crush et al. 2015).

The Zimbabwean-South African border, with its crop farms and residential labour compounds, attracts a still greater range of circuits. Traders capitalize on the large waged populations on the farms, tying together a border economy as they move between them each payday. Soldiers circulate between the garrisons along the national boundary fence, while police patrol from their base in the town of Musina. During my fieldwork, Doctors without Borders came to ensure access to healthcare, as the border area gained prominence as a zone of humanitarian intervention (see Rutherford 2011). Mobile clinics began intermittently touring the compounds. Here, then, is a setting that is literally made of mobility.

How do border farm dwellers' opportunities for physical mobility relate to their social mobility or immobility? John Urry (2007) provides a helpful conceptual starting point. He argues that scholarship on physical mobilities has an important contribution to make to understandings of social inequality and social mobility. Urry takes his cue from, and seeks to build on, Bourdieusian perspectives on class in which forms of capital confer advantage in social fields. Social space is defined primarily by the positioning of individuals in terms of their economic, social and cultural capital, through time. This approach is open to other relevant social properties, and Urry (2007) adds 'network capital', drawing attention to how advantage and disadvantage are produced through the differential access people have to flows of information, goods and travel. Network capital, in turn, has important effects in building support and status recognition (i.e. social and cultural capital), as well as facilitating material accumulation (i.e. economic capital).

Urry's framing offers a clear way to relate physical and social mobility. As we shall see, networks are a useful starting point for considering border farm dwellers' possibilities and strategies. The concept of network capital is, after all, intended to address a world of ever-greater movement. Yet, towards the end of the chapter, I consider whether network capital has limits for thinking through social advantage and disadvantage. How does it fare in a setting with the sheer amount and diversity of mobility that is in evidence on the Zimbabwean-South African border, where people's experiences of social mobility itself are inflected by their diverse trajectories?

In order to answer this question, we must first investigate the actual ways that farm dwellers are and are not able to move in the border landscape.

Living through Mobility and Immobility on the Border

Grootplaas's core labour force of 140, composed almost entirely of men, maintains the farm all year round. For the annual five-month harvest, this is augmented by 460 seasonal workers, who pick and pack fruit – pickers are mostly men, while graders and packers are mostly women. Core workers – often known simply as *mapermanent* (the permanent ones) – are permanent in more senses than simply their open-ended contracts (Bolt 2013). They occupy their own rooms, which they have adapted from bare barrack-like accommodation into congenial living spaces. They share knowledge of the landscape, such as earlier boundaries between estates, and earlier locations of worker homes. Place names memorialize the identities, behaviours and characteristics of former or current white farmers. Some residents, like Norman, have farm wives alongside other spouses back in Zimbabwe, in settled domestic relationships that may involve children, but are only treated as durable and legitimate on the farms.

Despite the fact that core workers lack real security of tenure, they experience their rootedness in a thoroughgoing way.

This is especially striking because the white farmers increasingly emphasize their own potential flexibility. In an era of market liberalization and redistributive land reform, they have done so by investing in portfolios of estates and other farm-related businesses in different places – even different countries. In this way, they ensure the means to move on if any particular enterprises fail or are expropriated (ibid.).

Recent arrivals from Zimbabwe stand in sharp contrast to this picture of settled life. Word of recruitment spreads along and across the border in the months following Easter. Many arrive on the farms, having worked their way 50 km west from Beitbridge, often in minibus taxis, and then having braved gangs and soldiers who extort and attack migrants in the Limpopo's dry riverbed. Once at Grootplaas, most are housed in groups (four for women, six for men), in rooms of the same size that permanent workers occupy individually. This is in a huge, exposed grid of thirty buildings, each of whose six rooms are marked by an external metal door and a small accompanying metal-framed window. The unlucky sleep in a building that is still more overcrowded – each room here accommodates twenty to thirty workers. The recruits cook on fires outside, and avoid their rooms as far as possible. The fact that documenting seasonal workers takes a long time – sometimes longer than the contract itself – means that they live a fugitive existence. Some therefore abandon their rooms altogether. Despite the freezing winter nights, they prefer to sleep in alcoves dug in dry streambeds in the bush to avoid detection by police deportation patrols.

There is a spectrum between these extremes. Repeat seasonal workers are not strangers when they come to the farm, and they are more likely to be housed with kin or friends. Regulars from the villages across the border share connections of kinship, friendship or sexual relationships with influential permanent workers. And twenty or so women are so well embedded that they are kept on for odd-jobs throughout the year, as 'semi-permanent' employees.

But, to schematize somewhat, permanent workers are remarkably settled, given the transience of the area in general. Their relatively privileged position, and their capacity to climb the recognizable social ladder of the labour hierarchy, seems to come precisely from their immobility. Seasonal workers, by contrast, are necessarily temporary. At first blush, their lives appear defined by involuntary mobility. But matters are more complex. Appreciating the rhythms and scales at which mobility operates for different farm-worker constituencies is key if we are to understand how these relate to the social possibilities available to them. What follows untangles the nexuses of mobility and immobility that set the terms of everyday life for members of each employment category.

Immobile Permanent Workers?

Permanent employees' open-ended residence on the border in fact underpins lives that require a great deal of local mobility – even setting aside for a moment the kind of trip to Zimbabwe described in this chapter's opening. Although working in fruit plantations, workers cannot derive sufficient food from the estates. There are options: workers keep gardens, and flocks of hens cross-bred with wild Guinea fowl; they snack on oranges in the orchards; farmers keep mango trees for non-commercial consumption. But, beyond this, acquiring sustenance means moving around. Women rove across the estates on foraging trips to pick wild spinach under the sprinklers that feed the citrus trees, or through the border fence to fish in the Limpopo River. Perhaps most important of all is access to Musina town, 50 kilometres to the east. People and groceries are ferried by informal taxi drivers with pickup trucks, for whom the farms' isolation represents a business opportunity (see Bolt 2012).

Permanent workers' social arrangements also rely in key ways on their capacity for movement. Each farm has a football team, and tournaments mean matches each weekend along the border. Trips to town may be simply to participate in a day out. Easy mobility is one way that permanent workers assert and experience their difference from their seasonal counterparts. One, a football player, suggested several times that I join him for his morning runs that tracked the border fence.

Networks of kinship, care and friendship criss-cross the various estates, sustained by weekend visits on bicycles or on foot. And children move unaccompanied between farms. The nearest school is on a neighbouring estate, and they walk the couple of kilometres along the border road each morning.[7] Social networks include the one remaining commercial farm on the Zimbabwean bank of the river. Residents cross the river each weekend, with soldiers' permission, for social calls and to buy Chibuku beer,[8] which is only available in Zimbabwe.

In fact, status hierarchies on the farms rely heavily on extraversion (see Bayart 2000) – the very capacity to be connected to other places. Marula, the foreman, is a good example. His close friend, the black manager of a game farm halfway to Musina, frequently turns up at Marula's house, stopping at the drinking area outside in his pickup truck. He provides lifts on the way, and on one occasion killed and *braaied* (barbecued) a goat in honour of the end of an inter-farm football tournament. Robert, a border clearing agent from Musina, comes each weekend to visit his girlfriend, a peer educator for the HIV/AIDS-awareness NGO based in the compound. He, too, pays his respects at Marula's drinking area, arriving with beer and leaving his sizeable saloon car parked close by with music still blaring. For Marula, a long career working his way up local farm hierarchies has produced ever-greater recognition along the border more generally.

Several senior workers are similarly recognized beyond the farm as important people worth visiting. One picking supervisor is a prophet in the United African Apostolic Church. On one occasion, a delegation arrived from Musina, seeking his guidance about transporting the body of a deceased church member back to Zimbabwe. A younger work supervisor, Hardship, runs the seasonal worker football team, which he founded with Robert's financial support for the purchase of uniforms. And, between them, Hardship and Robert organized a ticketed gig for the end of the 2007 harvest that involved the Venda region's two best known musical acts – the foremost reggae star and a highly regarded *tshingondo* (Zimbabwean jive) musician. This was not simply a money-making scheme; the arrival of two famous bands, through the orchards and in the middle of the night, clearly communicated Hardship's clout beyond the workforce.

All of this is enabled by the soldiers, who are themselves highly mobile. Hailing from other parts of South Africa, they are stationed on the border for three months at a time. During that period, they are transferred every two weeks between the small 'echo' garrisons along the fence. Their duties involve patrolling the border road, escorting police deportation raids, checking the fence and apprehending any 'border jumpers' they encounter. Soldiers are explicit about the futility of stopping large numbers of Zimbabweans crossing – one estimate was 100 daily when the riverbed is dry. Few are detained, and those who are come through again once they have been deposited in Beitbridge on the Zimbabwean side.

Yet the soldiers' roles are more complicated than merely as ineffective barriers. When they encounter people crossing, they have a range of responses. They detain those whom they consider 'border jumpers'. But women report that they are more likely to be released than men, since they can agree to provide sexual services. In that sense, asserted one group of recent women arrivals who waited in the orchards for employment, they have it easier than men. Soldiers also allow known farm residents through the fence, to fish or make visits to the farm or the villages on the other side. They develop a range of relationships with farm dwellers, as they frequent farm compounds to seek beer, company and sex, and during research in 2007 they even assembled a football team for the inter-farm tournament. Although they circulate between the border's garrisons, they may nevertheless remain attached to particular compounds and residents, including girlfriends.

Spending time in the compounds, the soldiers come to rely on local knowledge offered by male permanent workers, and they in turn mediate disputes. The border garrisons – themselves itinerant – are deeply implicated in dynamics of mobility. They corroborate Quirk and Vigneswaran's (2015) assertion that states should themselves be regarded in terms of mobility not sedentarism. They are made of institutions that channel mobility, rather than simply preventing it. And they represent portable forms of authority whose manifestations are constantly brokered as they move. It is through all this movement that established permanent workers' highly gendered positions as local notables are thrown into relief.

As we saw earlier in the chapter, periodic visits home constitute longer-term rhythms of mobility that extend away from the border area. These broader rhythms have multiple causes, that reflect both the familiar dynamics of labour migration and the exigencies of a zone of large-scale transience and displacement. I have argued elsewhere (Bolt 2014) that remittances become important not only because they sustain kin, but also because of the urgency of removing cash and other wealth from a border full of strangers.

More generally, permanent workers are mobile on the border, in arrangements that involve state personnel who are themselves highly mobile. Indeed, their permanence and status are built out of their networks and their movement within these. Physical mobility enables relatively comfortable lives, as well as performances of local influence and importance. Conversely, this relies on permanent residents' recognition as embedded in the social landscape.

Mobile Seasonal Workers?

If permanent workers rely on movement, one striking aspect of migrant seasonal workers' lives on the border is the degree to which they are characterized by waiting. Those who arrive on the estates between paydays – and therefore between rounds of recruitment – sit in the orchards by the access roads. They hope to be noticed, so that they will receive preferential treatment when gaps are left by pickers or packers who decide to move on. Once they are recruited, they lack the ready cash to frequent *shebeens* (unlicensed bars). One pastime is to stand back from *shebeens*, close enough to watch the music videos showing on televisions in open doorways. But most simply sit outside their rooms. On weekends, when their permanent counterparts move between farms to visit friends, or head to town, most seasonal workers stay in the compound – nervous about exposing themselves to police raids on the border road that links the estates. When raids come through the compound, they retreat further, to the bush. In the meantime, when not shuttling as directly as possible between packshed, orchards and compound, they express boredom and frustration.

There are good reasons to wait, however. Short-term stasis is juxta-posed with longer-term mobility. This is unavoidable, given that con-tracts run only until the end of the five-month harvest. But Grootplaas offers provisional stability. Deportation raids mean that life is far from settled. Yet the ID cards produced and distributed by farmers as proof of employment often keep state officials at bay, at least on the estates them-selves. And many workers do eventually receive official documentation. In any case, life off the farms is yet more fugitive than life on them, even if the latter means staying in the shadows where possible. Indeed, in the run-up to recruitment, even migrants without jobs experience a meas-ure of temporary protection. Unsure who will be employed and who left simply as a 'border jumper', the soldiers treat those waiting on the farm as between categories. Once recruited, seasonal workers are safer on the estates than on the border road beyond, with its police and army patrols.

Waiting is frustrating, even disempowering, but it also produces orien-tations to the future that require appreciating in their own terms. On the border farms, it enables people to maintain a stance of open-endedness and retain multiple future possibilities. This is especially key in a context of crisis. Crises like Zimbabwe's are marked by fragmentation, and the incoherence that comes from the breakdown of established ideas about actions' consequences (Mbembe and Roitman 1995, Vigh 2008). Faced with such radical uncertainty, forging elaborate plans makes little sense. Writing of Cameroon, Johnson-Hanks (2005) shows how young women respond to crisis with a stance of 'judicious opportunism'. This means holding options open by keeping connections in play. On the border, migrant workers open up possibilities for the present through farm employment. Suddenly, one can choose whether to keep moving or to stay for a few weeks, or a few months, or until the end of the harvest in September. Employment in cities to the south, such as Johannesburg, is imagined to be more dignified and better remunerated than farm labour. Yet it has to be weighed against the temporary certainties of a job, a roof and familiar faces. In the meantime, the costs of integrating in compound life (beer, for example) compete with saving for remittance or further travel. The timing of further travel competes with the timing of sending money and goods home.

Seasonal employment offers ways to balance these. Where possible, workers buy goods that ameliorate their living conditions in the compound yet would also constitute useful items of remittance. A camping stove enables a respectable life indoors, but can be taken with once contracts are finished. Equally, there is a sense in which seasonal workers bide their time through their access to shelter and pay. Many leave quickly after one or two paydays, unable or unwilling to tolerate long days of low-status labour and aggressive work dynamics. Talk of opportunities, in Johannesburg and other cities, draws especially young male employees away. But sufficient numbers return empty-handed, with stories of dangerous metropolitan centres full of job-seekers, to give pause to those still working on the farm. The temporal orientation of many seasonal workers is therefore to wait for a plan to unfold.

Each payday presents anew the possibilities and the risks of leaving, made distinctly concrete by acquaintances departing, trucks and informal taxis offering rides, and degrees of success contacting distant kin and friends by phone. What transpires in the meantime produces a steep learning curve. Jameson, the university-educated former teacher mentioned earlier, had come to the border with his wife. After picking cotton down the road, she secured a packshed job at Grootplaas with him. Initially, the plan was for him to head southwards after a period of work, seeking further employment in Pretoria while she waited at their small-town Zimbabwean home for the signal to follow. But they were quickly discouraged. They heard stories of adverse conditions in the cities. And Jameson's experience of everyday insecurity on the border, and the aggressive workplace masculinities forged in response, led him to discard the idea that they should be separated. After the harvest, they left for Zimbabwe together, and they would plan the next move from there. Anticipation and future-making here operate in relation to an expanding but indistinct horizon.

Moreover, waiting is socially productive. In India, Jeffrey (2010) shows, young unemployed men develop knowledge and a sense of common experience through the apparently 'purposeless' hanging around known as 'timepass'. In Jeffrey's analysis, waiting produces a shared structure of feeling – an orientation to current obstacles and future prospects. On the border farms, it constitutes a form of action despite significant differences in seasonal workers' expectations.

This is not simply temporal; it also produces a collective orientation to place. For many seasonal pickers, waiting – staying with a view to leaving – enables them to be on the farm without being of the farm. After all, in southern Africa agricultural employment is considered to be especially undesirable, so much so that the sector has long had to rely on migrants with limited options (Bradford 1993, Rutherford 2001). Many workers speak of hanging on for as long as they can put up with undigni-fied, dirty conditions. They spend their evenings secluded in their bare rooms, sharing stories about violent, uneducated work supervisors and an unthinking acceptance of racial hierarchy (see Bolt 2010). In doing so, they perform a degree of abstention. This preserves the sense that they remain better than farm work, even as they live under its protection.

Abstention from aspects of farm life in which the status of *mapermanent* is made visible – at the *shebeens* or on the football field, for example – constitutes a basic challenge to any unilineal notion of social stratification on the farm. This is true even though migrants who perform it vary in important respects. Among the recent wave of middle-class migrants, there are significant differences. Young recruits who have recently com-pleted their A-levels expect to be able to move onward and upward rela-tively quickly. Alex, for example, was a teenager picker in 2007, who hoped to save to buy a computer and then start a DVD business in his hometown of Bulawayo. Not having actually lost a job, he retained a sense of optimism. He and his friend Vusa, with whom he had travelled and who also had A-levels, underlined that their time on the farm was a delimited period of exile. With their new friend Simon (from Harare), they did so by exchanging observations that they would tell everyone about on their return home. Vusa even joked that he could write a great book – no one would believe it! Alex would flick through a family photo album, adding immediacy to their previous lives and their expectations of better futures. Such optimism was not shared by older middle-class migrants like Jameson. He, too, abstained from compound life, waiting at its margins and avoiding anything that smacked of nightlife. But he was clear that there was no perceptible end to his exile. The Zimbabwean economy would have to recover substantially for his previous life there to be imaginable.

Abstention, moreover, is an orientation that extends beyond work-ers of middle-class background. Indeed, during the period of fieldwork, an unwillingness to be incorporated into farm life, and an attachment instead to previous occupations, was shared across a range of seasonal workers. Charles, a close associate of Jameson's, had been an artisan who made street signs. Yet his and Jameson's generationally specific experi-ences cross-cut class background. Charles, too, saw his future in terms of indefinite exile, and the sense of futility that came from a career up in smoke.

As among Jeffrey's research participants, it is precisely the perfor-mance of staying-while-waiting-to-leave that produces a sense of shared experience in contrast to others in the same setting. But, at Grootplaas, this is institutionalized through the work process itself. The attempts of such men to maintain distance from workplace camaraderie makes them bad pickers. During the period of fieldwork, the least willing to integrate were grouped together in a 'special' team that cleared fallen and neglected fruit in the wake of the main workforce. Here, operating according to a slower rhythm, they affirmed an alternative source of status, grounded in education, by discussing Zimbabwe's politics and future prospects (see Bolt 2010).

What exactly is the foil in these performances? Permanent workers are one target. They are mocked as yokels now in charge, during pickers' long evenings with nothing to do. But the other point of contrast is provided by regular pickers and packers. The border has attracted ever more migrants and has become a site for journalism and humanitarianism. Yet such longer-term seasonal workers continue to join their permanent counterparts each year, just as they did before the idea of a crisis gained international currency. Their differences from recent arrivals, in terms of background and familiarity with the border farms, in turn mark integration versus abstention.

Those who lack education-related status tend to have greater experience of the border, clearer and better-worn plans, and local networks offering security. One of my neighbours in the compound, Hardship's younger cousin, makes her way to Marble Hall to the south after the Grootplaas harvest. There, she is employed on a short-term contract for another few months, bridging the gap to her next stint on the border (she hails from a village across the river). Such workers know that they will be picked for employment, because they have powerful relatives. Their connections also mean that they are documented more quickly once they begin work. They are thus quicker to avoid harassment by the police. As they wait for recruitment to start, and as they jostle for position with everyone else, they know that their experiences will diverge somewhat from more recent arrivals. The effect of vulnerability on them is less thoroughgoing. For those who wait to leave, and who deny being part of the farm, these are the real seasonal workers. Those who abstain are simply 'in exile'; their ill-suitedness is a badge of downward social mobility, which in turn claims an alternative basis for status and recognition even on the farm.

From Physical to Social Mobility: Social Space in a Place of Crisis

Settled permanent workers live lives of mobility and extraversion on the border. Many migrant seasonal workers spend their time waiting between fugitive episodes. Recent scholarship on mobilities offers useful tools for framing this multiplicity of temporal and spatial scales. Cresswell notes that paying attention to 'stillness' does not mean 'suggesting a return to a discipline based on boundedness and rootedness but rather to an alertness to how stillness is thoroughly incorporated into the practices of moving' (2012: 648). Mobility always contains moments of stasis. Yet stasis is itself relative and relationally produced. Adey (2006) departs from the notion of 'moorings'. Movement is always in relation to points perceived to be stable, but mobile entity and mooring, defined against each other, also often shift places. Both airport and aeroplane are composed of aggregations of constant movement, and they are the stable point in relation to each other at different times.

So, too, with permanent and seasonal workforces, however much the former appears to be the mooring for the latter. Migrant arrivals are partially incorporated into existing communities. These communities are nevertheless full of movement each day, settled in the middle term, and lack any certainty of permanence in the long term because of their employers' own flexible strategies. Some seasonal workers are incorporated in a thoroughgoing way, their earnings looked after by supervisors, and their leisure time organized by them. Given that *mapermanent* men enjoy overwhelming control of access to accommodation, some women become domestic workers for settled residents or join them in live-in sexual relationships in attempts to gain some kind of foothold, however precarious. Meanwhile, even seasonal workers who wait out their time as deliberate misfits benefit from protection, at the same time as they perform a degree of diffidence towards the farm community.

Yet permanent workers are also 'moored'. Their ability to travel back to Zimbabwe, as in the opening vignette, requires a secure base. Such mooring is relational; it often depends on those with less stable claims to farm residence. The dynamics of social mobility through rootedness are therefore, as already noted, often clearly gendered. Live-in sexual relationships or housekeeping arrangements (such as Lovely's and Pula's) enable permanently employed men to enjoy lives of congenial domesticity commensurate to their ideals of male seniority. The women in question are far less secure. I have argued elsewhere that men have a greater interest in having someone around than in persisting with a particular partner – under these conditions, their own domestic projects reproduce the vulnerability of mobile women (see Bolt 2013). Yet, in the short-term, domestic relationships are important moorings for them. They free up time, augmenting their capacity to move around and to engage in the micro-politics of extraversion that shapes workforce hierarchy.

The dynamics of mooring extend further still. The relative isolation of seasonal workers provides business opportunities not only to traders who set up markets on the farms each payday, but also to well-embedded residents (see Bolt 2012). Stable accommodation enables compound dwellers to establish enterprises, ranging from smuggling cigarettes across the border, to stocking groceries and beer from town and running *spazas* (general stores) and *shebeens*, to driving pickup trucks as informal taxis. A residential base is a first step towards a viable livelihood based on informal trade on the farm, largely the preserve of permanent workers' partners, or of the 'semi-permanent' women kept around for odd-jobs throughout the year. Here, then, is another layer of mooring built around workforce permanence.

Yet, here too, mooring works both ways. If business relies on residential permanence – however provisional – it also moves around a seasonal workforce that is fixed in place by degrees of isolation and vulnerability. Workers, residents and other traders move back and forth between town and farm, bringing goods to sell, while countless pickers and packers must simply wait for their needs to be met. Virtually everything is more mobile in day-to-day terms than seasonal workers. Goods, money, permanent workers and fruit conveyed each day by trucks to Durban – these all circulate around seasonal workers left stranded on the border's estates.

The mooring discussed here anchors social, not merely physical, positioning. Seasonal-worker isolation is key to the very way that senior workers build status. Indeed, it is in relation to the hundreds of seasonal workers that permanent employees are local notables. Whether guarding income, or running churches or football teams, or judging disputes, various roles beyond the labour process have pickers and packers as their audience. These roles are themselves grounded in the capacity for physical mobility: the capacity to draw musicians, sports funders or church followers to the farm all depends on extension beyond it. Yet their authority is challenged by the abstention of migrant arrivals, who use their very rootlessness to assert an alternative basis for social recognition and diminish the status of senior workers. This, even though migrants' isolation and temporary physical immobility sets limits; their lives, for now, are ultimately in the hands of their superordinates on the farm.

We are now in a position to take stock of connections between physical and social im/mobilities. The enormous diversity of physical mobilities and immobilities on the border – including the coexistence of apparently opposing tendencies among the very same people – are clearly socially produced. Moreover, people's capacities to move as well as settle shape not only social advantage or disadvantage, but also the notions of social status that co-exist on the border. Permanent workers' moorings, the results of upward career trajectories, demonstrate their connections. So do their movements, and so too the significance of their movements for their status. Seasonal workers' mobility is born of necessity, even if the most hopeful imagine some form of social mobility through future migratory opportunities in South Africa's cities. Armed with lists of phone numbers representing possible assistance elsewhere, they nevertheless have limited access to local networks on the border itself – those of the permanent workers, and the more formal membership constituted by stable employment. Seasonal workers' waiting, meanwhile, resembles the confinement characteristic of many undocumented or vulnerable migrants. They are on the move, but they are excluded locally from mechanisms that ensure safety, security and options for advancement – what Coutin (2003) refers to as 'nonexistence' (see also De Genova 2002).

Yet, adding further complexity, workers' diverse backgrounds and expectations mean that similar living and working conditions do not simply produce similar experiences on the farm. Physical mobility and immobility are the canvas for their social counterparts in important but indirect ways. If permanent workers rely on mobility for their successful farm careers, downwardly mobile seasonal workers interpret their isolation as an exile that leaves their self-understandings provisionally intact. Their expectations and experiences are entrenched by strategies of abstention, which preserve a form of 'school' status despite the border's power dynamics and labour hierarchies. All of this challenges us to broaden our conception of social space – a key aspect of a Bourdieusian approach to social positioning and mobility.

Physical im/mobilities inflect social mobility and people's capacities to operate in social space, in ways that appear well catered for by Urry's (2007) concept of network capital, described earlier. But his framing has its own limitations, which in turn expose an important aspect of social im/mobilities in the case discussed here. Urry places a particular emphasis on infrastructure. Access to mobility, for him, can be understood in terms of the economic resources required to move, the physical dimensions of movement, its organizational aspects, and people's temporal availability. None of these excludes settings like the Zimbabwean-South African border. Nor do the eight elements that constitute network capital, which has become 'a distinct stratification order that now sits alongside social class, social status and party' (2007: 197).[9] But their interplay is explored in a particular kind of narrative about the transformation of human social life: in an era of ever greater flows, network capital is about reproducing social position and life chances through non-proximate connections.

There is a bias here towards wealthier parts of the world, wealthier people and urban settings. We hear of multi-level systems and overlapping forms of technology, such as the fate of public transport and the rising trend of flexi-time. A narrative of 'the breakdown of predictably scheduled events' (ibid.: 193) refers to 'modern' life, not the crisis and fragmentation that affects people on the fringes, such as the Zimbabwean-South African border. Urry is not alone here. Cresswell extends mobilities scholarship into non-Western settings, but the expanding horizons are themselves about public infrastructure, technological innovation and urban life (2010: 555).

If recent framings of physical mobility betray bias towards the wealthy North, we must be equally careful in our conceptualizations of social mobility, which can smuggle in unduly uniform conceptions of social space and social stratification. As noted earlier, Urry builds on Bourdieu's multiple forms of capital. The social terrain on which these capitals operate is social space, in which games of social positioning unfold. Indeed, they have a crucial symbolic dimension, meaning that they can be taken to rely on thoroughgoing incorporation into systems of meaning characterized by substantial agreement. Even adherents of countercultures understand their marginal status in relation to high culture and the status quo (see Atkinson 2015: 59–80).

But in places of crisis that are themselves marginal, we need a more open conceptualization of social space. The sheer multiplicity of forms of movement, settlement and mutual evaluation on the Zimbabwean-South African border presents a challenge. It is not just that infrastructures are limited, raising questions about how we imagine physical mobility. More importantly, radical differences interact with the limited institutionalization of an overriding order. Agricultural work is of extremely low status across the region, but it produces influential people. Seasonal workers at the bottom of the hierarchy grew up embodying a dominant habitus characterized by education and professional employment. Under these conditions, there is little agreement about the terms of status and success. Some workers recognize their supervisors as local notables; others see them as jumped-up yokels. Middle-class pickers remain teachers, intellectuals or political dissidents in the eyes of some of their team-mates; in the eyes of others, they are simply deluded and maladapted. Workers are potential deportees. Farmers are protectors and colonial anachronisms. Soldiers are impersonal state officials and localized components of the farm order.

Urry's particular focus leaves plausible the idea that, when it comes to social mobility, there is agreement about what matters. Social, cultural and network capital all rely on a high degree of convention. Von Holdt (2012), writing of labour struggles in South Africa, offers a thought-provoking avenue for further consideration, in relation to more fragmentary settings. Bourdieu, he notes, imagines European societies in which people are pacified and arrangements sustained by the symbolic violence of naturalized hierarchy. By contrast, Fanon's conceptualization of the social order came from experience of a settler society whose status quo required upholding by undisguised brutality.

In South Africa, today and at least since the turbulence of late apartheid, what pertains is somewhere between the two. Symbolic orders are more fragile than Euro-American sociology assumes, with little in the status quo taken for granted. Alternative orders with their own rules persist, each with their own recourse to physical coercion (ibid.). Certainly, the Zimbabwean-South African border is a far cry from a Weberian monopoly of legitimate violence, and far from the far-reaching naturalized symbolic violence of Bourdieu. No one in the workforce is an unambiguous superior, and the unpredictability of crisis inflects attempts to produce hierarchy. Kicks and punches in the orchards, the use of soldiers and security guards as enforcers, and extreme vulnerability come to hold the hierarchy in place (in ways that nevertheless uphold the power of white farmers remarkably effectively – see Bolt 2016). But social scripts and status, and the terms of recognition, remain fragile here.

Work on the farm represents social mobilities of all sorts depending on preceding social trajectories. In a setting of crisis, farm work represents real advancement for some, while others try to make a living while retaining and performing a sharply contrasting form of cultural capital that we might call 'school capital'. The latter is subordinated to the everyday influence of workforce seniority – and the need for protection – but senior workers also need an audience to be notables, and the audience can be disparaging and even destabilizing. In such circumstances, social space is plural – far from any unilinear notion of stratification. Appreciating this is key for thinking about the complexity of status hierarchies and of social positions.

Maxim Bolt is Reader in Anthropology and African Studies at the University of Birmingham, and Research Associate at WISER, University of the Witwatersrand. He is author of *Zimbabwe's Migrants and South Africa's Border Farms: The Roots of Impermanence* (Cambridge University Press, 2015), which won the 2016 British Sociological Association / BBC Thinking Allowed Ethnography Award. An economic anthropologist, he has recently extended his interests in institutions and class reproduction into a study of property, inheritance and legal bureaucracy in Johannesburg, South Africa. Maxim is Co-Editor of *AFRICA: Journal of the International African Institute*.

Notes

1. High school finishing exams.
2. Actually his mother's sister, but she brought him up when his own mother passed away.
3. Basic level high school exams, the stage before A-level.
4. Hyperinflation eroded teachers' salaries and parents' capacities to pay school fees.
5. 'Spear of the Nation', the armed wing of the African National Congress in its struggle against the apartheid regime.
6. Although the longer-term effects of land reform have been far more complex. See Matondi 2012.
7. Mostly these are children from permanent families, but accompanied intermittently by more transient children because patrols generally leave minors alone.
8. Commercially produced 'traditional' beer.
9. 'Array of appropriate documents, visas, money, qualifications'; 'others (workmates, friends and family members) at-a-distance'; 'movement capacities'; 'location free information and contact points'; 'communication devices'; 'appropriate, safe and secure meeting places'; 'access [to transport and the means of communication]'; 'time and other resources to manage and coordinate 1–7' (Urry 2007: 197–98).

References

Adey, P. 2006. 'If Mobility is Everything then It is Nothing: Towards a Relational Politics of (Im)mobilities', *Mobilities* 1(1): 75–94.

Atkinson, W. 2015. *Class*. Cambridge: Polity.

Bayart, J.-F. 2000. 'Africa in the World: A History of Extraversion', *African Affairs* 99(395): 217–67.

Boeyens, J.C.A. 1994. '"Black Ivory": The Indenture System and Slavery in Zoutpansberg, 1848–1869', in E.A. Eldridge and F. Morton (eds), *Slavery in South Africa: Captive Labour on the Dutch Frontier*. Oxford: Westview Press, pp. 187–214.

Bolt, M. 2010. 'Camaraderie and its Discontents: Class Consciousness, Ethnicity and Divergent Masculinities among Zimbabwean Migrant Farmworkers in South Africa', *Journal of Southern African Studies* 36(2): 377–93.

_____. 2012. 'Waged Entrepreneurs, Policed Informality: Work, the Regulation of Space and the Economy of the Zimbabwean-South African Border', *Africa* 82(1): 111–30.

_____. 2013. 'Producing Permanence: Employment, Domesticity and the Flexible Future on a South African Border Farm', *Economy and Society* 42(1): 197–225.

_____. 2014 'The Sociality of the Wage: Money Rhythms, Wealth Circulation and the Problem with Cash on the Zimbabwean-South African Border', *Journal of the Royal Anthropological Institute* 20(1): 113–30.

_____. 2015. *Zimbabwean Migrants and South Africa's Border Farms: The Roots of Impermanence*. Cambridge: Cambridge University Press.

_____. 2016. 'Mediated Paternalism and Violent Incorporation: Enforcing Farm Hierarchies on the Zimbabwean–South African Border', *Journal of Southern African Studies* 42(5): 911–27.

Bonner, P., and E.J. Carruthers. 2003. *The Recent History of the Mapungubwe Area*. Mapungubwe Cultural Heritage Resources Survey. Commissioned by the South African Dept of Environmental Affairs & Tourism.

Bradford, H. 1993. 'Getting Away with Murder: "Mealie Kings", the State and Foreigners in the Eastern Transvaal, c. 1918–1950', in P. Bonner, P. Delius and D. Posel (eds), *Apartheid's Genesis, 1935–1962*. Johannesburg: Ravan Press, pp. 96–125.

Braun, L.F. 2013. 'The Returns of the King: The Case of Mphephu and Western Venda, 1899–1904', *Journal of Southern African Studies* 39(2): 271–91.

Coutin, S.B. 2003. 'Illegality, Borderlands, and the Space of Nonexistence', in R.W. Perry and B. Maurer (eds), *Globalization under Construction: Governmentality, Law, and Identity*. Minneapolis: University of Minnesota Press, pp. 171–202.

Coplan, D.B. 2001. 'A River Runs through It: The Meaning of the Lesotho-Free State Border', *African Affairs* 100: 81–116.

Cresswell, T. 2010. 'Mobilities I: Catching up', *Progress in Human Geography* 35(4): 550–58.

_____. 2012. 'Mobilities II: Still', *Progress in Human Geography* 36(5): 645–53.

Crush, J., A. Chikanda and G. Tawodzera. 2015. 'The Third Wave: Mixed Migration from Zimbabwe to South Africa', *Canadian Journal of African Studies* 49(2): 363–82.

De Genova, N.P. 2002. '"Illegality" and Deportability in Everyday Life', *Annual Review of Anthropology* 31: 419–47.

Donnan, H., and T.M. Wilson. 1999. *Borders: Frontiers of Identity, Nation and State*. Oxford: Berg.

Dorman, S.R. 2003. 'NGOs and the Constitutional Debate in Zimbabwe: From Inclusion to Exclusion', *Journal of Southern African Studies* 29(4): 845–63.

Flynn, D.K. 1997. '"We Are the Border": Identity, Exchange and the State along the Bénin-Nigeria Border', *American Ethnologist* 24(2): 311–30.

Heyman, J.M. 1990. 'The Emergence of a Waged Life Course on the United States-Mexico Border', *American Ethnologist* 17(2): 348–59.

Jeffrey, C. 2010. *Timepass: Youth, Class, and the Politics of Waiting in India*. Stanford: Stanford University Press.

Johnson-Hanks, J. 2005. 'When the Future Decides: Uncertainty and Intentional Action in Contemporary Cameroon', *Current Anthropology* 46(3): 363–85.

Matondi, P.B. 2012. *Zimbabwe's Fast Track Land Reform*. London: Zed Books.

Mbembe, A., and J. Roitman. 1995. 'Figures of the Subject in Times of Crisis', *Public Culture* 7(2): 323–52.

Muzondidya, J. 2009. 'From Buoyancy to Crisis, 1980–1997', in B. Raftopoulos and A.S. Mlambo (eds), *Becoming Zimbabwe: A History from the Pre-Colonial Period to 2008*. Harare: Weaver Press, pp. 167–200.

Pelkmans, M. 2006. *Defending the Border: Identity, Religion, and Modernity in the Republic of Georgia*. Ithaca: Cornell University Press.

Quirk, J., and D. Vigneswaran. 2015. 'Mobility Makes States', in D. Vigneswaran and J. Quirk (eds), *Mobility Makes States: Migration and Power in Africa*. Philadelphia: University of Pennsylvania Press, pp. 1–34.

Raftopoulos, B. 2009. 'The Crisis in Zimbabwe, 1998–2008', in B. Raftopoulos and A.S. Mlambo (eds), *Becoming Zimbabwe: A History from the Pre-Colonial Period to 2008*. Harare: Weaver Press, pp. 201–32.

Rutherford, B. 2001. *Working on the Margins: Black Workers, White Farmers in Post-Colonial Zimbabwe*. London: Zed Books.

_____. 2011. 'The Uneasy Ties of Working and Belonging: The Changing Situation for Undocumented Zimbabwean Migrants in Northern South Africa', *Ethnic and Racial Studies* 34(8): 1303–19.

Titeca, K., and T. de Herdt. 2010. 'Regulation, Cross-Border Trade and Practical Norms in West Nile, North-Western Uganda', *Africa* 80(4): 573–94.

Urry, J. 2007. *Mobilities*. Cambridge: Polity.

Vigh, H. 2008. 'Crisis and Chronicity: Anthropological Perspectives on Continuous Conflict and Decline', *Ethnos* 73(1): 5–24.

von Holdt, K. 2012. 'The Violence of Order, Orders of Violence: Between Fanon and Bourdieu', *Current Sociology* 61(2): 112–31.

Wagner, R. 1980. 'Zoutpansberg: The Dynamics of a Hunting Frontier, 1848–67', in S. Marks and A. Atmore (eds), *Economy and Society in Pre-Industrial South Africa*. London: Longman, pp. 313–49.

Chapter 8

Domestic Dramas
Class, Taste and Home Decoration in Buea, Cameroon

Ben Page

Prologue

If you wanted to touch upward social mobility and the 'new' African middle class what would you reach for? Setting aside (for now) anxieties about the empiricism that such a desire for tangibility implies, the range of answers is increasing all the time: shopping malls, work places, private schools, voting booths, restaurants, beach resorts, coffee shops, cupcake vendors, smoothie bars and cars are all productive sites for research not just about consumption patterns but also about how the middle classes relate to the state, to businesses, to 'Africa Rising', to politics and to history. Or how about reaching for a will – the site where an individual's assets are totted up ready to be passed to the next generation (Bolt 2016)? Does upward social mobility in Africa have to be as urban as this list suggests or is the separation of urban and rural another Eurocentric misreading of African everyday life (Ndjio 2009)? Would African upward social mobility even be 'in Africa' or is it in the transnational spaces of the airport lounge and diaspora meeting room? Wherever social researchers choose to look for the middle class in twenty-first-century Africa, it is now time to supplement the statistical story that has come from African economists (Ncube and Lufumpa 2015), political scientists (Cheeseman 2015) and investors (Deloitte 2014) with stories of everyday life in order to improve understanding of these social changes.

Notes for this chapter begin on page 196.

The domestic sphere is the acme of social positioning in Africa at this current moment. The middle class have no monopoly over using houses as markers of position, but it is one of their particular pre-occupations. Plots of land, the fences around them, the buildings on them and the cars outside are the best-lit stage on which the dramas of social boundary-making are being played out (Lentz 2015, Mercer 2014, 2016). Structurally the drama is fundamentally relational: stage, actors and audience work together to produce this new social scene. Class positioning is only one of the many jobs that such boundary-making does, but it is the focus of this particular analysis. These boundaries might distinguish between those who are prospering and those who are not but they could also be normative boundaries between the worthy meritocrats of the new business world and the more suspect political 'elite' some of whom ascend through the adept accumulation of rents. They could be boundaries between generations or genders or ethnicities or occupations or those with different levels of education. Or they could be understood as boundaries between different fractions within the emergent middle class. The central claim is that the desire for recognition among both the dominant and the dominated in these hierarchies is made visible in the material space of a 'well-decorated' living room or, to use the idiomatic term from Cameroon, parlour.

The claim that the home is a key site of social boundary-making is hardly novel. The domestic sphere is central to the analysis of the British middle class in the eighteenth and nineteenth centuries (Davidoff and Hall 1987, St George 2006, Tosh 1999). Similarly, it is the subject of current analysis around the world too (Cox 2016, Jacobs and Malpas 2013, Walsh 2006). Much of this work is framed by the ideas of the sociologist Pierre Bourdieu. He addressed economists on their home turf when he looked at the more-than-economic aspects of housing 'markets' in the *Social Structures of the Economy* (2005 [2000]). The book is a study of the transition from rented high-density housing to owner-occupied single-family homes in the 1980s in the Val d'Oise, north of Paris. It explores the way that the market is constructed by the state and shaped by the (sociological) contradiction between the tastes of a middle class (who aspire to the cultural capital of the dominant class) and their economic assets (their capacity to afford the house they desire). The households he analyses 'strive to content themselves... with the judgement reality has passed on their expectations' (Bourdieu 2005: 187). As often happens, the African story of boundary-making in the domestic sphere is not a simple revival of an old European production taken from the existing repertoire with the same characters, costumes and set-design. Rather this is a novel reinterpretation of the play's script: some of the speeches may be the same, but their significance is changed by the spatial and temporal context.

In the remainder of the chapter I will reflect on the analytical framing of the book as a whole by addressing Bourdieu's concept of 'the social space' in the context of a case study from Cameroon, describe and analyse three parlours in homes in Cameroon as examples of taste,[1] and use the conclusion to explore the internal diversity of the new middle class. The chapter continues to plough its (laboured) theatrical metaphor, not merely as a rhetorical indulgence, but to make an argument about the relational nature of class without dissolving into the short-cuts of overfamiliar academic jargon (terms like 'relational', for example). The idea that social boundary-making is a bit like a piece of theatre is part of a wider argument about social space as a dialogue between authors, actors and audience. As actors will tell you, there are good audiences and bad audiences. They will also explain how some scripts and some directors are much easier to work with than others. As audiences make clear, two people can watch the same performance and come away with very different thoughts and observations. Social boundary-making is theatrical in its concern with visibility, interpretation, thrill, repertoire, experiment, artifice and the suspension of disbelief. The arid vocabulary of social science often loses the vim of this dramatic creativity.

Before we continue, I want to make two quick comments on the position of judgement from which the chapter is written. First, the theatrical metaphor pre-supposes a familiarity among readers of the kind of theatre I am imagining. Ironically the obscure professional language of abstract analysis may have more universal salience than a culturally specific referent like theatre, though Africa's dramatic traditions are vigorous, diverse and relevant. Second, the descriptions of the three parlours that make up the core of the chapter overtly express my own emotional reactions to these rooms. However, I am clearly not the intended audience that their decorators imagined as a visitor, but a nosy interloper into this particular social universe. I cannot make an insider's judgement about the decoration. Rather, I have made my own reactions explicit in the hope that the reader can see them in order to see past them. In every parlour described here there were mass-produced decorative gee-gaws that I would not choose to display in my own home. By telling you this, my hope is you will be able to see beyond my patronizing metropolitan bourgeois snobbery.

The Proscenium Arch: The 'Social Space' as Analytical Frame for a Small Town in Cameroon

The distribution of social positions in the small town of Buea in Anglophone South-west Cameroon has been shaken up since the millennium by a distinct increase in prosperity for some households (Courade 1970, Page and Sunjo 2017).[2] What was once a sleepy administrative centre comprising a mix of civil servants and famers has become a dynamic and entrepreneurial town – a process led by the expansion of the university and the investments of transnational migrants.[3] On this basis it is conceivable to identify an emergent 'group' – the 'new middle class' (though this is a term that has no local salience). These households have, over the last few years, accelerated away from the bulk of the population in terms of wealth. But this simple assertion that there is a relationship between capital accumulation (a purely economic variable) and the formation of a new class does not capture the social dynamics at work in Buea. For example, the routes to prosperity are many and varied. Some households in Buea have capitalized on the new private sector business opportunities associated with economic growth across Africa, others use their position vis-à-vis the state, and others accumulate assets through international migration (Alpes 2013).[4] The strategies of distinction at work in these changes cannot be reduced to purely economic measures of average incomes, household wealth or property values.

Instead, in line with a major source of inspiration for this book, the goal is to think about social mobility in the context of Pierre Bourdieu's notion of 'social space'.

> The social world can be represented as a space (with several dimensions) constructed on the basis of principles of differentiation or distribution constituted by the set of properties active within the social universe in question, i.e., capable of conferring strength, power within that universe, on their holder. Agents and groups of agents are thus defined by their relative positions within that space. (Bourdieu 1985: 723–24)

The social space is in some ways a background idea in his larger conceptual scheme. It provides a way of thinking about the co-ordinates through which more familiar concepts (field, habitus, capital) can be positioned in order to understand relations of domination. For my purposes three key points arise from this idea.

Firstly, the social space obviously has multiple dimensions. Because this is Bourdieu, these are primarily expressed as different types of capital: usually economic capital (money and other monetized assets), cultural capital (culturally relevant knowledge and embodied know-how), and social capital (who we know).[5] But other forms of capital are available too: political, educational, informational, religious, technological. Crucially, when any form of capital becomes recognized as legitimate (and as a result confers benefits associated with that legitimacy), it also takes on the character of symbolic capital. So in Buea being educated is highly respected and titles like 'Professor' express legitimacy and can bring some social profits. In contrast, the relationship between wealth and symbolic capital is much more ambiguous. Whilst the pursuit of wealth and public displays of wealth are common and are seen as legitimate, they are often haunted by a miasma of rumour that casts doubt on whether that wealth is literally legitimate or has been accumulated by deviant spiritual or criminal means. So the extent to which economic capital in Buea is also symbolic capital is highly contextual. The accumulation of symbolic capital is expressed in an elevated social position, in the capacity to ensure others will pay attention to you. It also sometimes suggests an obligation to the community. It is not just about the capacity to have one's way, but also about being recognized as 'a somebody' (Menkiti 1984, 2004). This aspiration to personhood is central to house-building in Buea (Page and Sunjo 2017).

In relation to the wider discussion about the middle class in Africa (Ncube and Lufumpa 2015), Bourdieu's approach provides a means of breaking away from imagining a class hierarchy that falls along a single line measured in terms of wealth. Instead by using the device of the social space, this chapter seeks to add to existing accounts that present a more complicated picture of the disposition of actors across the stage of 'class relations' (Enaudeau 2013, Lentz 2015, Mercer 2014, Spronk 2012). Social mobility cannot be reduced to the 'economic' because other elements (say recognition) are relatively autonomous of wealth. As some households increase their economic capital, others whose income has not increased over the same time period (such as secondary school teachers) are at a relatively lower position within the social space when viewed economically. Yet those teachers can still be recognized as persons because of their higher level of education and symbolic capital. These schoolteachers can still contest the recognition of the newly prosperous as legitimately superior – not least by passing judgement on the aesthetic choices they make in their homes.

Second, Bourdieu's social space refers to 'the social universe in question' – that is to say, it is contextually specific. It has geographical edges (however messy such frontiers might be). The principles used to distribute individuals within the social space could vary between locations. For example, in *Distinction* (1984: 122–23 and 455), Bourdieu presents a graph showing different cultural choices, professions and political preferences in relation to the distribution of economic and cultural capital in 1970s France. His analysis is specific not only to that moment in time, but also to that place. In other places such a 'graph' might deploy different forms of capital in different ways. For example, in the Cameroonian context it might be more useful to incorporate social capital into the visualization because 'who you know' and ideas of 'personhood' are so closely associated with the practice of power in this particular social universe.[6] So, whilst the framework might assert universal utility, there is also something assertively idiographic about it. It has the merit of providing a framework for comparison between (and within) different African middle classes, which recognizes diverse histories and geographies at a time when notions like 'Africa Rising' risk erasing spatial differences (Jazeel 2019). Whilst the current wave of research on the new African middle class (Spronk 2012, Melber 2016, Mercer 2014, 2016) might have successfully addressed the historicity of its object, it has paid less attention to its spatiality.

The third point to take from Bourdieu's definition of the social space relates to the risks associated with visualization, particularly in relation to the term 'lifestyle'.

> The means one has to use to construct social space and to exhibit its structure risk concealing the results they enable one to reach. The groups that must be constructed in order to objectivize the positions they occupy hide those positions. Thus the chapter of *Distinction* devoted to the different fractions of the dominant class will be read as a description of the various lifestyles of these fractions, instead of an analysis of locations in the space of positions of power-what I call the field of power. (Bourdieu 1989: 16)

Bourdieu argues against the assumption that individuals who occupy a similar location in social space ('classes on paper') will necessarily come to exist as a united group ('real classes').[7] So whilst a class on paper might look like a particular group of lifestyles, it is not necessarily a real class. Dieter Neubert (2016) argues that the notion of 'the middle class' has little analytical salience in Kenya at the moment, and instead it is more useful to think about the multiple lifestyles of those on middle incomes (pragmatists, social climbers, young professionals, different religious milieu, neo-traditionalists and cosmopolitan liberals). It intuitively makes sense that in the absence of deliberate unity based on an awareness of shared self-interest, there is no tangible 'class', but interesting though these lifestyle typologies are, they should not be the endpoint of the analysis. Rather, for Bourdieu they are a precursor to more explicitly political questions about domination: who amongst these groups can assert their will?

What capacity do they have to challenge the existing structural relations of domination? Claire Mercer (2014, 2016) gets closer to these issues when she argues that the various different embodied and practised lifestyles of middle income households in Dar es Salaam agglomerate to have class effects relevant to other people even in the absence of a self-conscious middle class (for example in relation to the marketization of land in the city's suburbs). If analysis goes no further than listing 'lifestyles' on the grounds that there is no empirical real class, then Bourdieu's project of using lifestyles to unveil relations of power is lost.

The social space then is more-than-economic; it is a multidimensional, geographically specific means of locating social differences. However, it risks visualizing a social universe of lifestyles that can end the analysis prematurely by hiding the very thing it seeks to show: relations of power.

Some Scenes from a Play: Decorating Parlours in Twenty-First-Century Buea

Scene One

Walking into the parlour of an ambitious, upwardly mobile, politically active, male civil servant (whose salary is supplemented by multiple entrepreneurial activities such as market gardening, retail, transport, car sales, etc.), I am struck by the dramatic chiaroscuro of the scene. The rectangular room (5 × 8 m) has windows on two walls, but the one at the front allows little light in because of a low, wide balcony outside. Though the walls are white there is a general gloom because of the dark red rug, the bulky red velour furniture (embroidered with gold trim), and the heavy red drapes half-covering the windows (gathered loosely by tasselled yellow ropes). But glaring, mote-filled light slants through the louvres at the side and illuminates a colourful, carefully collated array of decorative objects. Most obviously there are bunches of pink, orange and yellow artificial gladioli and daisies, a collection of plastic toy animals arranged on a silky-embroidered tablecloth, a shiny red tin, and a two-metre high artificial apple tree in a decorative pot. A tiered trio of bowls, containing more plastic flowers, hangs down from the ceiling in a mac-ramé net. The colours of these objects are duplicated in the shiny surfaces of the imported aluminium-legged, glass-topped tables on which they sit. The tables have shelves underneath where more artificial flowers and photo albums are stacked.

Routes from the door to the seats are constrained by the volume of stuff in the centre of the room, so that choices about where to go are limited and only one person can move along them at a time. The bulky seats themselves are of a kind fabricated by local carpenters. There is no space to put down a glass (or fieldwork notebook) on this line of tables in the middle of the room, but small locally-made coffee-tables (with embroidered white cloths on them) are placed beside us as we sit down to talk. A large (100 × 50 cm) colour photograph of the man's wife (who decorated the room) shows her with her head resting on her forearms. It is mounted on card and looks down across the scene from the outside of a glass-fronted wooden dresser, which covers the whole of the back wall facing the door. It is filled with more photos, crockery, glassware and electronics. The photographs are of family members, the couple's wedding, important dinners, etc.

The second decorative layer of the room has more to do with the man of the house, though it too has been arranged by his wife. It weaves together political and religious iconography with assertions of his commitment to 'tradition'. There are photographs of him in a new, richly embroidered agbada (gown) meeting big-wigs in the ruling political party; in the grandstand on national day for the march past; with his wife in matching outfits made from fabric decorated with the party's logo. The commitment to the governing party is explicit, shameless. There are also almanacs and calendars from the mainstream Protestant church where he is an elder, small statuettes of crucifixes, twee ceramics of cherubs and saints, and decorative banners with embroidered biblical aphorisms. Adjacent to one such banner on the front interior wall, over the cramped (largely unused) dining table, hangs a bundle of 'traditional' objects: a raffia bag, a series of caps, an animal fur, a fly-whisk, a staff, a woven blue and white jerkin. These are ready to be taken down and worn or carried when he attends born-house or cry-die ceremonies or when he goes to meetings of his 'kontri-people' – his ethnic group. His group are 'strangers' (immigrants) in Buea but assemble every month to socialize and take care of each other (Mercer et al. 2008, Page 2011). But these traditional objects are also hung in this room to be seen, not merely because it is a convenient spot to store them. They are used to assert belonging – both to a specific ethnic group and to his 'African' heritage. He is a title holder among his people and I know that some of the objects signify that role as well as his membership of a secret society. These things have explicit spiritual significance and so it is easy for me to exoticize this dusty bundle and make them more earnest than they are. 'These are things we don't joke about' says their owner – before immediately laughing and asking me why I think they are more interesting than his Christian paraphernalia.

To my eyes the room is abundant, exuberant, snug, comic, gaudy, cluttered, claustrophobic, kitsch. Its decoration does a lot of work. It makes me nervous, guarded: will I knock something over and spoil the display?

Will I let my judgement about some of these 'naff' things show? Will I be able to find out about the politics, the traditional objects? The furnishing speaks to a dialogue between the showy, homely aesthetic of the wife and the more self-consciously weighty, self-aggrandizing display of the husband. In terms of proportion of the space, the wife dominates, but her husband's contributions are more diverse (less coherent?) and demand more of my attention because of the more obvious social work that they do. Both sets of objects are externally-facing statements in this semi-public part of the house's interior.

The dialogue between husband and wife continues in terms of how the room is used. At some times this room is more public than at others. On days when the household hosts events much will happen outside: on the balcony and in the courtyard where there is space for dancing, marquees, large crowds. But this room will be where 'notables' – persons of significance – will sit and be entertained. When there are no big occasions, this is where people come in the afternoon and evening to ask for the husband's help and advice. He conducts business here. His wife greets these visitors (a mix of men and women) and provides drinks and food before generally either withdrawing to the kitchen or sitting in the corner of the parlour perched on the arm of a chair. She is no mere stagehand though and interjects when she can. Before her husband had become socially established, he had drawn from the credibility of her family – her father is a senior government official. Much of the time (when her husband is out) this is her space, where she meets with her friends, church groups and other networks. She is among her things and her stylistic choices. She also uses this space for 'business' – trading in cosmetics. Some of my interviews are with the husband and wife in here together, but the husband also prefers to talk to us elsewhere – in his car for example.

Scene Two

Parlour Two belongs to an unmarried Cameroonian woman who works in logistics for an international humanitarian organization, and who travels the world both for work and leisure. She is globally mobile. Her work is tough and has taken her to sites of extreme violence, but has also secured her an enhanced financial position that reflects the demands of her job and her extensive experience and professional skills. This house in Buea is brand new and is her 'sanctuary' – the place she comes to seek relief from her intense, upsetting work.

The L-shaped parlour is larger than Parlour One, with distinct areas for sitting and eating. The two spaces are separated by the use of different large, stone floor tiles. The whole room feels spacious with generous windows on two walls, which (though covered in anti-burglar bars) allow light as well as air to spill in. The curtains are made of two fabrics (one red, one tartan) and hung on simple rails and were well clear of the windows when pulled back. The house is built close to the edge of the building plot and surrounded by a high wall, so there is no view as such but, even so, there is a fresh breeze and a feeling of openness.

The bright white suspended ceilings over the two living spaces are clean and have been decorated with restrained prefabricated 'staff' plasterwork.[8] There is a ceiling rose where the main light fittings are supported, another oval decorative ring around that, then two more rectangular lines of decoration before the final ornamental flourish at the edge. There is then quite a wide gap between the ceiling and the edge of the actual room, which is left plain, drawing attention to the way the ceiling hangs above us. The complex ceiling arrangements create an effect that speaks to an ambition for grandeur, modernity and sophistication, yet they are not too ostentatious. Tucked into the ceiling decorations are dozens of recessed halogen lights, whilst the new matching central chandeliers are in a stylized floral form mixing black metal work with a dozen small, opaque glass shades. There are a number of uplighters on the wall, which match the glass fittings of the central light.

The seating arrangement combines two brand new small sofas and two more new single armchairs – all four seats are from a matching set: brown leather, supplemented by lighter cushion backs and a mix of decorative beige cushions made up from the same fabrics. They had been purchased in the UK and imported along with much of the other furniture in the house via sea in a container. They are arranged around three sides of a simple dark wooden coffee table, which could have come from the same furniture range – it certainly harmonizes with the chairs. It is unblemished and entirely clear of stuff except for the remote controls that pointed neatly towards the big flat screen TV (where CNN was running silently). The seating area is defined by a simple red rug. There is abundant space to move easily between and behind the chairs, which are a comfortable distance from the TV. The dining table and its six matching chairs are also an imported set: a strong almost art deco, geometric design with a thick black wooden table top, shiny metal legs and chairs with a wide flat circular shiny metal ring for backs. There are quite a number of decorative objects in the room, but it is not at all cluttered: a large glossy sculpture of a treble-clef, three matching African-made candlesticks on the dining room sideboard, one small framed photo beside the TV, a globe tucked into the corner of the room, an East or Southern African style bead table runner decorated with zebras.

There are four pictures on the wall – all of which were assertively 'African' in their aesthetic – all are figurative, showing semi-abstract, elongated, stylized women dancing or carrying water or children. The frames of three of them are decorated with leather and cowries. The fourth (which was also the largest) is surrounded by a bold mirrored frame and contains three shallow relief female figures formed from metal. They are all the kind of images sold to tourists in African craft markets or airports: sympathetic, sentimental, generic, depersonalized, undemanding representations of poverty and female labour and stoicism. The home's owner told us she had collected the pictures and other *objets d'art* on her travels around Africa for work. They are entirely decorative images in the sense that they do not threaten the easiness of the room with magical powers unlike the traditional objects in Parlour One. These are commodities that could have been bought by any traveller. Even if they announce a kind of pan-African pride, they also seemed to speak to a social distancing from the Africans in the images. This was someone who could be a patron of the African arts and perhaps also patronize the Africans who still carried water on their heads and babies on their backs. There seemed to be a gulf between these images and the way of life of their owner – but there are plenty of families living nearby within Buea who could have been real models for these pictures, for whom poverty was not aestheticized in this way. I was enjoying sitting there drinking her South African fruit juice, chatting about decor and catching up on world news from the TV so I felt a bit shabby about judging the pictures on the wall so harshly.

For me, the whole effect of the room is comfortable, confident, easy, smart, insipid and safe. The comfort is bodily (good chairs to sink into) as well as emotional (familiarity). It feels as though we are in sure hands here. The room could easily have been in a British show home in a new-build development (though a bit more generous in space than most of those). The pseudo-ascetic neutrality of the overall scheme – careful colour palette, coherent design, high-quality materials and imported furniture – gave the room a studied restraint (albeit with flashes of glamour) that spoke to a language of bourgeois propriety. This was someone who had a secure comprehension of the rules of cosmopolitan 'good taste'. We could have been almost anywhere. Nothing too vulgar, nothing ironic, more suburban than hip. Perhaps the whole room was too new to be really comfortable yet. It seemed almost impersonal in some ways – there was an overall meaning to the whole space (security, relaxation, calm, withdrawal), but no significant accretion of memories: it is yet-to-be-fully-personalized.

Compared to many of the houses I visited this one was smaller in scale overall, but had a higher standard of finishing. The owner spoke clearly of her aim of building something for her specific needs, rather than because she wanted to make a big visible statement (although I had just missed the house-warming party). Not making a statement is surely a classic way of making a statement for some within the middle class. The relationship between scale and quality was one that generally tipped the other way in Buea (just to be clear this was not a small house by local standards, just a smaller one than many others I visited) and, given that it was built for a woman, I was hoping the owner might explain this difference in gender terms – but this was a suggestion she refused flatly. It was more, she said, about 'understanding' – a far-sightedness that came from her travels. She had seen the world and knew that it was easier to manage and maintain a smaller house, and that high-quality finishing was ultimately of more value than flashy excess that would look shabby in a year or two and need repairs. It was a big enough house to host the guests she wanted, but did not invite the extended family to take up residence. It was what she wanted.

Scene Three

Parlour Three was created by a man who had accumulated wealth as a senior officer in the merchant marine – navigating the ports of West Africa as a senior employee of an expanding commercial shipping company. He comes from a world of commerce. His wife, who worked as a junior civil servant, made it clear the house was primarily her husband's project. In a region of increased average economic growth rates, the commercial trade of goods along the coast was doing well and that had lifted this family well above their immediate neighbours in economic terms. Externally their home reflected this difference in a very literal, visible sense. It is very tall and quite thin, because the fairly small (inherited) plot of land on which it is built is hemmed in on all sides by neighbours – many of whom are also relatives. It stands proud on its sloping site: three and half storeys high. It has a complicated façade combining bays, balconies, pillars and pediments. The house stands out from the neighbours in scale, materials and orientation: it is large, complex, glossy and vertical, whereas it is surrounded on all sides by generally shabby, matt, wooden-walled horizntal bungalows made from planks and topped with rusting corrugated sheets. The house was built to its owner's own design (helped by a draftsman and a builder). Unlike the owner of Parlour One, he is a member of Buea's indigenous ethnic group (the Bakweri) and is explicitly concerned with their lack of social mobility vis-à-vis incomers. As we stood on his highest balcony looking down on his neighbours' homes, he explained to me that he wanted to use his house to inspire other members of his family and encourage his own ethnic group about what they could achieve through hard work. Both the exterior and the interior related specifically to his immediate family who were also his neighbours – this was his audience.

Parlour Three runs the whole depth of the house (4 × 16 m) and is on a raised ground-floor level. There is something paradoxical about the geometry of this room; it is a challenge to describe its shapes. The room is divided into three sections: a seating area at the front, a bar area in the middle and a dining area to the rear. The seating area is separated from the bar area (wooden with stools, mirror and shelves for the bottles of spirits) by the top part of a (not quite perfectly round) white plaster arch, which rests on two ornate white pilasters with Corinthian-style capitals (some of the decoration has been picked out in gold). The pilasters do not seem to be structural because there are also separate supporting pillars right beside them. The ends of the arch come quite low (about chest height), so that the route to the rear of the parlour through the arch looks somewhat restricted. This visual impediment is significantly compounded by a sofa that sits under the arch and by a staircase (going up to the floors above) that rises from the bar area and cuts through the arch at about 30 degrees, so that one side of the space is almost entirely blocked by the underside of the stairs.

The seating area at the front of the parlour is one and a half storeys high. Looking up you can see an open wooden balustrade beside a landing leading to the bedrooms, but you can't see the top of the landing because the ornate ceiling of the parlour is a metre or so lower than the ceiling of the landing– so you see people's legs walking along the landing above you, but not their faces.. The dominant feature of the interior decoration are the ceramic tiles. The walls and floor of the seating area are entirely lined with a melange of tiles: there are grey tiles that are the shape and size of bricks on the side you enter from; heavily textured, larger white tiles from floor to ceiling (4–5 m?) on the opposite side wall; and very small horizontal mosaic-style tiles (dark brown, pale brown and beige) on the arch end and in the windowed front bay of this part of the room. The floor tiles are a sandy brown. The ceiling is white with a big white plaster rose in the centre (with more details picked out in gold) and a similar cornice. The big chandelier is gold and crystal and cylindrical.

There are imported black leather sofas and chairs on three sides and a vast TV suspended high on one wall. There is also an array of locally-made tables, cupboards and display units made from glossy reddish wood (bobinga?) with spindly decorative legs turned on a lathe. The imported dining table has flecks of gold embedded in the glass top. The six matching dining chairs are backed with a gold and black animal print (more giraffe than leopard). Every surface in the room has a decorative object placed on it: a large double photo-portrait of the owners, ceramic animals (including quite a large dolphin), a carved hippo, some wooden maps of Cameroon on the bar, and crochet work on the backs of the seats. Many things were made in Africa but none had an overtly African aesthetic. In our discussions the origins of these objects are unremembered, they do not seem to carry precise memories. In interviews the husband insisted that he had taken control of the interior decoration because women tended to introduce too much clutter when decorating and he wanted a simpler, less fussy look. He spoke with great earnestness: decoration was a very serious thing for him. Unlike the owner of Parlour Two who could relate easily to global cosmopolitan rules of good taste, this house felt as though the owner was trying too hard. But he wasn't anxious about it; it didn't matter because that wasn't where this social boundary was being drawn. The house collected locally-made and imported objects, just as the owner connected a family in which some are socially mobile and some are not. The house spoke not to power in any political sense as in Parlour One, but to power in the form of the intensely local desire to advance.

The whole effect was joyous and impressive, but also slightly alarming and giddying. One part of the room was higher than it was wide. Others almost made you feel you had to duck to enter. Sitting in the parlour it was beautifully bright, but somehow the light did not find its way around the whole house. Every surface was shiny with ceramics, but there were so many different colours, textures and shapes that my eyes kept moving all the time – every time they settled, something else caught their attention. To my eyes the room (and indeed the whole house) is quirky, individual, charming, disorienting, disjointed, awkward, amateurish, uninhibited, gleeful. It is all genial and eager to please – if, unwittingly, crazed: a bit of a mess, but impossible not to love as an expression of its author's creativity. It is more than I have ever managed to build and I admire its creator and am a bit jealous of what they have achieved even if I like to think I would never decorate a room quite like this.

The Curtain Call

The immersion into the world of any play is harder to sustain as the end approaches and the audience await a summing up speech and prepares to leave the theatre. As our actors from these three parlours all gather on one comparative stage for the start of the denouement, it is inevitable that we have to try and array them across Bourdieu's 'social space'.

   Our three parlours have been chosen to represent three versions of
upward social mobility in Buea: state-led, migration-led and business-
led. What dimensions (capitals) would we use in this particular social
universe to lay out principles of differentiation? Bourdieu's visualization (1984: 122–23 and 455) used capital volume, economic capital and
cultural capital. In this chapter the three households considered were
deliberately chosen to have broadly similar economic capital. But where
they differ is in relation to their taste in home furnishings (the culturally relevant knowledge and embodied know-how of cultural capital);
their personal networks (social capital); and the acquisition of prestige,
recognition and legitimation (symbolic capital). The incorporation of
social capital is central to the geographical specificity of this case study.
In Parlour One a civil servant who has built his social mobility out of
party loyalty is part of a national network of those who depend on him
and to whom he himself looks for further advancement. It is part of a
joint endeavour with his wife, who takes a supporting role. In Parlour
Two the scale of the network is far more global, reaching into the diaspora and the professional networks of humanitarian practice and the
leisure activities of a global traveller. The cultural know-how relates
to the people encountered across that experience and is expressed in a
form of 'good taste' that is indexed against a global aesthetic. Parlour
Three is about a more assertively local, vernacular network, concerned
with addressing the extended family and co-ethnics in the immediate vicinity of the new home. However, it is the incorporation of symbolic capital that takes us beyond a typology of three different lifestyles
and into a discussion of the dynamics of power, domination and class
relations.
   The legitimate exercise of power requires the possession of symbolic
capital, which gives a person the authority to act. Becoming a somebody
in Buea is not about having a well decorated parlour; it is about being
recognized as someone with the capacity to dispense patronage (political, commercial, familial, communitarian). Symbolic capital 'is the power
granted to those who have obtained sufficient recognition to be in a position to impose recognition' (Bourdieu 1989: 23). The owner of Parlour
Three had the capacity to demand that his family members acknowledge
his views of what constituted success and how it is achieved because they
saw his house adjacent to their own, towering over them. They had to
recognize his claim that they too could do better in life (or their children
could) if they emulated his example and worked hard in business. The
individuals whose parlours I visited depend on the recognition of those
they dominate; there is a mutual inter-dependence here. They only have
symbolic capital because people believe in them, because they are held in

esteem. Showing good taste is part of earning that confidence. How then do you show good taste in Buea?

An enthusiasm for the novel and the unique (new furniture, new geometries, new technologies) is often a sign of culturally relevant knowledge and embodied know-how. Multiple builders claimed that they were the first to use some new material (mirror glass for example), others would draw attention to the uniqueness of the multifaceted roofline on their home. This would be the dominant means of earning the admiration of visitors or passers-by. Neophilia speaks not only to a sign of being able to afford new things but also to a rupture in time, which endorses the 'newness' of the 'new' African middle class. Yet an enthusiasm for the new in Cameroon is not really a new thing (Ardener 1970, Fardon 2006), nor is it limited to the middle class, as the ubiquity of new technical gadgets across society shows. This temporal break does social work. It asserts a boundary between the old and the new that marks out the socially mobile from the immobile. This admiration for the new is also a displacement of social newness (becoming a new person, being *nouveaux riches*) onto tangible things (decorative objects). The visible accumulation of new stuff can be seen as a means of becoming a recognized, creative somebody within a particular set of social relationships in this context (as in many others).

There is a spatial iteration of this neophilia too: an admiration for imported manufactured furniture and decorations were seen by many interviewees as showing better taste than those produced by local craftsmen. There is little valorization of the vernacular or craft. Italian imports were valued over those from China; tiles from Dubai had a particular cachet when compared to those from Nigeria. But there are contradictions here, because such imported objects are often mass produced (the artificial apple tree in Parlour One for example was seen in lots of houses and was available in roadside stores too). The ability to assert individuality through uniqueness is also seen as an expression of good taste. It is easier to show such originality through commissioning local craftsman, yet this was a rarity. Yet in contradiction to the broad principle, certain craft materials (bobinga wood in particular) which are 'local' are at the peak of the pyramid of taste when it comes to selecting doors. Negotiating your way through good imports and bad imports, good craft and bad craft is another opportunity to show a capacity to be discriminating.

Another means of showing good taste in home furnishings is successfully navigating your relationship to the timespace of the African past. Locally crafted objects can be tasteful if they suggest a capacity for discernment. This might actually be about specific exclusions when decorating – I was frequently told that it was inappropriate to put African masks on your wall as they might offend Christians because they contained spiritual power. However, demystified, commodified African carvings (as found in Parlour Two) were fine. A capacity for managing Africa by not simply turning your back on it in your decorative schema (as had happened in Parlour Three) speaks to a higher level of cultural capital – a capacity for knowingness, for knowing how to incorporate Africa in an appropriate way. Given the close links between politics and neo-traditionalism in Cameroon, the display of 'cultural' objects in Parlour One would be seen as a perfectly legitimate assertion of a particular form of power for an individual whose mobility and authority depends on the state and the ruling party. But by carefully balancing these objects with an array of Christian iconography, questions of whether they are appropriate (or even offensive) do not arise.

It is also a measure of elevated know-how if you can design your parlour to meet the challenge of property maintenance in the physical environment of Buea (high humidity, torrential rain, dust, insects). The wise builder shows restraint and focuses on quality not quantity. This is a good example of something that is autonomous from wealth. Whereas the owner of Parlour Two had given considerable thought to the question of maintainability, the owner of Parlour Three had not really done so. A house is never finished, but will need to be renovated from time to time just as earning recognition from your peers is also a never-ending process.

The parlours described are clearly highly relational: they were constructed in front of and for the viewing 'pleasure' of other people. More research is needed to make strong claims about how this audience reads these scenes (Alpes 2013, Pelican 2010). However, wider discussions in Buea suggested that the people who build new houses are recognized as successful by those who are less successful, which is to say that everyone agrees what success looks like when it looks like a house. However, several people cast doubt on the legitimacy of the means by which success was achieved by implying that criminality or witchcraft was involved. The symbolism of Parlour One's gloom is, in this respect, a felicitous contrast to the transparency and illumination of Parlours Two and Three. Different actors agree about the rules of the drama – even if everyone also recognizes that, as it is a play, it is a bit of an illusion. Even those (such as the teachers mentioned earlier) who accuse the new middle class of vulgar excess also recognize that, as 'the old middle class', they do not currently possess the capacity to effectively assert any alternative.

But the picture being painted here is too certain – it risks suggesting a settled field that seems empirically inappropriate in Cameroon. Violent protests across this part of Cameroon starting in October 2016 suggest that, at least in the political sphere, there is an ongoing struggle over legitimate forms of domination. The owner of Parlour One looks less secure in retaining recognition than the owner of Parlour Two because his symbolic capital rests on the universal recognition of the social hierarchy arranged by the current ruling party, whereas hers is drawn from her profession and transnational experience. Whilst he is currently seen as more useful for those wishing to navigate the Cameroonian system, she does not have the same immediate capacity to solve other people's (non-monetary) problems and is content to be less visible, except within her diaspora networks. But all this could change in the event of the ruling party losing its grip. The owner of Parlour Three seeks recognition at a different scale: within his family and ethnic group, here too the vicissitudes of national politics, while not irrelevant to his symbolic capital are, at best secondary.

Through this analysis I have sought to show how qualitative accounts of middle-class life can be translated into more ambitious analyses that go beyond wealth and income to address questions of recognition, power, domination and personhood. Differences within the category 'African middle class' emerge. Dialogues are opened within families, amongst economic peers and between those who are thriving and those who are not. Certainly, Bourdieu's framework provides tools that shift analyses away from unilinear accounts of class measured in terms of wealth towards a more diverse set of measures of social difference. However, Bourdieu also identified the risk of empiricism when connecting these ideas to empirical research materials:

> people who are very distant from each other in social space can encounter one another and interact, if only briefly and intermittently, in physical space. Interactions, which bring immediate gratification to those with empiricist dispositions – they can be observed, recorded, filmed, in sum, they are tangible, one can 'reach out and touch them' – mask the structures that are realized in them. This is one of those cases where the visible, that which is immediately given, hides the invisible which determines it. (Bourdieu 1989: 16)

Bourdieu's strained relationship with the idea of the unconscious (Steinmetz 2006) is expressed here in terms of the challenge of focusing not on the visible but on the 'invisible which determines it'. Habitus functions somewhere other than in consciousness or language. This is what really seems to concern him about the idea of a social space, and to this extent he was caught up in the challenge of balancing the temptation to represent social mobility and social positions with the view that such representations actively mask the real drama underneath the public play of class, taste and boundary-making. In that context the more empirical parts of this chapter seem perhaps to wilfully ignore his warnings. But my argument is that the play is all we have to go on if we are searching for something underneath that cannot be spoken. Like dreams or Freudian slips, the fantastical homes of the new middle class hint at the invisible forces that determine the unfolding social dynamics in this small town in Africa.

Ben Page is Associate Professor of Human Geography and African Studies at University College London. He has undertaken research in Cameroon for over twenty years. His interests fall broadly within the field of the migration-development nexus, with a specific interest in the role of international migrants in class formation and urban transformations in their countries of origin. He recently edited a volume on time, temporalities and mobility called *Timespace and International Migration* (2017).

Notes

1. These descriptions are based on a large set of photographs as well as research notes. However, I have deliberately made a choice not to use photographs in the chapter. This is partly a simple practical consequence of not getting permissions, but it is also an ethical preference because I have tried to leave out some aspects of the description, which could identify specific individuals.
2. This research is based on fieldwork in Buea between February and April 2013 and in April 2015 and July 2016. The qualitative data is based on twenty-nine interviews and walk-round tours undertaken with homeowners, building contractors, officials, politicians, architects and the regional manager of the government's mortgage bank. All interviews were undertaken in English (or Pidgin) by the author and by Emile Sunjo, from the University of Buea. I am grateful to Claire Mercer, James Kneale and Claire Dwyer for comments on a draft of this chapter as well as to an anonymous referee.
3. Tragically, much of this chapter now seems like an anachronism as violent conflict has consumed Buea and the surrounding region since the fieldwork was undertaken. The future is uncertain.
4. The boom is of course not continent wide, despite frequent uses of aggregate data about GDP. Even setting aside the sluggish growth in South Africa and very slow growth in northern Africa, there is considerable variation between regions, countries and cities across the sub-continent.
5. I am grateful to Joël Noret for reminding me that 'social capital' plays a far less prominent role in the argument of *Distinction* than economic, cultural and symbolic capitals (along with many other helpful comments).
6. 'Who you know' is crucial to the practice of power in many other places too.
7. In other conceptual lexicons this would be called 'class consciousness' and is key to the analytical distinction between 'class in itself' and 'class for itself'. The difference, however, is that in Bourdieu's framework there is no 'telos'. Classes on paper are nothing more than similar conditions of existence, they will not necessarily be mobilized as a real class.

8. This is the French term for decorative plasterwork or stucco, but it is used widely in the construction trade in Anglophone Cameroon.

References

Alpes, M. 2013. 'Imagining a Future in "Bush": Migration Aspirations at Times of Crisis in Anglophone Cameroon', *Identities: Global studies in Culture and Power* 21(3): 259–74.

Ardener, E. 1970. 'Witchcraft, Economics and the Continuity of Belief', in M. Douglas (ed.), *Witchcraft Confessions and Accusations*. London: Tavistock, pp. 141–60.

Bolt, M. 2016. 'Making Wills and Making Futures: Inheritance and the Formal Process of Middle-Class Reproduction in South Africa', ASAUK Conference, Robinson College, Cambridge, June 2016.

Bourdieu, P. 1984 [1979]. *Distinction: A Social Critique of the Judgment of Taste*. London: Routledge.

_____. 1985. 'The Social Space and the Genesis of Groups', *Theory and Society* 14(6): 723–44.

_____. 1989. 'Social Space and Symbolic Power', *Sociological Theory* 7(1): 14–25.

_____. 2005 [2000]. *The Social Structures of the Economy*. Cambridge: Polity.

Cheeseman, N. 2015. '"No Bourgeoisie, No Democracy?" The Political Attitudes of the Kenyan Middle Class', *Journal of International Development* 27: 647–64.

Courade, G. 1970. 'The Urban Development of Buea: An Essay in Social Geography', International Colloquium of the Centre National de la Recherche Scientifique -Social Science, Centre d'Etudes de Géographie Tropicale, Bordeaux.

Cox, R. 2016. 'What are Homes Made of? Building Materials, DIY and the Homeyness of Homes', *Home Cultures* 13(1): 63–82.

Davidoff, L., and C. Hall. 1987. *Family Fortunes*. London: Routledge.

Deloitte. 2014. *The Deloitte Consumer Review – Africa: A 21st Century View*. Retrieved 18 February 2019 from https://www2.deloitte.com/ng/en/pages/consumer-business/articles/consumer-review-africa.html.

Enaudeau, J. 2013. *In Search of the 'African Middle Class'*. Retrieved 18 February 2019 from http://africasacountry.com/tag/african-middle-classes/.

Fardon, R. 2006. *Lela in Bali: History through Ceremony in Cameroon*. Oxford: Berghahn.

Jacobs, K., and J. Malpas. 2013. 'Material Objects, Identity and the Home: Towards a Relational Housing Research Agenda', *Housing, Theory and Society* 30(3): 281–92.

Jazeel, T. 2019. 'Singularity. A Manifesto for Incomparable Geographies', *Singapore Journal of Tropical Geography* 40(1): 5–21.

Lentz, C. 2015. 'Elites or Middle Classes? Lessons from Transnational Research for the Study of Social Stratification in Africa', Working Papers of the Department of Anthropology and African Studies of the Johannes Gutenberg University Mainz, 161.

Melber, H. (ed.). 2016. *The Rise of Africa's Middle Class: Myths, Realities and Critical Engagements*. London: Zed Books.

Menkiti, I. 1984. 'Person and Community in African Traditional Thought', in R. Wright (ed.), *African Philosophy: An Introduction*. Lanham: University Press of America, pp. 171–81.

_____. 2004. 'On the Normative Conception of a Person', in K. Wiredu (ed.), *A Companion to African Philosophy*. Oxford: Blackwell, pp. 324–31.

Mercer, C. 2014. 'Middle Class Construction: Domestic Architecture, Aesthetics and Anxieties in Tanzania', *The Journal of Modern African Studies* 52(2): 227–50.

_____. 2016. 'Suburbs of Distinction: Middle Class Boundary Work in Dar es Salaam', ASAUK Conference, Robinson College, Cambridge, June 2016.

Mercer, C., B. Page and M. Evans. 2008. *Development and the African Diaspora: Place and the Politics of Home*. London: Zed Books.

Ncube, M., and C. Lufumpa (eds). 2015. *The Emerging Middle Class in Africa*. London: Routledge.

Ndjio, B. 2009. 'Migration, Architecture, and the Transformation of the Landscape in the Bamileke Grassfields of West Cameroon', *African Diaspora* 2: 73–100.

Neubert, D. 2016. 'Kenya – An Unconscious Middle Class? Between Regional Ethnic-Political Mobilization and Middle Class Lifestyles', in H. Melber (ed.), *The Rise of Africa's Middle Class: Myths, Realities and Critical Engagements*. London: Zed Books, pp. 110–27.

Page, B. 2011. 'Fear of Small Distances: Home Associations in Douala, Dar es Salaam and London', in K. Brickell and A. Datta (eds), *Translocal Geographies: Spaces, Places, Connections*. Farnham: Ashgate, pp. 127–44.

Page, B., and E. Sunjo. 2017. 'Africa's Middle Class: Building Houses and Constructing Identities in the Small Town of Buea, Cameroon', *Urban Geography* 39(1): 75–103.

Pelican, M. 2010. 'Local Perspectives on Transnational Relations of Cameroonian Migrants', in T. Grätz (ed.), *Mobility, Transnationalism and Contemporary African Societies*. Cambridge: Cambridge Scholars Publishing, pp. 178–91.

Spronk, R. 2012. *Ambiguous Pleasures: Sexuality and Middle Class Self-Perceptions in Nairobi*. Oxford: Berghahn.

Steinmetz, G. 2006. 'Bourdieu's Disavowal of Lacan: Psychoanalytic Theory and the Concepts of "Habitus" and "Symbolic Capital"', *Constellations* 13(4): 445–64.

St George, R. 2006. 'Home Furnishings and Domestic Interiors', in C. Tilley et al. (eds), *Handbook of Material Culture*. London: SAGE, pp. 221–29.

Tosh, J. 1999. *A Man's Place: Masculinity and the Middle Class Home in Victorian England*. New Haven: Yale University Press.

Walsh, K. 2006. 'British Expatriate Belongings: Mobile Homes and Transnational Homing', *Home Cultures* 3(2): 123–44.

Conclusion
A Multidimensional Approach to Social Positionality in Africa

Joël Noret

How can we account for the dynamics of African societies today, and, perhaps more prospectively, for the directions they are currently taking? In this book, we have argued that any attempt to answer these multifaceted issues must involve close attention to social positionality and social im/mobilities. Building on Bourdieu's notion of 'social space', we have suggested that an approach which pays attention to both the objective and subjective sides of social positionality, as well as to its multidimensionality and relational character, can shed light on key aspects of the dynamics of social im/mobility on the continent. In this regard, the volume has offered a theoretical perspective on, rather than a survey of, the multiple issues and challenges faced today by African societies. Before returning to some key aspects of this perspective, I will now briefly discuss the quantitative approaches to social mobilities in Africa that have emerged in the last decade. They bring to light some statistical 'evidence'. As such, they account for what can be known of evolutions in major 'objective structures' of the social world, as changes in occupational structures, or in levels of education. Yet, at the same time, they raise new questions.

Africa and the Measurement of Social Mobility

Some readers, especially those with a concern for the unity of the social sciences, might be surprised to have encountered so little discussion

---

Notes for this chapter begin on page 209.

of quantitative research up to now. Indeed, in the last decade, a few sociologically-minded development economists have produced attempts at measuring social mobility in different African settings throughout the colonial and postcolonial periods. Originating with the works of Pitirim Sorokin (1959 [1927]),[1] mobility tables exploring the patterns of transmission of social positions – of occupations, in fact – have attracted significant interest in sociology for decades. In the last forty years, they have played a notable role in quantitative debates around class analysis in the West (notably Goldthorpe 1980, Erikson and Goldthorpe 1992). They have also, since then, been echoed in research conducted in other parts of the world. And indeed, quantitative studies of intergenerational social mobility have multiplied across the global South in the last decades. Yet, for reasons diversely related to the weakness of statistical data available for most African countries and the relative absence of quantitative sociological research on the continent (with the notable exception of South Africa, for instance Seekings and Nattrass 2008), such research designs are still relatively recent and sparse in African studies.[2]

In Africa, the broadest move in this direction has probably been the comparative project of Bossuroy and Cogneau, who have attempted to measure social mobility in four different continental African countries and Madagascar. Relying on surveys designed (or inspired) by the World Bank since the 1980s, they compare the changes in occupational structures between generations, how the occupations of fathers and sons and levels of education are more or less closely related, and how different degrees of social mobility between countries can be interpreted. Fundamentally, they conclude, a more important political centralization in former French colonies, combined with different growth trajectories between countries, as well as with the importance of income dualism between 'farm' and 'non-farm' activities, result in different patterns of social mobility. In the end, 'Ghana and Uganda stand out as more fluid societies' when compared to Ivory Coast and Guinea, themselves more 'fluid' than Madagscar (2013: S107). Deploying an original research design in a continent where there has been very little quantitative research addressing intergenerational mobility, Bossuroy and Cogneau indisputably fill an important gap, and make a significant contribution to social research in Africa.

Yet, despite the pioneering dimension of their work, the methodological virtuosity of their statistical analysis, and their impressive command of a considerable mass of data, there are a few dead angles to such an exclusively quantitative approach. An extensive discussion would take us far beyond the format of these concluding remarks. Still, I would like to point a few issues, beyond the fact that they explicitly acknowledge a focus on the masculine population only, and that they work with data concerning cohorts almost exclusively born before 1970, which accounts for just above 20 per cent of the adult population of the continent today.

Firstly, as they themselves point out, Bossuroy and Cogneau's research design relies on surveys that have not made room for heterogeneity within the 'farm sector'. In addition, much of their research effort bears on the dynamics between 'farm' and 'non-farm' activities. This has different consequences. For instance, other strands of work – actually dating back to the 1970s' class analysis of African peasant worlds – have pointed out significant heterogeneity within the 'farm sector', and the importance of wage employment in African rural worlds (Rizzo, Kilama and Wuyts 2015). Some have even shown how rural labour dynamics were sometimes key in accounting for major political undercurrents – to say nothing of major dramas, such as the genocide in Rwanda (Vidal 1998, Verwimp 2005). Then there are questions, such as which rural actors have sons moving to which segments of the non-farm economy? Or, what are the most significant dynamics of social mobility in the 'non-farm sector'? These key questions remain largely unanswered. In fact, in the same way as some commentators on the recently revived 'middle class' debate in social theory have pointed out that the emphasis put on exploring the contours of the middle classes in Africa (or elsewhere) has left some key dynamics of capital accumulation out of the picture,[3] the extensive discussion of the farm/non-farm passages might well end up masking key dynamics of (re)production of an elite in the upper tiers of social space. In other words, we should remain vigilant about the fact that the focus on the dynamics between the farm and non-farm sectors does not turn into blinkers obliterating other crucial dynamics.

Secondly, another issue raised by such a measurement of social mobility resides in the unstable value over time of the occupational categories that are mobilized. Quantitative explorations of social mobility relying on nominal or categorical variables (as occupational or socio-professional categories) can indeed easily presuppose the stability of the value of the categories of analysis (as the farm/non-farm divide), while their significance can actually change as time passes. In other words, did the peasant condition mean the same thing fifty or sixty years ago on the one hand, and one or two decades ago on the other? Is being active in the farm sector when it encompasses the majority of a country's population the same as when the peasant condition is more clearly declining, both demographically and in terms of social recognition? In a nutshell, what part of social mobility do we account for when we focus exclusively on the objective side of social positionality – i.e. in recording peoples' objective occupation – without exploring its subjective side – i.e. the social recognition (or lack of) attached to these various positions? Obviously, being an

African peasant fifty or sixty years ago and nowadays is not equivalent in terms of social positionality, and remaining a peasant today can probably be considered as a downward move and a degraded status rather than as an absence of social mobility and the reproduction of a position.

In fact, social mobility – in the sense of altered 'life chances' – does not automatically follow from changes in sector of activity, nor can social immobility be easily equated with the intergenerational transmission of an occupation. Bourdieu's famous study of the social relegation of farmers from south-western France becoming 'unmarriageable' – unable to find wives on the local matrimonial market – in a generation, following the process of the local rural exodus (Bourdieu 2002 [1962]), provides one telling example of the importance of accounting for social positionality and social im/mobilities in a relational way, that is in considering the structural transformations of the social space in which people deploy their social strategies, or that they 'navigate', to borrow Vigh's metaphor (2009). Teachers provide an exemplary African case of how the value of occupational categories can change over generations. Indeed, in the decades after the African independences, primary and secondary school teachers were generally seen as an intellectual elite. By comparison, in the post-adjustment Africa of the last two decades, the social conditions and status of teachers have significantly diversified, and, overall, declined. Those with the status of full civil servant now represent a minority in many countries, while the – younger – heirs of the Structural Adjustment Programmes form a kind of teaching 'precariat' – to borrow Standing's term (2011) – without much brighter economic prospects.

In fact, some quantitative studies conducted at the national level have partly avoided the difficulties derived from a reliance on nominal or categorical variables alone, and also provide information on intergenerational linkages of social positionalities. Building on data produced on descendants of the first generations of pupils of the colonial era, Wantchekon, Klašnja and Novta (2015) have recently shown the multidimensional effects of education 'on living standards, occupation and political participation' over generations in Benin. Lambert, Ravallion and van de Walle (2014) have explored intergenerational social mobility in Senegal, analysing the economic importance of the intergenerational transmission of education, inheritance and occupation, and their effects on expenditure levels in the current generation. Azomahou and Yitbarek (2016) have estimated the importance of intergenerational linkages in educational levels in some African countries, highlighting the weight of parents' educational experience on children's educational outcomes.[4]

These studies remain focused on the objective side of social positionality, and rely almost exclusively on statistical regressions – which

tend to insist on the weight of specific variables rather than on structural causalities and effects of structures (Bourdieu 1979: 113–21). Yet, as
with Bossuroy and Cogneau's comparative project, these works document important changes, for instance on educational levels or (less convincingly perhaps) occupational structures. Critically, some of these
researches also explore intergenerational connexions. In this volume, we
have offered nothing comparable to these massive statistical enterprises
of measurement of 'social mobility'.[5] Yet, by emphasizing the necessity to
hold together the objective and the subjective sides of social positionality,
as well as its relationality and multidimensionality, our perspective offers
productive lines of thought along which dynamics of social im/mobilies
on the continent can be explored. On this note, let us return to the chapters and look back at what insights emerge from the volume.

For a Multidimensional Approach to Social Positionality

The variegated dynamics of social im/mobilies outlined throughout
this book largely point to the interest of a multidimensional approach to
social positionality. In overall ascending or descending social trajectories,
different forms of capital are regularly entwined, and combine to make
social groups move in different upper or lower regions of the social space.

Let's start with a Central African case. In Benjamin Rubbers' account
of the mirroring trajectories of white businessmen and (black) workers
of the Congolese national mining company sacked after the company's
bankruptcy at the turn of the 2000s, the contrasting economic routes of the
two groups cannot be understood without considering the intersection of
their respective economic and social capitals. The resources of extraversion of the white entrepreneurs – the strength of their racial 'weak ties', to
put it a bit differently, and their ability to rely on trustworthy partners –
on the one hand, and the reliance on state wages and company-bound
social networks on the other, produced quite different outcomes. While
the former have benefited from the Congolese state's partial collapse in
the 1990s and are now trusting economically dominant positions in the
upper tiers of the regional social space, the latter have experienced more
or less acute social downgrading. Yet, the different amounts of the compensations in cash that former managers and former workers received
when their contracts were terminated resulted in different capacities to
invest, and in diverging 'reconversion strategies' (Bourdieu 1979: 145–85)
amidst the changing circumstances they were facing (see also Rubbers
2017). Furthermore, as Rubbers goes on to explore, a multidimensional
analysis of social positions also sheds new light on the internal dynamic

of the white community itself. The new white elite of the last decades is made of businessmen and no longer of colonial executives and other professionals. Subsequently, the importance of cultural capital has now declined in the white 'community'. In Rubbers' words, distinction practices in this social world now revolve 'around houses, cars, mobile phones, holiday destinations, dinner invitations, parties and the size of domestic staff'.

Conversion processes between forms of capitals and distinction practices also figure prominently in Ben Page's chapter on the cultural production of domestic architecture and design in Western Cameroon. As he points out in his study of Buea's house owners, the social trajectories and structures of capitals of upwardly mobile subjects can differ in notable ways. In a region where, as in many other places throughout Africa,[6] building a house represents an emblematic social achievement and sign of economic success, prosperous individuals reveal different levels of connection to the State, of political capital, of autochthony and of (transnational) 'network capital', in John Urry's terms (Urry 2007). They represent different possible routes to the upper regions of the space of social positions, where their variegated ways of inhabiting these upper strata are reflected in different domestic architectures and interior design.

Approaching the social world from the perspective of a multidimensional social space also draws attention to the uncertainty of some social hierarchies. Continuing a conversation begun by Burawoy and Von Holdt (2012) about the relevance of Bourdieu's theoretical apparatus to explore the South African situation, Max Bolt explores the fragility of 'symbolic orders' on the Zimbabwean-South African border. Here, the education and cultural capital of some urban, middle class migrants who have been students or teachers in a former life is confronted with the economic uncertainty grounded in their new condition as temporary workers. On the border farms, the black labour force is, indeed, dominated by older, more settled male workers, with Bolt not losing sight of the local forms of a gender bar. These men are better paid, benefit from more economic stability and enjoy more freedom of movement on the border, as well as more comfortable lifestyles, even though they might lack a proper school education. Unlike seasonal workers who make a virtue out of necessity by contemplating more open-ended economic strategies, these permanent farm workers can also plan for the future from more stable ground.

Cultural capital plays a key role in Bourdieu's argument on class analysis. Not only is it one of the essential social powers that Bourdieu identifies as a differentiating force in French society, but it has also inspired the (debatable) framing of Bourdieu's contribution to class analysis as a 'cultural turn'. Yet, the salience of cultural capital in the production and distribution of social positions in Africa appears less immediately obvious in different respects. Not only, however, does a multidimensional approach to social positionality allow the unpacking of the complexity of social moves and the changes in the terms of trade between forms of capital. It also helps to theorize multidimensional dynamics of domination, where objective, material conditions of existence on the one hand, and subjective processes of categorization on the other, can reinforce each other in the making of social divisions. In Kano, as Hannah Hoechner demonstrates, the social immobility of students in the 'traditional' Qur'anic schools at the bottom of the urban social hierarchy stems from both their social origins and objective economic poverty – most coming from poor rural households – and the social contempt for their style of religious education, now imbued with images of backwardness. In different respects, this is yet another instance of a much wider phenomenon: African rural worlds are now commonly both marked by economic deprivation and considered with a sense of distance by the more urban, educated and less poor or more prosperous (if only moderately) segments of the population. This story has been told many times, from the growing 'distance (and inequality) between village and city' (Geschiere 1995: 59) in Cameroonian funerals to the backward connotation that rural 'tradition' has among young Nairobian professionals cultivating a sense of cultural *avant-garde* (Spronk 2012: 83–86), to mention just two among many other possible cases.[7] In all these instances, a comprehensive account of the dynamics of social positions and social im/mobilities actually requires the holding together of the objective and subjective sides of social positionality, as both a set of conditions of existence, and a sense of one's place (and of the others' place) in the social world.

What is more, working against a 'reproductionist bias' in Bourdieu's reception (Gorski 2013, cf also the introduction to this volume), a multidimensional approach to the space of social positions allows us to address structural social transformations such as the emergence of new social 'regions'. In their chapters, Gabriella Körling and Fawzia Mazanderani explore in different ways how the expansion of school education has affected the production of social space in Niger and in South Africa. For different historical reasons, the provision of education in both countries was limited until the last decades, when the end of Apartheid in the South African case, and the 'Education for All' agenda in Niger's case, led to a new scramble for education. Besides the specificities of each country, there is a more general dynamic at play here. Africa is now regularly considered to have entered another phase of school expansion, with a general increase in both the number of pupils and overall education level (Charton 2015).

Against this backdrop, as more and more graduates progressively enter the labour market, we see the relationship between education and social mobility becoming more sinuous, and the trajectories of youth endowed with some educational capital becoming more diverse. School titles remain important in framing 'life chances', in Weber's words. In this volume, however, Körling, Mazanderani, as well as Rubbers analyse how convoluted the relationship of education to upward social trajectories can be. As Mazanderani shows in her chapter, only a small proportion of secondary school graduates from poor, rural backgrounds end up graduating from universities in South Africa, even though their educational achievements largely surpass those of their parents. Yet, the imaginary of upward social mobility that is embedded in a school career leaves those who do not achieve a sufficient upward social move with a feeling of failure, and an urge to leave their rural homesteads, in order to avoid being seen doing 'township maintenance' in the locality where they grew up. Unsurprisingly, the increase in the number of graduates goes together with a diversification of their social trajectories. In fact, in recent decades this has not only led to a form of relative devaluation of school titles, already well-documented, but also to the emergence of a new (and growing) 'region' in African social spaces – that of precarious graduates (also see Mains 2007).

Indeed, in the first decades of postcolonial Africa, school and even more so university graduates were unambiguously engaged in upward mobility. They populated the upper regions of the new national social spaces. Yet, along with the expansion of education and the banalization of school titles, less prosperous and upwardly mobile school graduates became more common and salient figures of African societies. In a nutshell, African social spaces witnessed the emergence of (young) literate poor, or those achieving only 'fleeting social mobility', to use Camfield and Monteith's formula in this volume, or a form of 'moderate prosperity', as Dominique Darbon (2014) puts it in a perhaps slightly euphemizing way in his characterization of the lower segments of the so-called African middle classes. These precarious school graduates can still present a notable difference with the illiterate poor in terms of cultural capital, yet their social move towards literacy also diverges from clear-cut upward social mobility and cannot be easily represented in terms of a unidimensional social ladder. On the Zimbabwe-South African border, some of these Zimbabwean graduates end up picking fruit alongside less educated workers. Yet, they continue to display a sense of cultural distance towards manual work, as Bolt evokes in his contribution.

Still, despite mitigated 'generational conditions' (Chauvel 1998), university graduates retain better economic chances than less educated youth in many African countries, as development economists have shown with some consistency (for instance Kuepie et al. 2009, De Herdt et al. 2008). The situations of mere school graduates are more diverse. Obviously, some school graduates continue onto a career in the civil service, as was the case for one of the main figures in Körling's case study, who finally became a policeman after a few unsuccessful attempts. However, others will only access the more precarious jobs created in public administrations in the wake of the Structural Adjustment Programmes, typically in the education sector. Here we find the new teaching 'precariat', with much less employment security, supporting the current expansion of education throughout the continent. Others again will try their luck as small businessmen, as in Camfield and Monteith's study of Kampalan entrepreneurs. However, here the possibility to draw on social capital – especially within kin networks – proves key in starting viable businesses that have a chance to resist the regular turbulences of economic careers in the difficult environment of African informal economies.

In fact, education still represents a significant resource insofar as it can be converted to access formal, qualified employment. This indeed eases social subjects' access to profitable forms of economic straddling, allowing them to combine diverse sources of income, a widespread economic strategy deployed for decades at different scales, 'both at the top and the bottom of the heap' (Cooper 1981: 43), throughout African social spaces. However, besides the straddling practices and open-ended strategies of the self-employed that Camfield and Monteith report, the economic possibilities of men and women also differ sometimes significantly. For women especially, access to income-generating activities can depend on forms of marital union. In Maputo, a 'divided city' with a sharp spatialization of social inequalities (see also Tvedten 2018), Inge Tvedten reminds us that the analysis of African urban spaces and the interpretation of the distribution of social positions cannot be carried out without sustained attention to gender dynamics. Here, the progressive emergence of women in the Mozambican public sphere and their growing economic independence progress hand in hand (also Archambault 2017: 92–94). Women who can be counted as household heads tend to benefit more from this dynamic, as their economic strategies and daily activities are not impeded by the mundane workings of masculine domination in everyday domestic life.

As such, Tvedten reminds us that categorical differences must be considered seriously when we attempt to account for the distribution and the dynamics of social positions and life chances. The multi-layered workings of masculine domination – which can operate at both institutional levels, for instance when women have less rights than men, and in everyday practice – provide a telling scene of this phenomenon. However, this book has also hinted at other categories of difference which play major roles in the dynamics of social positionality across African social spaces. The racial barrier is evoked in the chapters by Max Bolt and Benjamin Rubbers. The Congolese copperbelt evoked by Rubbers is, furthermore, a region where – as in so many others – ethnicity can represent a significant social division (Vinckel 2015). The importance of citizenship, as well as autochthony-related issues, are in fact hinted at in different contributions. Max Bolt's chapter probably provides the most exemplary instance in this volume of the excluding side of citizenship, 'a inherited property' (Brubaker 2015: 19–21) which regularly works as 'capital' too in a world where borders remain crucial economic barriers. Indeed, the lack of regular South African citizenship largely contributes to the precariousness of Zimbabwean fruit pickers and packers on the South African farms immediately south of the border, in a national space where the divide between citizens and those excluded from national citizenship intersects in complex ways with 'ultra-rapid class differentiation' (Fourchard and Segatti 2015: 7; also Monson 2015). In the last chapter, however, returning to the integrative dimension of categories of belonging, Ben Page exemplifies with true verve how autochthony and quests of political notability grounded in ethnicity matter when it comes to understanding local domestic architectures and to account for some of the possible ways in which middle classness is deployed in Western Cameroon. Here, as in other parts of Africa, interior space and furniture to accommodate guests (and clients) properly represent key dimensions of notables' displays of social status, and a *sine qua non* condition of their political ambitions.

The question of social mobility and immobility represents a central issue for the social sciences, as it is intimately woven in with the crucial problem represented by how the social is (re)produced and perpetuated, as well as altered and changed. In this volume, we have argued that treating societies as social spaces, produced by different, intersecting systems of differences and inequalities, provided a productive lens with which to explore social im/mobilities. 'Individuals do not move about in social space in a random way' (Bourdieu 1984 [1979]: 104), and their possible moves are grounded in, and framed by their positionality. In this view, deploying a multidimensional and relational approach to social positionality, where one is also attentive to both its objective and subjective sides, represents a fruitful analytical path to explore social im/mobilities on the African continent today. As the different chapters in this volume have shown, the idea of a multidimensional social space helps to theorize the intersection of social powers in the production of social positionality, processes of conversion between forms of capitals, changing terms of trade between them over time, as well as 'reconversion strategies'. As a correlate, accounting for social space as multidimensional also helps to unpack social differentiation beyond the idea of a unilinear, or unidimensional social ladder. Next, a relational approach to social positionality and im/mobilities proves essential to think about positions as a system of differences, and to consider their value and their meaning relationally: being a peasant when it represents the condition of the majority and a well-regarded occupation can be very different to being a peasant when it represents a socially and demographically declining status, looked down upon by an educated 'elite'. Finally, an approach bridging the objective and the subjective sides to social positionality draws attention to the relationships between conditions of existence and subjectivities, objective inequalities and meanings, and their possible reinforcements or contrapuntal expressions. The contributions to this volume have explored diverse possible routes in this direction.

Joël Noret is Associate Professor of Anthropology at the Université libre Bruxelles. He has conducted most of his fieldwork in southern Benin, where he worked on funerals, religious change and the memory of slavery. In the last few years, he has started investigating social inequalities in education, combining ethnography with survey research to explore the making of unequal lives. His publications include *Deuil et Funérailles dans le Bénin Méridional: Enterrer à Tout Prix* (2010), *Mort et Dynamiques Sociales au Katanga* (co-authored with Pierre Petit, 2011), and *Funerals in Africa: Explorations of a Social Phenomenon* (co-edited with Michael Jindra, 2011).

Notes

1. Pitirim Sorokin was the founder of the sociology of social mobility, and it is perhaps worth remembering here that he was also the first to make a systematic use of the notions of 'social position', 'social space', and to characterize the social world as 'a universe of many dimensions' (Sorokin 1959: 7), within which both vertical and horizontal moves are possible.
2. I would like to thank Pierre Desmarez for his help on this particular (short) section of discussion of quantitative studies.
3. This has been a recurring argument in the recent sociology of class (for instance Savage et al. 2015, Therborn 2012). In Africa, variants of this point have been made notably by Melber 2017 or Southall 2018.
4. Additionally, there are also a few quantitative studies of intergenerational mobility specifically dedicated to South Africa (e.g. Lam 1999, Louw et al. 2007, Nimubona and Vencatachellum 2007). See, however, Louw et al. (2007) on intergenerational educational

mobility in South Africa, Lambert et al. (2014) on intergenerational social mobility and inequality in Senegal, and Wantchekon et al. (2015) on the intergenerational economic and educational effects of unequal school provision in colonial Dahomey (now Benin).
5. And we certainly have our own dead angles. We have for instance not addressed demographic issues and the debate around the 'demographic dividend', the social differentiation of fertility rates, and the current evolutions of 'dependency ratios' on the continent.
6. See for instance Mercer (2014) on Tanzania, Tall (1994) and Dia (2007) on Senegal, van der Geest (1998) or Pellow (2003) on Ghana.
7. This should not obliterate the fact that imaginations of and actual relations to the countryside among urban dwellers also need to be understood in view of social positionality. In Maputo for instance, those poorer and less educated groups that are less able to identify with the modernity of the city and the urban also hold different views of the rural (Tvedten 2018). Simultaneously, however, some disenfranchised urban social identities are also constructed in direct opposition to the rural, as in Abidjan youth's famous opposition between the two social prototypes of the – astute – urban *nouchi* and the – naïve – rural *gaou* (Newell 2012).

References

Archambault, J. 2017. *Mobile Secrets: Youth, Intimacy and the Politics of Pretense in Mozambique*. Chicago: The University of Chicago Press.
Azomahou, T., and E. Yitbarek. 2016. 'Intergenerational Education Mobility in Africa. Has Progress Been Inclusive?', World Bank Group, Policy Research Working Paper 7843.
Bossuroy, T., and D. Cogneau. 2013. 'Social Mobility in Five African Countries', *Review of Income and Wealth* 59(1): 84–110.
Bourdieu, P. 1979. *La Distinction*. Paris: Éditions de Minuit.
_____. 1984 [1979]. *Distinction: A Social Critique of the Judgement of Taste*, trad. R. Nice. London: Routledge & Kegan Paul.
_____. 2002 [1962]. *Le Bal des Célibataires: Crise de la Société Paysanne en Béarn*. Paris: Seuil.
Brubaker, R. 2015. *Grounds for Difference*. Harvard: Harvard University Press.
Burawoy, M., and K. von Holdt. 2012. *Conversations with Bourdieu: The Johannesburg Moment*. Johannesburg: Wits University Press.
Charton, H. 2015. 'Penser la Fabrique de l'Ecole comme un Objet Politique', *Politique Africaine* 139: 7–21.
Chauvel, L. 1998. *Le Destin des Générations: Structure Sociale et Cohortes en France au XXe Siècle*. Paris: Presses Universitaires de France.
Cooper, F. 1981. 'Africa and the World Economy', *Social Science and Humanistic Research on Africa* 24(2–3): 1–86.
Darbon, D. 2014. 'Nom de Code "Classes Moyennes en Afrique": Les Enjeux Politiques d'une Labellisation de Groupes Invisibles et Vulnérables', in D. Darbon and C. Toulabor (eds), *L'Invention des Classes Moyennes Africaines: Enjeux Politiques d'une Catégorie Incertaine*. Paris: Karthala, pp. 15–59.
De Herdt, T., W. Marivoet and S. Marysse. 2008. 'Political Transition in DRC: How Did Kinshasa's Households Fare?', *African Development Review* 20(3): 400–25.

Dia, H. 2007. 'Les Investissements des Migrants dans la Vallée du Fleuve Sénégal: Confiance et Conflits d'Intérêt', *Revue Européenne des Migrations Internationales* 23(3): 29–49.

Erikson, R., and J.H. Goldthorpe. 1992. *The Constant Flux: A Study of Class Mobility in Industrial Societies*. Oxford: Clarendon Press.

Fourchard, L., and A. Segatti. 2015. 'Introduction: Of Xenophobia and Citizenship: The Everyday Politics of Exclusion and Inclusion in Africa', *Africa* 85(1): 2–12.

Geschiere, P. 1995. 'Funerals and Belonging: Different Patterns in South Cameroon', *African Studies Review* 48(2): 45–64.

Goldstone, B., and J. Obarrio (eds). 2017. *African Futures: Essays on Crisis, Emergence, and Possibility*. Chicago: The University of Chicago Press.

Goldthorpe, J.H. 1980. *Social Mobility and Class Structure in Modern Britain*. Oxford: Clarendon Press.

Gorski, P. 2013. 'Bourdieu as a Theorist of Change', in P. Gorski (ed.), *Bourdieu and Historical Analysis*. Durham: Duke University Press, pp. 1–18.

Kuepie, M., C.J. Nordman and F. Roubaud. 2009. 'Education and Earnings in Urban West Africa', *Journal of Comparative Economics* 37: 491–515.

Lam, D. 1999. *Generating Extreme Inequality: Schooling, Earnings, and Intergenerational Transmission of Human Capital in South Africa and Brazil*. Report 99–439, Michigan University. Ann Arbor: Population Studies Center.

Lambert, S., M. Ravallion and D. van de Walle. 2014. 'Intergenerational Mobility and Interpersonal Inequality in an African Economy', *Journal of Development Economics* 110: 327–44.

Louw, M., S. van der Berg and D. Yu. 2007. 'Convergence of a Kind: Educational Attainment and Intergenerational Social Mobility in South Africa', *South African Journal of Economics* 75(3): 548–71.

Mains, D. 2007. 'Neoliberal Times: Progress, Boredom, and Shame among Young Men in Urban Ethiopia', *American Ethnologist* 34(4): 659–73.

Melber, H. 2017. 'The African Middle Class(es) – In the Middle of What?', *Review of African Political Economy* 44(151): 142–54.

Mercer, C. 2014. 'Middle Class Construction: Domestic Architecture, Aesthetics and Anxieties in Tanzania', *The Journal of Modern African Studies* 52(2): 227–50.

Monson, T. 2015. 'Everyday Politics and Collective Mobilization Against Foreigners in a South African Shack Settlement', *Africa* 85(1): 131–53.

Newell, S. 2012. *The Modernity Bluff: Crime, Consumption and Citizenship in Côte d'Ivoire*. Chicago: The University of Chicago Press.

Nimubona, A.-D., and D. Vencatachellum. 2007. 'Intergenerational Education Mobility of Black and White South Africans', *Journal of Population Economics* 20: 149–82.

Page, B., and E. Sunjo. 2018. 'Africa's Middle Class: Building Houses and Constructing Identities in the Small Town of Buea, Cameroon', *Urban Geography* 39(1): 75–103.

Pellow, D. 2003. 'New Spaces in Accra: Transnational Houses', *City & Society* 15(1): 59–86.

Rizzo, M., B. Kilama and M. Wuyts. 2015. 'The Invisibility of Wage Employment in Statistics on the Informal Economy in Africa: Causes and Consequences', *The Journal of Development Studies* 51(2): 149–61.

Rubbers, B. 2017. 'Towards a Life of Poverty and Uncertainty? The Livelihoods Strategies of Gécamines Workers after Retrenchment in the DRC', *Review of African Political Economy* 152: 189–203.

Savage, M. et al. 2015. *Social Class in the 21ˢᵗ Century*. London: Pelican.

Seekings, J., and N. Nattrass. 2008. *Class, Race, and Inequality in South Africa*. New Haven: Yale University Press.

Sorokin, P. 1959 [1927]. *Social and Cultural Mobility*. Glencoe: The Free Press.

Southall, R. 2018. '(Middle-)Class Analysis in Africa: Does it Work?', *Review of African Political Economy* 157: 467–77.

Spronk, R. 2012. *Ambiguous Pleasures: Sexuality and Middle Class Self Perceptions in Nairobi*. Oxford: Berghahn.

Standing, G. 2011. *The Precariat: The New Dangerous Class*. London: Bloomsbury.

Tall, S.M. 1994. 'Les Investissements Immobiliers à Dakar des Émigrants Sénégalais', *Revue Européenne des Migrations Internationales* 10(3): 137–51.

Therborn, G. 2012. 'Class in the 21st Century', *New Left Review* 78: 5–29.

Tvedten, I. 2018. '"It's All about Money": Urban-Rural Spaces and Relations in Maputo, Mozambique', *Canadian Journal of African Studies* 13: 1–16.

Urry, John. 2007. *Mobilities*. Cambridge: Polity Press.

Van der Geest, S. 1998. '"Yebisa Wo Fie": Growing Old and Building a House in the Akan Culture of Ghana', *Journal of Cross-Cultural Gerontology* 13(4): 333–59.

Verwimp, P. 2005. 'An Economic Profile of Peasant Perpetrators of Genocide: Micro-Level Evidence from Rwanda', *Journal of Development Economics* 77(2): 297–323.

Vidal, C. 1998. 'Questions sur le Rôle des Paysans durant le Génocide des Rwandais Tutsis', *Cahiers d'Etudes Africaines* 150/152, 38(2–4): 331–45.

Vigh, H. 2009. 'Motion Squared: A Second Look at the Concept of Social Navigation', *Anthropological Theory* 9(4): 419–38.

Vinckel, S. 2015. 'Violence and Everyday Interactions between Katangese and Kasaians: Memory and Elections in Two Katanga Cities', *Africa: The Journal of the International African Institute* 85(1): 78–101.

Wantchekon, L., M. Klašnja and N. Novta. 2015. 'Education and Human Capital Externalities: Evidence from Colonial Benin', *The Quarterly Journal of Economics* 130(2): 703–57.

Appendix 1
Sample Characteristics

Name / Pseudonym	Education	Source of capital/assets/ savings/employees	Marital status in 2012	Marital status in 2016	Occupation in 2012	Occupation in 2015	Constraints
Market vendors							
Hadija Nikuze (F, 26, Rwandan and Kenyan parents)	Never went to school	**Capital:** husband (5000 UGX) **Assets:** household goods only **Savings:** 2,000 to ROSCA every Thursday and Saturday for supplies; 'Small debts', feels too risky to take loan to develop business **Employees/ apprentices:** no	Married (polyg)	Separated (partner returned to wife), one child (with another man who died)	Market vendor – fruit, tomatoes, cabbage, sells silverfish and homemade groundnut sauce	Stall given away by landlord so works two days on friend's stall making 15,000 UGX per day	Own and daughter's respiratory problems; daughter struggling in education after she repeated a year; house demolished by KCCA as part of slum clearance and possessions stolen. No place to sell produce.
Joan Nyamugisha (F, 24)	Completed primary	**Capital:** mother (first business), step-father (second business) **Assets:** household goods only **Savings:** saves in kind in a ROSCA for soap and sugar **Employees/ apprentices:** no	Married (two children)	Separated (husband mistreating her) and staying with female friend (two children)	Market vendor – bananas and tomatoes (moved to Kampala as house girl to her aunt then started own business)	Sells oranges, lemons and tangerines wholesale	Can only work at night if it isn't raining as she doesn't have a stall and has no space to sell in or store goods. She sometimes gets chased away and has heard the market will be sold. Competition is high and quality of goods variable. Husband doesn't support children.

Monica Awor (F, 26, Kenyan parents)	Completed O-level	**Capital**: uncle, mother (took over stall) **Assets**: mother's house, grandparents' land in Kenya **Savings**: saves 1,000 UGX per day but does not give it to a group **Employees/ apprentices**: no	Single	Single (moved to sister's house after father died in 2014)	Market vendor – fish, inherited stall from mother	Market vendor – fish. Rents land at home for a tomato stall.	Business was supported by maternal uncle (50,000 UGX per month) but this stopped in 2015; reduction in fish stocks and previous supplier arrested; death of mother who was funding her food processing course, which she had to stop; death of father who accommodated her and gave her 80,000 UGX per year.
Mariam Mutesi (F, 23)	Completed O-level	**Capital**: husband, savings **Assets**: 3 goats and 50 chickens looked after by her mother **Savings**: doesn't save in a group or take loans **Employees/ apprentices**: no	Married (one child)	Married (two children – one 7 months)	Market vendor – bananas (previously sold clothes in her uncle's shop and worked for one year in a restaurant)	Market vendor – bananas (now sells 20–25 bunches rather than 5 each day), other fruit and veg, charcoal	Prices for bananas have gone up (changing climate) and charcoal (forestry laws). Lost 80,000 UGX of Matoke when she took a week off to give birth to her daughter.

Name / Pseudonym	Education	Source of capital/assets/ savings/employees	Marital status in 2012	Marital status in 2016	Occupation in 2012	Occupation in 2015	Constraints
Agnes Uwamahoro (F, 30, Rwandan)	Completed A-level	**Capital**: first husband, loan from 'Silver Association' (household goods collateral) **Assets**: household goods only **Savings**: used to save every month in a market cash around **Employees/apprentices**: no	Married (one child)	Separated from husband and temporarily moved back to Rwanda after father's death (one child and pregnant with second), then met wealthy new husband, remarried and moved to a prosperous area	Market vendor – selling tomatoes, onions, beans, and cabbage (previously sold clothes in Rwanda, but business was less profitable than her current one as it was heavily taxed)	Gave up stall on moving to Rwanda and then to look after child. Now they have a new maid she considered finding a new stall but doesn't need to work.	
Shops							
Janet Mukamwezi (F, 31, born Tanzania, studied in Rwanda and Tanzania)	Started primary (stopped in P7)	**Capital**: loan from friends, including fridge, husband supported household expenses while business getting going **Assets**: fridge **Savings**: doesn't save as income not stable, but member of cash around **Employees/apprentices**: no	Married (four children)	Separated (four children went with the father as she couldn't afford to support them, new baby remained with her – looked after by niece)	Dairy shop in home selling milk and bread; also sells homemade yoghurt and juice and boiled water for drinking	Sells tea on the road to Busega	Her big freezer broke and she got a smaller one which broke too so had to stop selling cold drinks and yoghurt. Milk is expensive during dry season so profits reduce. Rarely sees children and worries about them.

Name	Education	Capital / Assets / Savings / Employees	Marriage	Children	Business	Second business / other	Notes
Rose Mbagudde (F, 32)	Completed primary	**Capital:** aunt (inherited store), brother, loans/ stock on credit. **Assets:** equipment, store, chicken rearing. **Savings:** saves 10,000 UGX per week in a SACCO and is a member of a burial society. **Employees/ apprentices:** yes	Married to Jimmy who already had a wife and children	Married to Jimmy (five children, two from this marriage, three from her previous marriage)	Runs poultry feed business and rears chickens – has 3,300 layers and 600 broilers (started selling bananas and making banana juice, then worked in a salon and as a waitress, but stopped due to chest pain, finally worked with her aunt in her poultry feed business before starting her own)	Runs poultry feed business and rears chickens (has a second store which she owns outright)	Fire destroyed everything and it took one month before they could reopen. Needs to borrow to pay off debts and only had three-month lease on current shop as her landlord plans to sell it. Rent is high and premises not secure. Mother paralysed after boda boda accident – can't work in shop and needs constant care.
Jimmy Muwoya (M, 28)	Completed primary (n.b. in first interview he said he studied to S4, in second to P7)	**Capital:** uncle (inherited store), bank loans. **Assets:** equipment, plot of land. **Savings:** saves regularly. **Employees/ apprentices:** yes	Married to Rose and another woman (four children)	Married (five children aged 3–15)	Runs poultry and animal feed business which he took over from his uncle, including milling and mixing, and rears chickens in Wakiso district	Runs reduced poultry and animal feed business with Rose, frequently borrowing from neighbours. Sold chickens to replace one of the machines.	Fire in old market in 2013 (second time this had happened), lost all his stock and 3 machines. Moved to smaller space with higher rent, off main road so no passing trade. SACCO collapsed after fire as everyone withdrew funds.
Amina Sserwanga (F, 29)	Batchelors	**Capital:** n/a **Assets:** none **Savings:** none mentioned **Employees/ apprentices:** n/a	Married to Moses	Married (two children)	Husband runs an electronics shop (see below)	Husband runs an electronics shop (see below)	Cost of funeral and closing shop for one week affected business. Electricity frequently goes off.

Name / Pseudonym	Education	Source of capital/assets/ savings/employees	Marital status in 2012	Marital status in 2016	Occupation in 2012	Occupation in 2015	Constraints
Moses Sserwanga (M, 28)	Completed A-level and trained in electronics	**Capital:** friend, mother, bank loan **Assets:** equipment and goods, plot of land with rentals **Savings:** saves in a ROSCA every week **Employees/ apprentices:** yes	Married	Married (one year old son died in an accident at the shop; now has twin girls aged 6 months)	Runs an electronics sale and repair shop (sold radios with his uncle while growing up and then worked in a repair shop while studying before buying his own with financial support from a friend and his mother)	Runs an electronics sale and repair shop and has taken on the adjoining shop so space 4–5 times bigger and can display higher value goods. Selling mobile money and air time.	
Musa Kyingi (M, 40)	Completed primary and the first two years of secondary school	**Capital:** uncle, savings **Assets:** eight rentals, lorry, motorcycle, car, one goat and two kids **Savings:** has two savings groups where they save 5,000 UGX per day and 50,000 UGX per week respectively **Employees/ apprentices:** yes	Married (four children?)	Married (six children aged 1.5–19 years, two from his first marriage and four from his second)	Butcher – set up business with paternal uncle after doing casual labour, trading offal and working as a boda boda driver	Butcher – business has expanded as he used to sell 40–45 kg per day and now sells 50 kg and 100 kg on Saturday. Rents eight rooms. Has one goat and two kids. Owns a lorry, which is managed by a driver, a motorcycle and car.	Currently not experiencing any problems but in the past reported theft, fraud (land title), KCCA regulations around handling meat and the increasing cost of meat

Name	Education	Capital/Assets/Savings/Employees	Marital	Marital	Business (start)	Business (now)	Problems/needs
Regina Mukalubiga (F, 37)	Completed primary	**Capital**: brother (100,000 UGX), husband (100,000 UGX), BRAC loans (×4). **Assets**: has bought a plot and wants to build rental properties. Has 10 goats with husband's family. **Savings**: has a savings group. **Employees/apprentices**: no	Married (four children)	Separated – little support from husband (five children, two from first husband)	Runs 'House of Plastics' roadside kiosk which sells plastics, wooden spoons, glasses, and clay plates. Start-up capital from brother and husband).	Runs 'House of Plastics' from a room she built in a building behind the kiosk. Business is better as she has more space to display different and higher value stock, e.g. stoves.	Too many people selling plastics and Kenyan plastics are poor quality. Interest for credit from BRAC now too high.
Services							
Juliet Nakiwala (F, 37)	Completed O-level	**Capital**: brother (500,000 UGX), husband found premises and sewing machine to rent. **Assets**: equipment, poultry business, own home with three rentals attached, plot of land. **Savings**: members of savings group and saves 50,000 UGX per month. **Employees/apprentices**: yes	Married	Married (four children – three are husband's)	Tailor (started working by her roadside with her sister-in-law, then her husband rented her a verandah and then her own room)	Tailor – expanded premises when tenant next door left, giving her a new area to fit clients and display materials. Bought a sewing machine to do finishing. Runs a poultry business with stepson's help. Currently building a house and has three rooms to rent.	Historical problems with theft and electricity costs, now resolved. Needs to look further for customers now business has expanded and currently very seasonal with peaks at Christmas and school start times. Needs to pay gatekeeper to get tenders.

Name / Pseudonym	Education	Source of capital/assets/ savings/employees	Marital status in 2012	Marital status in 2016	Occupation in 2012	Occupation in 2015	Constraints
Aida Nassozi (F, 26)	Completed primary and studied to S2, but stopped when pregnant	**Capital:** father, aunt lent sewing machine **Assets:** cow and two calves, sewing machine. Plans to soon buy a large plot to build rental accommodation. **Savings:** in two ROSCAs – 3,500 UGX per day **Employees/ apprentices:** no (planning to take on)	Divorced (2009)	Divorced (two children aged 7 and 10 with different fathers – no support from them)	Tailor (repairs and second-hand shoes), learned tailoring from her aunt after having her first child and started own business after divorce	Tailor – has added dresses, Bitengi for holidays, and new shoes so feels business is growing. Owns cow with two calves in the village.	Youngest child fell ill and cost 300,000 UGX to treat
Eria Kato (M, 24)	Completed O-level and did a vocational course in welding and fabrication	**Capital:** brother, friend, group loan from Pride microfinance **Assets:** equipment, incl. welding machine **Savings:** has pension and is part of savings group with colleagues from work (saves 100,000 UGX per month) **Employees/ apprentices:** yes	Married	Married (two daughters aged 2 and 7 months)	Runs a salon inherited from his brother (could not find a secure, well-paid welding job)	Has formal sector employment at Martplex as a welder during the day and runs salon in evenings and Sundays with help from a friend (they profit-share)	Currently not experiencing any problems but in the past has had to move his salon due to fire, theft and KCCA laws and taxes.

Appendix 1 221

Name	Education	Finance	Marital status		Business		Challenges
Mbabazi Scovia (F, 38)	Completed O-level	**Capital**: brother in Kampala **Assets**: equipment **Savings**: saves small amounts on her own and with women's group **Employees/apprentices**: yes	Single	Married (four children, youngest aged three)	Runs a salon (started in 2009 and moved three times till she found the best spot)	Runs a salon, bought big dryer to offer new services such as steaming and a TV for customers to watch while they wait. Had training from hair product company, which increased styles she could offer. Has a plot of land.	Rent and Council taxes increasing; electricity frequently cut off so she can't work. Premises too small and water seeps through the wall.

Appendix 2
Summary of Entrepreneurs' Directions of Social Mobility

Entrepreneur	Direction	Events since 2013	Future plans
Hadija	Downwards	She has lost her stall and works two days per week on a friend's stall earning $4 per day.	She plans to regain her stall through selling a plot of forested land, she still holds a coffee plantation, and wants to secure NGO support for her daughter's education by paying for coaching to improve her performance.
Joan	Downwards	She has lost her stall, which was outside her home and is staying with a female friend after her husband mistreated her. Now selling citrus fruit wholesale at night and without a permanent location.	She plans to expand her business by getting a stall in the market and selling carrots. Long-term, she wants to acquire another retail stall in the suburbs.
Monica	Downwards	Although she still has her fish stall, she has lost three family members who were providing financial support and is struggling with government constraints on the fish trade.	She plans to expand her business and add new lines such as tomatoes. Wants to build a house and farm animals in her village.

Entrepreneur	Direction	Events since 2013	Future plans
Mariam	Stable/ upwards	She has moved to a new site, which allows her to sell four or five times as many bananas each day and has expanded into other fruit, vegetables, and charcoal, in addition to the animals her mother looks after.	She wants to start a cosmetics shop or salon, but first plans to buy land and build a house in town.
Agnes	Downwards, but moving upwards?	She separated from her husband and lost her market stall. However, she has since remarried and moved to a prosperous area, which has changed her future aspirations.	Although heavily pregnant, she plans to return to trading in the future but with a 'better business' such as a shop.
Janat	Downwards	She separated from her husband and he took four of their five children, leaving her to manage the baby alone. Without financial support, she has been unable to repair the fridge. This was central to running the dairy and she now sells tea on the road to Busega.	Even though her previous dreams around buying land and building a house are on hold, she still plans to expand her business by including porridge and buns.
Regina	Upwards	Despite separating from her husband and receiving little support for her five children, she has moved to new premises and expanded her stock.	Plans to build rental properties and has livestock with family in a rural area.
Juliet	Upwards	She has expanded her business and bought new machinery and is running a poultry business with help from her stepson. She is building a house and renting three rooms.	She plans to get more tenders for school uniform, although she laments the informal payments that are needed to secure these.
Aida	Upwards	Despite the costly illness of her youngest child, she has expanded her business. She owns a cow with two calves in the village.	She plans to buy a large plot to build rental accommodation and breed chickens.

Entrepreneur	Direction	Events since 2013	Future plans
Scovia	Upwards	She has bought new machinery and added new services to her salon, she also has a plot of land. As she rents she has little control over the premises and the electricity is unreliable as the landlord obtains it illegally.	She plans to build her own salon to give her more security and enable her to take on more paid trainees.

Index

.

www.ingramcontent.com/pod-product-compliance
Lightning Source LLC
Chambersburg PA
CBHW070619030426
42337CB00020B/3850